Innovation and the Growth of Cities

To Annabel, Ashley and Jane

Innovation and the Growth of Cities

Zoltan. J. Acs

Doris E. and Robert V. McCurdy Distinguished Professor of Entrepreneurship and Innovation, Robert G. Merrick School of Business, University of Baltimore and US Bureau of the Census

Edward Elgar
Cheltenham, UK • Northampton, MA, USA

Published by
Edward Elgar Publishing Limited
Glensanda House
Montpellier Parade
Cheltenham
Glos GL50 1UA
UK

Edward Elgar Publishing, Inc.
136 West Street
Suite 202
Northampton
Massachusetts 01060
USA

A catalogue record for this book
is available from the British Library

Library of Congress Cataloguing in Publication Data

Acs, Zoltán J.
    Innovation and the growth of cities/Zoltan J. Acs.
        p.; cm.
        1. Technological innovations – Economic aspects. 2. Industrial management.
    3. Urban economics. 4. Economic development. I. Title.
HC79.T4 A26 2002
307.1'416—dc21   2002018836

ISBN   1 84064 936 4 (cased)

Typeset by Cambrian Typesetters, Frimley, Surrey
Printed and bound in Britain by Biddles Ltd, *www.biddles.co.uk*

Contents

List of figures

List of tables

Foreword

Zoltan Acs, as my students might say, 'gets it'. He is the kind of scholar who does not get hemmed in by disciplinary boundaries. He does not get bound up in conceptual mumbo-jumbo. He takes on real-world problems: what kinds of firms innovate? Where do they do it? And, what does this mean for cities and regions? When the real world looks different than theory, Acs is likely to think that maybe it's the theory that's got it wrong. To help get it right, he goes out and takes a good hard look at what's really going on, collects new and unique data, and then tries to figure out just what causes what.

Such is the case with *Innovation and the Growth of Cities*. The geography of the United States is being reshaped, Acs argues, and innovation holds the key. The book opens with the story of Dayton Ohio's rise and decline – a metaphor for the rise and decline of the once-great American industrial heartland and the seismic shift in the landscape of innovation and economic growth. These shifts are more than mere facts for Acs who hails from Cleveland and lived the very transformations of which he writes.

Acs has long been a disciple of Schumpeter. In this book, he brings Schumpeter to geography, while bringing geography to Schumpeter. *Innovation and the Growth of Cities* situates Acs within a long and distinguished intellectual tradition of thinkers who care about the connection of innovation and geography – from Alfred Marshall to Jane Jacobs. The great contribution of this tradition is that it marries geography to the long-held notion, established by both Schumpeter and Marx, that innovation is the driving force of economic growth. Innovation is not just an abstract economic process, nor one that is purely the province of firms. It does not emerge out of nowhere. In a very real sense, it comes from 'somewhere'. The 'new combinations' that lie at the heart of innovation do not come from thin air; rather they are the product of pools of resources and interactions that are themselves concentrated in particular places.

The great Jane Jacobs – who Robert Lucas has rightly suggested should be nominated for a Nobel Prize – showed long ago that innovation results from the creativity and diversity that concentrate in particular places. Cities, as Wilbur Thompson used to say, are the 'incubators' of innovation. And as the long sweep of economic history has shown, creative places – from Athens and Florence, to Manchester and Detroit, and more recently the Silicon Valley – are the cauldrons of innovation and economic growth.

Acs understands this. The new geography, he argues, is not the result of natural endowments of land, labor and capital, as economists have long thought. Rather, he suggests, it is powered by innovation and entrepreneurship; and this in turn is the product of real people acting in real places. In other words, the factors that really matter are the ones we create for ourselves. We do this by recombining the knowledge and other resources in new and novel ways. What is more, some places are better than others at doing this. That is because they are able to attract, mobilize and connect the factors that really matter – innovative people and creative entrepreneurs.

Innovation is indeed a very concentrated activity, as Acs shows. In the 60-year period between 1935 and 1995, the industrial heartland saw its share of patents drop from 85 percent to less than half; California overtook New York in innovative activity, while Texas surged past Illinois. Innovative centers like Silicon Valley, Seattle and Austin overtook older industrial cities like Cleveland, Buffalo and Pittsburgh as new centers for technology, entrepreneurship and economic growth. All of this in turns continues to exert a powerful effect on American economic, political and cultural life.

Acs notes that we met in Montreal a little more than a decade ago. I recall that meeting with delight. I had long had an interest in economic geography and regional development and had conducted studies of venture capital and high-tech industry with Martin Kenney. It was clear to me and to others that innovation is a geographically concentrated process; and there were certainly studies of this. But no one had really nailed it down. A big piece of the problem was that the field lacked the kinds of measures required to probe this issue. Acs brought a missing piece to the puzzle: he had the measures. Indeed, I was already familiar with Acs's pioneering work with Audretsch on the economics of innovation. They had been looking at the relative roles played by firms of various sizes, and were doing so with an incredible data set on real innovations. So when we sat down to lunch, the first question I asked was: 'Does it contain the required geographic detail?' When Acs responded: 'Yes', it was clear to both of us that a door had opened – that progress could be made. So we started to talk it out then and there; and we laid out an agenda of sorts for how one might look at the geography of innovation.

I went back home to Carnegie Mellon University where I teach, and told one of our graduate students at the time, Maryann Feldman, about this energetic fellow I had met and the wonderful data set that he was working with. The rest, as they say, is history. Acs and Feldman began to work together, and later in combination with David Audretsch and others, and went on to make path-breaking and much-cited contributions to the field. Working together, they did what good scholars are supposed to do. They developed a theory, collected the data, structured the analysis, and came up with new and original results.

I am honored that Zoltan Acs thinks our conversation that day played a role in stimulating this important line of research. But I am much more delighted to see this volume and to note the incredible contribution of this research in helping to bring geography to the study of innovation, and innovation to the field of geography. And, I am confident that *Innovation and the Growth of Cities* will help to stimulate even more.

Richard Florida
Heinz Professor of Regional Economic Development
Carnegie Mellon University, US
7 September 2001

Preface

In May of 1990 I met Richard Florida at a conference in Montreal, Canada on 'Networks of Innovators'. Over lunch Richard and I sketched out an idea for a research agenda on regional innovation. I had not previously considered doing research on regional innovation but was intrigued by developments in the 1980s that had a regional focus. Two graduate students that I had the pleasure of working with over the years, Maryann Feldman at Carnegie Mellon University and Attila Varga at West Virginia University made the ensuing research possible.

Adam Jaffe was the first to identify the extent to which university research spills over into the generation of commercial activity. His statistical results provided evidence that corporate patent activity responds positively to commercial spillovers from university research. Building on Jaffe's work Feldman (1994) expanded the knowledge production function to innovative activity and incorporated aspects of the regional knowledge infrastructure. She found that innovative activity is conditioned by the knowledge infrastructure, and responds favorably to spillovers from university research at the state level, strengthening Jaffe's findings.

Attila Varga (1998) built on this solid foundation. His main concern was whether university-generated economic growth observed in certain regions and for selected industries can be achieved by other regions. He extends the Jaffe–Feldman approach by focusing on a more precise measure of local geographic spillovers. Varga approaches the issue of knowledge spillovers from an explicit spatial econometric perspective and for the first time implements the classic knowledge production function for 125 Metropolitan Statistical Areas (MSAs), yielding more precise insights into the range of spatial externalities between innovation and research and development (R&D). The Jaffe–Feldman–Varga research into R&D spillovers takes us a long way toward understanding the role of R&D spillovers in knowledge-based economic development.

This book is the result of a long and fruitful research endeavor with several other colleagues. During the summer of 1990 and 1991 I returned to the WZB in Berlin to continue research with David B. Audretsch on small firms and innovation. In 1991 Steve Isberg and I at the University of Baltimore started doing research on the financing of innovative firms. Sharon Gifford and I also started collaborating shortly thereafter on entrepreneurship and innovation. In

1993 I spent the summer at St Andrews University in Scotland with Felix R. FitzRoy and started a long-term collaboration on employment and wages. In 1995 I had two long visits to the University of Ottawa to start work with John de la Mothe on regional innovation. A year at the University of Maryland, two years at the US Small Business Administration and one year at the Center for Economic Studies at the US Bureau of the Census took me away from this work. However, after returning to the University of Baltimore in the fall of 1999 I decided to pull this research together.

Most of the chapters of this book were co-authored. David B. Audretsch and Maryann Feldman were the co-authors on Chapter 2. Attila Varga and Luc Anselin were the co-authors on Chapters 3 and 4. Sharon Gifford was the co-author on Chapter 5, Steven Isberg was the co-author on Chapter 6 and Adrian Nikamwaudi was the co-author on Chapter 7. Chapters 8 and 9 were co-authored with Felix R. FitzRoy and Ian Smith. Finally, Chapter 9 was co-authored with John de la Mothe and Gilles Paquet. I was also fortunate to have had discussion with and assistance or comments from Richard Nelson, Mike Scherer, Bo Carlsson, Richard Florida, Daniel Gerlowski, Michael Conte, Catherine Armington, Adam Jaffe, Bernard Yeung, Gavin C. Reid, Paul Gompers, Alan Hughes, Roy Thurik, John Haltiwanger, Paul Reynolds, Andy Iserman, Wesley Cohen, Steven Klepper, Lemma W. Senbet, Stephen A. Ross, Edgar Norton, Bruce Kogut and Hun-Gay Fung.

I wish to thank participants at seminars and conferences at the American Economic Association, EARIE, International Joseph A. Schumpeter Society Meetings, R&D Decisions conference at the University of Keele, the ERSC conference on R&D, Technology and Policy at the London Business School, international conference on Entrepreneurship, Small and Medium-Sized Enterprises and the Macroeconomy at Jonkiping International Business School, international conference on Innovation and Performance of SMEs at Cambridge University, workshop on 'Endogenous Growth Policy and Regional Development: A Comparative Approach on the Role of Government and Institutions' at the Tinbergen Institute, University of Amsterdam, conference on Implication of Knowledge-Based Growth for Microeconomic Policies, Industry Canada, North American Meetings of the International Regional Science Association, Third Global Workshop on Small Business Economics at Erasmus University, WZB, University of Baltimore, University of Pennsylvania, Babson College, Harvard University, Georgetown University, St Andrews University, Carnegie Mellon University, Université d'Aix Marseille, Rutgers University, Milken Institute, Johns Hopkins University, University of Maryland at College Park, University of Ottawa, Prime Lecture for valuable comments. Clark Cui, Brett Salazar, Gisele Giles, Olga Korobkova, She-Fen Tsai, and especially Adrian Nikamwaudi provided excellent research assistance over the years.

Slightly different versions of these chapters have been previously published. Parts of Chapter 2 were published in the *American Economic Review* (1992), **82**, (1), 363–7, and the *Review of Economics and Statistics* (1994), **76**, 336–40. Chapter 3 was published in *Journal of Urban Economics* (1997), **42**, 422–48. Chapter 4 was published in *Growth and Change* (2000), **31**, (4), 501–15. Chapter 5 was published in *Small Business Economics* (1996), **8**, (3), 303–18. Chapter 6 was published in *Behavioral Norms, Technological Progress and Economic Dynamics*, University of Michigan Press, (1996), pp. 285–300. Chapter 7 was published in *Small Business Economics* (1998), **10**, (1), 47–59. Chapter 8 was published in *Economics of Innovation and New Technology* (1999), **8**, 57–78. Chapter 9 was published in *Papers in Regional Science* (2002). Chapter 10 was published in *The Implications of Knowledge-Based Growth for Micro-Economic Policies*, University of Calgary Press, (1996), pp. 339–58.

I would like to express my gratitude to the following organizations, which provided financial and technical support for the research underlying the book. I am grateful to the University of Baltimore for supporting my research over the years, as have the Harry Y. Wright Professorship and the Doris and Robert McCurdy Distinguished Professorship at the University of Baltimore. The May Wong Smith Fellowship at the University of St Andrews, a post as visiting professor at the Université d'Aix-Marseille, France, and the Wissenschaftszentrum Berlin für Sozialforschung (WZB) where I was a visiting Research Professor during the summer of 1990 and 1991, all provided valuable support.

I would like to thank Blackwell Publishers, The University of Michigan Press, The University of Calgary Press, Springer-Verlag GmbH & Co. KG, the MIT Press, The American Economic Association and Taylor & Francis Ltd for permission to reprint previously published material.

1. Technology and entrepreneurship

1.1 INTRODUCTION

In 1874 James Ritty invented the mechanical cash register in Dayton, Ohio. For most of the twentieth century to Wall Street and the world, Dayton, Ohio was the home of the National Cash Register Company. National Cash Register got rich as it sold its machines all over the world, and it rewarded its workers with high wages and benefits, and its home town with a firm hand of civic guidance. However, Dayton's dominance in cash registers and numerous other industrial innovations did not last forever. The information revolution led to a shift in the knowledge base, and the mechanical cash register was replaced with optical scanners and computers at the checkout counter in virtually every retail establishment. After a hostile takeover of National Cash Register by ATT in 1991, the financially strapped company was downsized, and finally spun off. Today, Dayton finds itself between two worlds: the old economy of making things and job security and the new economy of services, technology and job insecurity (*New York Times*, 1996).

The experience of Dayton is by no means unique. Early in the twentieth century the great bulk of traditional industrial strength of the United States was concentrated in a relatively small part of the northeast and the eastern part of the American midwest: roughly speaking, within the approximate parallelogram of Green Bay, Wisconsin–St Louis–Baltimore–Portland, Maine. This manufacturing belt took shape in the second half of the nineteenth century and proved remarkably persistent. As late as 1957, this manufacturing belt still contained 64 percent of total US manufacturing employment (only slightly down from the 74 percent share which it held at the turn of the century (Perloff et al. 1960)).

The strength of this legendary manufacturing belt was built on the existence of iron ore in the Masabi Range in Minnesota, abundant coal in the Appalachian Mountains and cheap water transportation. As a young boy growing up in Cleveland, Ohio, I used to watch the great ore carriers work their way up the Cuyahoga River to the steel mills. This combination created an economic miracle that was the envy of the world for over a hundred years. 'Why did the manufacturing region play such a dominant role for so long', asked Paul Krugman (1991: 13)? 'It was clearly not a case of an enduring

1

comparative advantage in natural resources: the manufacturing belt persisted even as the center of gravity of agricultural and mineral production shifted far to the west.' Once the regional knowledge base had been established it was not in the interest of any individual producer to move out of it.

However enduring this region its supremacy was not to last. As we have just seen, in the last quarter of the twentieth century – the time span of this book – the information revolution shifted the epicenter of the knowledge base, and therefore trade and commerce, from the industrial parallelogram to the west and the southeast. Today high-technology clusters are emerging outside of the traditional industrial heartland. This high-technology revolution became identified first with Silicon Valley, in and around San Jose, California. Other high-tech clusters are dispersed thoughout the south, the southwest and the west, far from the manufacturing belt of Cleveland, Detroit and Dayton. Why did the epicenter of economic activity shift away from its traditional location? One answer to this question is that the knowledge base of the economy shifted and economic activity motivated by entrepreneurial discovery followed the opportunity.

The long-run evidence in the shift of the knowledge base is found in the patent statistics. The patenting trend of the American sunbelt states stands in deep contrast with that of the old industrial heartland. Between 1935 and 1995, the industrial heartland's proportion of total domestic patenting declined from 83 percent to 48 percent, while the sunbelt states' proportion increased from 16 percent to equal the heartland's proportion. By 1985 the share of patents granted to the two regions were at parity. Most striking was that while New York State as late as 1940 has received twice as many patents as Illinois, by 1970, California had overtaken New York State in patents received and Texas had surpassed Illinois (Suarez Villa 2000: 136–47). The economic knowledge base had shifted west and south, and with it economic growth, income and wealth creation. According to Business Week (25 August 1997: 66):

> Who could have dreamed 40 years ago, that the eight disgruntled engineers who marched out of Shockley Semiconductor Labs in Mountain View California, would set in motion one of the most amazing chains of events in American Business History. . . . Look at what they've wrought. Noyce and Moore went on to found mighty chipmaker Intel Corporation, which led to at least eight more spin-offs, and Kleiner helped stoke the Valley's money machine when he launched the region's premier venture-capital firm, Kleiner Perkins Caufield & Beyers. Today, there are some 7,000 electronics and software companies and thousands of start-ups, with 11 companies being created every week – all crammed into a 50 mile long corridor, like transistors on a powerful chip.

Silicon Valley is home to 33 of the 100 largest high-tech firms launched since 1965 including Oracle, Sun Microsystems, Netscape, 3Com, Cisco Systems, Intel, National Semiconductor, Fairchild Semiconductor, Seagate,

Excite, and Yahoo. It also has one of the highest shares of small high-tech firms with fewer than 20 employees – 55.9 percent, and one of the highest shares of locally owned high-tech firms – 65.19 percent. In 1989 San Jose had 260 065 people employed in the high-tech sector, the highest on a per capita basis. Average high-tech wages in 1989 were $43 320, second highest in the nation after Houston. The ratio of high-technology earnings per job to non-high technology earnings per job in 1989 was 50 percent higher in San Jose, the largest differential in the country. Its university research and development expenditures at $280 493 in 1989 were third in the nation for an index of 22 cities (Acs 1996, chapter 8). Finally, as shown in Table 1.1 San Jose County had 386 industrial innovations in 1982, one for each day of the year, outdistancing the next closest county Los Angeles by over 100 innovations.

When one asked the question, 'What makes Silicon Valley unique?' the discussion usually comes back to one great institution – Stanford University. 'It is conventional wisdom that Silicon Valley and Route 128 owe their status as centers of commercial innovation and entrepreneurship to their proximity to Stanford and MIT' (Jaffe 1989: 957). Stanford built a community of technical scholars and a world-class network. Its graduates have been responsible for the founding of many of the greatest high-tech companies in the world, including Silicon Graphics 1982 (James Clark and six others), Excite 1993 (Ben Lutch, Ryan McIntyre, Graham Spencer, Mark Van Haren), Hewlett Packard 1939 (William Hewlett and David Packard), Cisco Systems 1984 (Leonard Bosack and Sandra Lerner), and many others.

How important is technical knowledge to innovation and regional growth? More specifically, 'How important are universities to economic growth?' and 'How important was Stanford University to the growth of Silicon Valley?' As a first step to probe this question, 32 relatively high-technology industries were identified. Next we selected 22 of the most important cities for these industries, most of which have major research universities. For sample variation, we also added 15 additional cities with only minor university research.

The relationship between university research and development (R&D) and high-technology employment can be analysed in a preliminary fashion using scatter diagrams. Both variables display great variation across metropolitan areas though there is a clear positive association between them. Since size of city may be a factor inducing spurious correlation, Figure 1.1 plots high-technology employment as a proportion of the (Standard Metropolitan Statistical Area SMSA) population in 1989 against research expenditures. The simple correlation drops markedly to 0.15 controlling for city size, our major SMSAs now generate few high-tech jobs relative to their university research expenditures. Rather it is medium-sized cities like San Jose, California, Raleigh-Durham, North Carolina, Seattle, Washington and Austin Texas, that emerge as benefiting most from university research spillovers.

Innovation and the growth of cities

Table 1.1   Number of innovations by county (top 26 counties, 1982)

No	County	State	Innovation
1	Santa Clara	California	386
2	Los Angeles	California	178
3	Cook	Illinois	155
4	Middlesex	Massachusetts	145
5	Norfolk	Massachusetts	121
6	Orange	California	117
7	Bergen	New Jersey	90
8	New York	New York	82
9	Fairfield	Connecticut	76
10	Nassau	New York	73
11	Dallas	Texas	64
12	San Diego	California	63
13	Suffolk	New York	62
14	Cuyahoga	Ohio	62
15	Essex	New Jersey	57
16	Westchester	New Jersey	54
17	Ramsey	Minnesota	49
18	Montgomery	Pennsylvania	45
19	Philadelphia	Pennsylvania	44
20	Hennepin	Minnesota	42
21	Morris	New Jersey	42
22	Alameda	California	39
23	Middlesex	New Jersey	36
24	Harris	Texas	35
25	Somerset	New Jersey	34
26	Monroe	New York	34

Source: Innovation Database

Figure 1.2 plots a scatter diagram of high-technology employment in the population against the number of scientists and engineers per 100 workers by SMSA. The motivation is that the supply of university science graduates with good general and specific skills influences the location of a high-technology cluster. In the whole sample, the correlation with the proportion of engineers and scientists is 0.73. Significantly, San Jose, California, Austin, Texas, Raleigh, North Carolina, Seattle, Washington and San Diego, California not only have a high proportion of the population in high-technology employment but also a high share of engineers and scientists. The simple evidence suggests

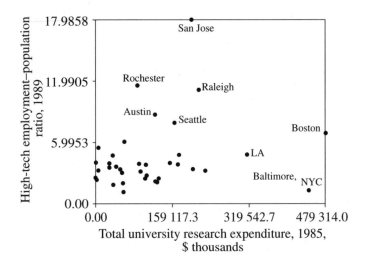

Figure 1.1   Plot of the high-tech employment–population ratio, 1989 and university research expenditure, 1985

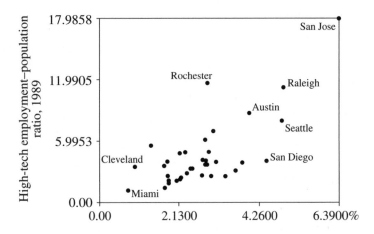

Figure 1.2   Plot of employment ratio against the proportion of scientists and engineers in each MSA, 1989

that both the employment of scientists and engineers and university research is important for high-technology employment.

While regional issues of convergence still exist, the impact of the information revolution on the US economy has been nothing but spectacular. According to Acs, Carlsson and Karlsson (1999: 3):

As the United States reelected President Clinton in 1996, the economic anxiety of four years earlier was no longer to be found in the electorate. After a quarter century of painful ups and downs, the U. S. economy appeared to be doing extraordinarily well. According to Lawrence H. Summers, Deputy Treasury Secretary, 'The economy seems better balanced than at any time in my professional lifetime.' In 1997 unemployment was just over 5 percent, the economy was growing at 3 percent a year, inflation was at bay, manufacturing productivity was rising by 4 percent a year, the dollar was strong, and the Dow Jones industrial average was breaking records as a matter of course. It seemed that the U. S. economy had restructured, moving from an industrial economy to an information one, and made the transition to the twenty-first century.

The stellar performance of the US economy in the closing years of the twentieth century has continued with two additional caveats. First, income growth that had been diverging for decades has again started to grow at all levels of society. In fact, between 1998–2000 the largest gains in wages were at the very bottom of the income scale. Second, the federal deficits of the 1980s and early 1990s have finally turned to surpluses and the enviable question for the twenty-first century is, 'How best to spend the money: reduce the federal debt or cut taxes?' As President George W. Bush, the first president of the twenty-first century, prepares to take office the domestic economy is barely an issue.

The purpose of this book is to explore the relationship between industrial innovation and economic growth at the regional level. We are interested in understanding why some regions grow and others decline. There are many ways in which to study this subject. Different disciplines as well as different fields have different strengths in shedding light on certain aspects of the subject. The approach taken in this book, as in much of my previous research, is eclectic (Acs 1984). The analysis draws on industrial organization, labor economics, regional science, geography, entrepreneurship and growth theory. However, since we are interested in the big picture, the lens through which we need to focus on innovation and the growth of cities is endogenous growth theory (Aghion and Howitt 1998).

1.2   ENDOGENOUS TECHNICAL CHANGE

In the eighteenth century, the avant-garde theories of Adam Smith concerning the wealth of nations provided a cheery alternative to the dismal science of Thomas Malthus. However, for over a century, from Marx to Jorgenson, the prospects of diminishing returns were central to our understanding of economic growth. Today, the new growth theory provides a more optimistic alternative to the conventional wisdom that counsels diminished expectations when it comes to future growth. 'Ideas don't obey the law of diminishing returns', according to Paul M. Romer. In economics saying that you have found the way around the law of diminishing returns is akin to saying you have discovered the Fountain of Youth. Above all, advances in technology and interdependencies between new ideas and new investment ultimately saves the day, yielding brighter prospects for long-run prosperity.[1]

We begin with a short survey of endogenous growth theory to bring out its strengths and weaknesses for regional analysis.[2] The distinguishing feature of endogenous economic growth theory as compared to the neoclassical growth model is in its modeling of technological change as a result of profit-motivated investments in knowledge creation by private economic agents. Schmookler (1966) argued in great detail that it is the expected profitability of inventive activity, reflecting conditions in the relevant factor and product markets, that determines the pace and direction of industrial innovation. If scientific advances operated within the profit sector of the economy, technological progress is a subject for economic analysis. The novel formulation of technological knowledge in economic theory in Romer (1990) is the key in establishing this new and rapidly evolving field of economic growth theory. According to this formulation, technological knowledge is a non-rival, partially excludable good. Such formulation of technological knowledge as a key factor in the production function results in a departure from the constant returns to scale, perfectly competitive world of the neoclassical growth theory.

Central to the neoclassical theory of economic growth as formulated in Solow (1956) is the production function. Assuming that capital does not depreciate, the labor force does not grow and technology does not change over time, the production function has the form of

$$Y = F(K, L) \tag{1.1}$$

where Y represents aggregate production, K the capital stock and L the labor force. $F(.)$ is the constant returns to scale production function. It is assumed that the capital stock grows without bounds. However, the growth rate of per capita income is bounded. Growth rate of per capita income is

$$g = s F_K(K, L) \tag{1.2}$$

where g is the growth rate of per capita income, s is the savings rate and F_K is the marginal product of capital. Equation (1.2) says that per capita income grows as long as the marginal product of capital exceeds zero. However, assuming constant growth in the capital stock, per capita income approaches zero. Relaxing the assumptions of stable labor force and no depreciation of capital does not change essentially the main point of the model. The condition for a sustained per capita income growth in the long run is that, resulting from continuous capital accumulation, the marginal product of capital should not decrease below a positive lower bound.

Development in the state of technology is an essential force to offset the effect of capital accumulation on per capita income leading to a decline in the neoclassical model of economic growth. Introducing technological progress in the production function, it takes the form

$$Y = F\,(A, K, L) \tag{1.3}$$

where A stands for the state of technology. Assuming that A increases, it will increase the marginal product of capital which will lead to a higher per capita income. As a result, in steady state the rate of technical development equals the rate of capital accumulation.

The essential role of technological progress in economic growth has been emphasized above. However, technological development remains unexplained in the neoclassical theory of economic growth. As a public good, it is considered exogenously determined although (as data in Solow 1957 and Maddison 1987 show) the major portion of economic growth can be attributed to technological change whereas capital accumulation (the main concern in the neoclassical model) explains only a fraction of it.

Primary attempts in the literature to endogenize technological progress include Arrow (1962) by introducing 'learning by doing' in technological development, Lucas (1988) by modeling human capital as the determinant factor in technical change and Romer (1986) by explicitly including research in the production function. In Arrow's formulation

$$Y_i = A(K)\,F(K_i, L_i) \tag{1.4}$$

the state of technology depends on the aggregate capital stock in the economy. Subscript i denotes individual firms. According to Lucas's model of endogenous technological change, spillovers resulted from human capital accumulation instead of the accumulation of physical capital increasing the technological level in the economy:

$$Y_i = A(H)\,F(K_i, L_i) \tag{1.5}$$

where H stands for the general level of human capital in the economy. In Romer (1986) it is assumed that spillovers from private research efforts lead to development in the public stock of knowledge. It could be written as

$$Y_i = A(R)\,F(R_i, K_i, L_i) \tag{1.6}$$

where R_i stands for the results of private research and development efforts by firm i and R denotes the aggregate stock of research results in the economy.

As summarized in Romer (1990), the major conceptual problem with the formulation of endogenous growth in equations (1.4)–(1.6) is that in those models the entire stock of technological knowledge is considered to be a public good. However, as daily evidence suggests, new technological knowledge can become partially excludable (at least for a limited length of time) by means of patenting. Not until the formulation of monopolistic competition in Dixit and Stiglitz (1977), applied in the dynamic context by Judd (1985), had modeling economic growth within an imperfectly competitive market structure become attainable. In Romer (1990) the approach by Judd was combined with learning by doing in innovation to create the first model of endogenously determined technical change with imperfectly competing firms.

Consequently, each firm developing new technological knowledge has some market power and earns monopoly profits on its discoveries. The 'new theory of economic growth' which follows from this first in Romer (1990) builds on a more suitable view of the available stock of technological knowledge as well as formulating the economy within the framework of imperfect competition.

At the core of the 'new' growth theory is the concept of technological knowledge as a non-rival, partially excludable good, as opposed to the neoclassical view of knowledge as an entirely public good. Knowledge is a non-rival good because it can be used by one agent without limiting its use by others. This distinguishes technology from, say a piece of capital equipment, which can only be used in one place at a time. Technology in many cases is partially excludable because it is possible to prevent its use by others to a certain extent. The excludability reflects both technological and legal consideration. Knowledge can be made partially excludable by the patent system and commercial secrecy. However as Arrow (1962: 615) suggests:

> With suitable legal measures, information may become an appropriable commodity. Then the monopoly power can indeed be exerted. However, no amount of legal protection can make a thoroughly appropriable commodity of something so intangible as information. The very use of the information in any productive way is bound to reveal it, at least in part.

This partial non-excludability of knowledge suggests that industrial R&D may generate technological spillovers. According to Grossman and Helpman (1991: 16):

> By technological spillovers we mean that (1) firms can acquire information created by others without paying for that information in a market transaction, and (2) the creators or current owners of the information have no effective recourse, under prevailing laws, if other firms utilize information so acquired.

There are many ways in which spillovers take place, for example, the mobility of highly skilled personnel between firms represents one such mechanism.

The Valley has a regional network-based industrial system that promotes learning and mutual adjustment among specialist producers of complex technologies. The region's dense social networks and open labor markets encourage entrepreneurship and experimentation resulting in knowledge spillovers (Saxenian 1994). Innovative activity may flourish the most in environments free of bureaucratic constraints. A number of small-firm ventures have benefited from the exodus of researchers who felt thwarted by the managerial restraints as in the case of Shockley Semiconductor Labs. These small firms exploit the knowledge and experience accrued from the R&D laboratories of their previous employers.[3]

Knowledge enters production in two ways. First, newly developed technological knowledge is used in production by the firm which has invested in the development of this new set of technological knowledge to produce output. In this role, knowledge can be protected from being used by others in producing the same type of output. However, this new set of knowledge increases the total stock of publicly available knowledge through being spilled over to other researchers who study its patent documentation (Romer 1990). As such, it increases the productivity of creating further inventions in the research sector. This second role of knowledge in production can be formalized as

$$dA = G(H, A) \qquad (1.7)$$

where H stands for human capital used in research and development, A is the total stock of technological knowledge available at a certain point in time whereas dA is the change in technological knowledge resulting from private efforts to invest in research and development. Human capital creates new knowledge, whereas at the same time, the productivity of human capital depends on the total stock of already available knowledge (A). The larger A the higher the productivity of H and the less expensive it is to create new technological knowledge. In the words of Grossman and Helpman (1991: 18), 'The technological spillovers that result from commercial research may add to a pool of public knowledge, thereby lowering the cost to later generations of achieving a technological breakthrough of some given magnitude. Such cost reductions can offset any tendency for the private returns to invention to fall as a result of increases in the number of competing technologies.'

A principal assumption in the theory of endogenous growth is that for creating new sets of technological knowledge the total stock of knowledge (A in equation (1.7)) is freely accessible for anyone engaged in research. However, this assumption is not verified in the growing literature of geographic knowledge spillovers. New technological knowledge (the most valuable type of knowledge in innovation) is usually in such a tacit form that its accessibility is bounded by geographic proximity and/or by the nature and extent of the interactions among actors in an innovation system (Edquist 1997).

Similar to the case of relaxing the neoclassical assumption of equal availability of technological opportunities in all countries of the world (Romer 1994), a relaxation of the assumption that the term A in equation (1.7) is evenly distributed across space within countries seems to be also necessary. The non-excludable part of the total stock of knowledge seems rather to be correctly classified if it is assumed to have two portions: a perfectly accessible part consisting of already established knowledge elements (obtainable via scientific publications, patent applications etc.) and a novel, tacit element, accessible by interactions among actors in the innovation system. While the first part is available without restrictions, accessibility of the second one is bounded by the nature of interactions among actors in a system of innovation.[4]

The implication of the fact that knowledge producing inputs are not evenly distributed across space is that regions may not grow at the same rate. A significant body of research suggests that because of increasing returns regions may not converge (Nijkamp and Stough 2000). The empirical work on convergence (notably the development of the notion of conditional β-convergence was primarily stimulated by improved data series and provides a more rigorous method of quantifying relative spatial economic performance. The initial findings of Barro and Sala-I-Martin (1992) indicated that regional convergence over recent years had taken place albeit at a very slow pace. The evidence suggests that if there is convergence across regions it is very slow. Convergence one would hypothesize depends on investment in knowledge creation and on the systematic exploitation of knowledge by entrepreneurs.

1.3 ENTREPRENEURIAL DISCOVERY

Even if the total stock of knowledge (in equation (1.7)) was freely available, including the tacit and non-tacit parts, knowledge about it existence would not be. In an important paper, Hayek (1945) pointed out that the central feature of a market economy is the partitioning of knowledge among individuals, such that no two individuals share the same knowledge or information about the economy. The key is that this knowledge is diffused in the economy and is not a given or at everyone's disposal. Thus, only a few know about a particular scarcity, or a new invention, or a particular resource lying fallow, or its not being put to best use. This knowledge is typically idiosyncratic because it is acquired through each individual's own circumstances including occupation, on-the-job routines, social relationships, and daily life. It is this particular knowledge, obtained in a particular knowledge base that leads to some profit-making insight. The dispersion of information among different economic agents who do not have access to the same observations, interpretations or experiences has two fundamental implications for entrepreneurship.

First, opportunities for discovering or creating goods and services in the future exist precisely because of the dispersion of information. This dispersion created the opportunity in the first place. Second, the very same dispersion presents hurdles for exploiting the opportunity profitably, because of the absence or failure of current markets for future goods and services. It is therefore necessary to understand, (1) how opportunities for the creation of new goods and services arise in a market economy; and (2) how and in what ways individual differences determine whether hurdles in the process of discovering, creating and exploiting opportunities are overcome. Thus, entrepreneurship, 'seeks to understand how opportunities to bring into existence "future" goods and services are discovered, created, and exploited, by whom and with what consequences' (Shane and Venkataraman 2000).

How do opportunities arise in the economy? In most societies, markets are inefficient most of the time, thus providing opportunities for enterprising individuals to enhance wealth by exploiting these inefficiencies. This is most clearly articulated in the work of Kirzner (1997) where most markets are in disequilibrium. A second premise suggests that even if markets are in equilibrium, the human condition of enterprise combined with the lure of profits and advancing knowledge and technology will destroy the equilibrium eventually. This premise is probably most familiar as Schumpeter's Creative Destruction. These two premises are based on the underlying assumption that change is a fact of life. And the result of this natural process is both a continuous supply of lucrative opportunities to enhance personal wealth, and a continuous supply of enterprising individuals seeking such opportunities.

There are at least four classes of opportunities. The first is inefficiencies within existing markets due either to information asymmetries among market participants or to the limitations of technology in satisfying certain known but unfulfilled market needs. The second is the emergence of significant changes in social, political, demographic and economic forces that are largely outside the control of individual agents. The third source of opportunity is the accumulated stock of knowledge (A) that exists in society. The fourth source is inventions and discoveries that produce new knowledge (dA) in equation (1.7).

It is one thing for opportunities to exist, but an entirely different matter for them to be discovered and exploited. Even new technology needs to have opportunities in which to exploit the new technology. Opportunity discovery is a function of the distribution of knowledge in society. Opportunities rarely present themselves in neat packages. They almost always have to be discovered and packaged. Thus, the nexus of opportunity and enterprising individuals is critical to understanding entrepreneurship.

The role of specific knowledge and technical knowledge in motivating the search for profitable opportunities is critical to our understanding of what triggers the search for and exploitation of opportunities by some individuals but not others. The possession of useful knowledge varies among individuals and these differences matter. This variable strongly influences the search for and the decision to exploit an opportunity, and it also influences the relative success of the exploitation process.

Specific knowledge (*A*) by itself may only be a sufficient condition for the exercise of successful enterprise in a growth model. The ability to make the connection between specific knowledge and a commercial opportunity requires a set of skills, aptitudes, insight and circumstances that is not either uniformly or widely distributed in the population. Thus, two people with the same knowledge may put it to very different uses. It is one thing to have an insight, but an entirely different matter to profit from it. The incentive, capability and specific behaviors needed to profit from useful knowledge or insight all vary among individuals and these differences matter for explaining the exercise of enterprise.

Bringing new products and markets into existence usually involves an element of downside risk. By definition, entrepreneurship requires making investments today without knowing what the distribution of the returns will be tomorrow. There is a fundamental uncertainty that cannot be insured against or diversified away (Knight 1921). Individuals vary in their perception of such downside risk, and in their aptitudes and capabilities to deal with and manage it. The significant issue is that individuals vary in how they process and interpret statistical generalities and these variations may have significant but systematic impact on the decision to become an entrepreneur and the relative success of the endeavor.

While idiosyncratic insight and the ability to convert knowledge to commercial profit leads to successful enterprise, these same qualities also present the entrepreneur with problems. The process of creating products and markets implies that much of the information required by potential stakeholders – for example, technology, price, quality tastes, supply networked, distributor networks and strategy – is not reliably available. Relevant information will only exist once the market has been successfully created. Potential stakeholders thus have to rely on the entrepreneur for information, but without the benefit of the entrepreneurs special insight. In almost every project entrepreneur's have more information about the true qualities of the project and themselves than any other parties. Because of this information asymmetry, neither buyers nor suppliers may be willing to make the necessary investment in specialized assets or formal cooperative arrangements to develop the business.

Despite the absence of current markets for future goods and services, some individuals do indeed create new markets and products. In fact, entrepreneurs are funded by venture capitalists to discover new knowledge to create future goods and services. According to Venkataraman (1997: 126):

> The significant point is that despite the existence of adverse selection and moral hazard problems, some individuals are able to successfully overcome these hurdles and achieve success. Thus, the ability to overcome adverse selection and moral hazard problems varies among individuals, and these differences matter for explaining successful enterprises. The interesting issue is not that such problems exist, but that in spite of them, some individuals are able to secure resources form different resource controllers, often at very favorable terms, whereby considerable risk is shifted from the entrepreneur to other stakeholders.

A critical decision for the entrepreneur is how to organize relationships with resource suppliers in order to foster the development and execution of a new business. Stated differently, when there are several possible institutional arrangements for creating a future product or service (such as a new firm, a franchise or license arrangement, a joint venture, or a simple contractual agreement), why do entrepreneurs choose a particular mode? Moreover, what are the consequences of this choice on the distribution of risks and rewards among the various stakeholders? The usual assumption about the execution of entrepreneurial activity has been that most (if not all) new business creation occurs within a hierarchical framework, either as novel start-ups or as new entities within an existing corporate body. However, much evidence suggests that indeed this may not be the case. Many new firms follow some different organizational form. Therefore, the most fundamental question in entrepreneurship research is, 'Why are any new entrepreneurial ventures organized as a start-up?'

Economics has an answer to this question. In the absence of monopoly rents being earned by the incumbent firm, perfect information with no agency costs, any positive economies of scale or scope will ensure that no incentive exists for an agent to start a new firm. If an agent had an idea for something different than is currently being practiced by the incumbent enterprise, in terms of a new product or process idea, which we will term here as an innovation, it will be presented to an incumbent enterprise. Because of the assumption of perfect information, both the firm and the agent will agree on the expected value of the innovation. However, to the degree that any economies of scale or scope exist, the expected value of implementing the innovation within the incumbent enterprise will exceed that of taking the innovation outside of the incumbent firm to start a new enterprise. Thus, the incumbent firm and the inventor of the idea would be expected to reach a bargain splitting the value added to the firm by the innovation (Acs and Audretsch 1994).

But, of course, as Knight (1921) and others emphasized, new economic knowledge is anything but certain. Not only is new economic knowledge inherently risky, but substantial asymmetries exist across agents both between and within firms. Which is to say that the assessment of the expected value of a new idea, or innovation, is likely to be anything but unanimous between the inventor of the idea and the decision-makers of the firm confronted with proposed innovations. In fact, it is because information is uncertain that leads Knight (1921: 268) to argue that the primary task of the firm is to process imperfect information in order to reach a decision. According to Audretsch (1995):

> Combined with the bureaucratic organization of incumbent firms to make a decision, the asymmetry of knowledge leads to a host of agency problems, spanning incentive structures, monitoring and transaction costs. It is the existence of such agency costs, combined with asymmetric information that not only provides an incentive for agents with new ideas to start their own firms, but also at a rate that varies from industry to industry, depending upon the underlying knowledge conditions of the industry.

The degree to which incumbent firms are confronted with agency problems with respect to new knowledge and (potential) innovative activity would not be expected to be constant across industries or regions. This is because the underlying knowledge conditions vary from region to region and from industry to industry. In some industries new knowledge-generating innovative activity tends to be relatively routine and can be processed within the context of incumbent hierarchical bureaucracies. In other industries, however, innovations tend to come from knowledge that is not of a routine nature and therefore tends to be rejected by the hierarchical bureaucracies of incumbent corporations. Nelson and Winter (1982) described these different underlying knowledge conditions as reflecting two distinct technological regimes – the entrepreneurial and routinized technological regimes: 'An entrepreneurial regime is one that is favorable to innovative entry and unfavorable to innovative activity by established firms; a routinized regime is one in which the conditions are the other way around' (Winter 1984: 297). At least some empirical evidence was provided by Acs and Audretsch (1988) supporting the existence of these two distinct technological regimes.

When the underlying knowledge conditions are better characterized by the routinized technological regime, there is likely to be relatively little divergence between the evaluation of the expected value of a (potential) innovation between the inventor and the decision-making bureaucracy of the firm. Under the routinized regime there will not exist a great incentive for agents to start their own firm, or at least not for the reason of doing something differently. However, when the underlying knowledge conditions more closely adhere to the entrepreneurial regime, divergent beliefs between agent and the principal regarding the expected value of a (potential) innovation is more likely to emerge. Therefore, it is under the entrepreneurial regime where the start-up of a new firm is likely to play a more important role, presumably as a result of the motivation to appropriate the value of economic knowledge, which due to agency problems, cannot be easily and costlessly transferred to the incumbent enterprise. As Audretsch has pointed out, 'This shifts the emphasis from firms and institutions to individuals – agents with endowments of new economic knowledge'.

1.4   WHERE IS THE KNOWLEDGE AND WHO KNOWS IT?

The fundamental insight of the new growth theory is that economic growth is non-diminishing because technological knowledge is a non-rival, partially excludable good. There are technological spillovers and the profit motive ensures that entrepreneurs will continue to search out opportunities. The key feature of Austrian economics is that the market is an entrepreneurially driven evolutionary process. Entrepreneurship plays an important role in the discovery of knowledge and the turning of that knowledge into future goods and services through industrial innovation.

The starting point for most theories of innovation is the firm. In such theories the firm is assumed to be exogenous and its performance in generating technological change is endogenous. For example, in the most prevalent model in the literature on technological change, the knowledge production function, the firm exists exogenously and then engages in the pursuit of new knowledge as an input into the process of generating innovative activity (Griliches 1979). The most important source of new knowledge is generally considered to be research and development.

This model of innovation is questionable because in many industries small firms serve as the engine of innovation. This is startling because the bulk of industrial R&D is undertaken in the largest corporations. Small enterprises account for only a minor share of R&D. Thus the knowledge production function suggests that innovative activity favor large firms. However, many smaller firms and entrepreneurs innovate (Acs and Audretsch 1990b). This leads to a fundamental question, 'Where do entrepreneurs get the innovation producing inputs, that is the knowledge?'

One suggested answer is that although the model of the knowledge production function may certainly be valid, the implicitly assumed *unit of observation* which links the knowledge inputs with the innovative outputs – at the level of the establishment or firm – may be less valid. Instead, a new literature suggests that knowledge spills over from the firm or research institute producing it, to a different firm commercializing that knowledge. This view is supported by theoretical models which have focused on the role that spillovers of knowledge across firms play in generating increasing returns and ultimately economic growth (Romer 1990).

An important theoretical development is that geography may provide a relevant unit of observation within which knowledge spillovers occur (Feldman 1994). The theory of localization suggests that geographic proximity is needed to transmit knowledge and especially tacit knowledge.[5] According to Krugman (1998: 172):

> It would not be surprising if it turns out that the market-size effects emphasized by the current generation of new geography models are a less important source of agglomeration, at least at the level of urban areas, than other kinds of external economies. It is, for example, a well-documented empirical regularity that both plants and firms in large cities tend to be smaller than those in small cities; this suggests that big cities may be sustained by increasing returns that are due to thick labor markets, or to localized knowledge spillovers, rather than those that emerge from the interaction of transport costs and scale economies at the plant level.

Knowledge spillovers tend to be localized within a geographic region. Jaffe (1989); Jaffe, Trajtenberg and Henderson (1993); Audretsch and Feldman (1996); Audretsch and Stephan (1996); Anselin, Varga and Ács (1997, 2000a) have supported the importance of geographic proximity for knowledge spillovers in a wave of recent empirical studies. For a critical survey of the literature on spillovers see Karlsson and Manduchi (2001).

1.5 ORGANIZATION OF THE REST OF THIS BOOK

This book casts industrial innovation as the engine of long-run regional growth. What we are looking for from this new evolving literature are insights that would help us develop a clear analytical framework which integrates economic growth, spatial interdependencies and the creation of new technology as an explicit production process to formulate production-oriented regional policies (Nijkamp and Poot 1997). This book is an empirical investigation. Each chapter uses the same innovation database to explore issues of how technology and entrepreneurship foster and promote growth at the regional level.

A new learning has recently emerged in the economics literature regarding the source of innovative activity and technological change. The conventional wisdom that giant corporations able to exercise market power are the engine of technological change is derived from the theories of Schumpeter and empirical verification is based on measures of inputs in the process of technological change, such as R&D, and intermediate inputs such as patented inventions.

The new learning emanates from new insights into the process of technological change as well as new measures, which are designed to reflect innovative output. Central to the new learning is that small firms, as well as large enterprises, play an important role in innovative activity. The relative innovative advantage of large and small firms apparently varies across industries, depending upon industry-specific characteristics, such as scale economies, market concentration, the technological environment and firm-size distribution (Acs and Audretsch, 1993b).

Measures of technological change have typically involved one of three aspects of the innovation process: (1) a measure of the inputs into the innovation process, such as R&D expenditures, or else the share of the labor force accounted for by employees involved in R&D activities; (2) an intermediate output, such as the number of inventions which have been patented; or (3) a direct measure of innovative output. A clear limitation in using R&D activity as a proxy measure for innovation activity is that R&D reflects only the resources allocated toward trying to produce innovative output, but not the actual amount of resulting innovative activity. That is, R&D is an input and not an output in the innovation process. The reliability of the patent measure has also been questioned. Not only are many innovations never patented, but also not all patented inventions result in innovations.

Chapter 2 uses this direct measure of innovation to examine the manner by which R&D 'spills over' from university laboratories and the R&D laboratories of industrial corporations to third-party firms at the state level. This chapter builds on Jaffe's 1989 article using patents as a measure of innovative output at the state level. Of particular interest is to identify the comparative advantages of large and small enterprises in taking advantage of such R&D spillovers in generating innovative activity. To empirically identify the role that spillovers in R&D play in the innovative activity of private firms, we apply a production function model relating knowledge-generating inputs to innovative output for units of observation at the geographical level. There is considerable evidence that, in fact, spillovers are facilitated by the geographic coincidence of universities and research laboratories within a state. In addition, corporate R&D is a relatively more important source of innovation in large firms, while spillovers from university research laboratories are more important in producing innovative activity in small firms.

Chapter 3 re-examines the empirical evidence on the degree of spatial spillover between university research and high-technology innovations. It extends the empirical evidence in three important respects. It broadens the cross-sectional basis for empirical analysis by utilizing data for 43 states (compared to 29 in Chapter 2) and for 125 metropolitan statistical areas (MSAs). This is the first time MSA-level data are used in this type of analysis, which avoids the problems associated with the inappropriate spatial scale of a state as the unit of analysis. MSA-level results are obtained by using R&D laboratory employment as a proxy for R&D activity, based on a specially compiled data set.

The chapter focuses on more precise measures of local geographic spillovers. At the state level, it introduces several alternatives to Jaffe's (1989) 'geographic coincidence index' that are more tightly integrated with the existing body of spatial interaction theory, and are able to significantly improve on his results. At the MSA scale, we formalize the spatial extent of the geographic spillovers by means of so-called spatial lag variables that capture the research activities in concentric rings around the MSA as well as in the MSA itself.

Finally, we explicitly consider the potential for spatial effects such as spatial autocorrelation that may invalidate the interpretations of econometric analysis based on contiguous cross-sectional data. In the existing literature, these effects are typically ignored or treated inappropriately. We implement a spatial econometric approach by both testing for the presence of spatial effects, and when needed, by implementing models that incorporate them explicitly.

Chapter 4 extends the empirical evidence in Chapter 3 in three important respects. The cross-sectional basis for empirical analysis is broadened by utilizing data for four high-technology sectors. The disaggregated approach followed in this chapter opens up the possibility to study likely variations across industries. Specific measures of local geographic spillovers are developed. These measures are based on a modification of the spatial lag variable used in Chapter 2. They are intended to capture research activities in concentric rings around the MSA as well as in the MSA itself. In the analysis of the sectorally disaggregated data, the potential for spatial effects such as spatial autocorrelation and spatial heterogeneity that may invalidate the interpretations of econometric analysis based on contiguous cross-sectional data was explicitly considered. Very strong and significant university research slipovers are evident in the electronics (SIC 36) and the instruments (SIC 38) industries. These spillovers extend beyond the boundary of the MSA within a 75-mile range from the central city.

In the previous three chapters, the unit of analysis was the region as we focused on R&D spillovers in the framework of a knowledge production function. In the next two chapters, we examine the firms that innovated within these regions using innovation data at the firm level. Both of these chapters build on the data developed in Acs and Audretsch (1991). The purpose of Chapter 5 is to test the effect of the degree of obsolescence on the rate of new product innovation and its significance for tests of the Schumpeterian Hypotheses. Carrying out this test is made difficult by the fact that the degree of obsolescence is difficult to measure. However, since the firm conducts product improvement only if the degree of obsolescence is low, we test the effect of product improvement on profits. Although these preliminary results are weak, they suggest that product improvement reduces the positive effective of firm size on new product innovation and at least partially offsets the negative effect of monopoly profits on new product innovations. This suggests that the degree of obsolescence may be an important determinant of the validity of the Schumpeterian Hypothesis.

The main focus here is the decision to attempt new product innovation at all, considering the opportunity cost embodied in the neglect of current operations. By focusing on the implications of limited entrepreneurial attention, the model ignores other aspects of the innovation production process, such as patent races, optimal timing of innovation and other decision problems which must be addressed once the firm has decided to try to innovate new products. We find preliminary support for the hypothesis that product improvement reduces the positive effect of firm size on new product innovation and sufficient product improvement may reverse the negative effect of monopoly profits on new product innovations. In addition, product improvement reduces the positive effect of technological opportunity on new product innovation.

Chapter 6 examines the impact of innovation-producing firm-specific assets on capital structure in the context of corporate governance. There are reasons to suspect that despite the presence of venture capital funds, there still might be attractive companies that cannot raise capital (Lerner 1998). A growing body of empirical research suggests that new firms, especially technology-intensive ones, may receive insufficient capital. The literature on capital constraints documents that an inability to obtain external finance limits many forms of business investment. Particularly relevant are works by Hall (1992) and Himmelbert and Petersen (1994). These show that capital constraints appear to limit research-and-development expenditures, especially in smaller firms.

This chapter extends research on capital structure in two ways: (1) by introducing innovation as a more complete measure of new investment and asset specificity; and (2) by examining how the relationship between investment, asset specificity and capital structure varies across firm size for a broad spectrum of publicly traded companies. It presents a model that investigates the degree to which capital structure is conditioned by asset specificity, and the extent to which large and small firms respond to different stimuli. The econometric analysis enables the testing of two hypotheses: (1) that innovation is negatively related to capital structure; and (2) that innovation will have a disparate effect on small- and large-firm capital structure choice. The results suggest that innovation is an important determinant of capital structure choice. For large firms, asset specificity is consistent with discretionary governance, but for small firms innovation is associated with a rules-based governance structure.

In the next three chapters, the emphasis shifts from firms back to cities, but no longer in the context of a knowledge production function. The question now is not the effect of spillovers on innovation but, 'How do knowledge spillovers affect high-technology employment growth in cities?' In addition to favorable effects on international competitiveness and their role in structural change, high technology clusters generate considerable regional benefits in terms of jobs, income and economic development. All three chapters use specialized data runs from the US. Department of Labor, Bureau of Labor Statistics to construct data series for 36 cities and six high-technology clusters.

As a way of introducing these data Chapter 7 uses shift-share analysis to examine employment growth for 36 SMSAs between 1988 and 1991. The chapter has two objectives: (1) to utilize the traditional shift-share technique in both absolute and relative terms and illustrate why both are necessary, and (2) to give the first account of the recent trend of high-technology industries in US metropolitan areas. It finds that shift-share analysis is a useful tool to study employment gains and losses in metropolitan areas. Most of the gains and losses in a metropolitan area can be explained by the region's competitiveness component. Moreover, industrial performance varies by size of MSA. In biotechnology and information technology and services small-sized MSAs perform better than medium and large-sized ones. In defense and Aerospace medium-sized MSAs perform better than small- and large-sized MSAs. Finally, in energy and chemicals, large MSAs perform better than medium-sized and small-sized MSAs.

Chapter 8 presents the first estimates of university R&D spillover effects on employment at this level of disaggregation, while controlling for wages, prior innovations, state fixed effects and sample selection bias. There is robust evidence that lagged and disaggregated university R&D is a significant determinant of city high-technology employment. The results also suggest that no non-regional spillover from university research can be detected. Second, real wages and employment are positively related, ceteris paribus. At first blush, these results are quite surprising. However, it is quite consistent with two important features of high-technology industries: that output markets with continual product innovation and imperfect information are far from the traditional model of perfect competition, and that specialized skills are often required in high technology sectors. These within-industry specific skills may not be transferable across industries leading to a positive relationship between wages and employment. This is consistent with increasing returns. Third, we find evidence that innovation is positively related to high-technology employment. However, these results vary by sector. Innovation had the greatest impact on employment in the information and technology sector and the smallest impact in energy and chemicals.

Chapter 9 extends the research in the previous chapter to ask the question, 'What type of economic activity will promote positive externalities and, therefore, economic growth'. This question is important given the debate in the literature about the nature of economic activity and how it affects economic growth. The Marshall–Arrow–Romer (MAR) externality concerns knowledge spillovers between firms in an industry. Arrow (1962) presented an early formulation. The paper by Romer (1986) is a recent and influential statement. Applied to cities by Marshall (1961 [orig. 1890]), this view says that the concentration of an industry in a city facilitates knowledge spillovers between firms and therefore the growth of that industry. According to this approach externalities work within industries. A very different position has been attributed to Jacobs (1969). Jacobs perceives information spillovers between industry clusters to be more important for the firm than within-industry information flows. Heterogeneity, not specialization, is seen as the most important regional growth factor. The MAR hypothesis that industrial R&D does not spill over across regional industry clusters is tested. The results suggest that the channels of knowledge spillover are similar for university and industrial R&D. Both university and industry R&D spillovers operate within, but certainly do not operate across, narrow three-digit industry groupings, thus supporting the specialization thesis in this context.

Chapter 10 looks at the question of whether innovation policy should attempt to be sector-neutral or whether it should be targeted at strategic groups of inter-linked industries, regions or firms that generate synergies through technological spillovers and other externalities. The chapter argues that Nelson's concept of a national system of innovation should be replaced by a concept based more on the importance of local networks. It discusses the origins of local networks, provides evidence of their growing importance and argues that networks often internalize the externalities of the innovation process. The main policy implications of the analysis are that the 'centralized mindset' should be replaced by a bottom-up approach, and that a sub-national infrastructure should be provided to support local interactions.

The final chapter presents a framework for theoretical work that would combine the theoretical work on the new geography with endogenous growth theory and the institutional development of innovation systems.

NOTES

1. Simultaneously and independently several books have appeared that try to identify the underlying processes and interconnections that govern regional innovation (Braczyk et al. 1998; de la Mothe and Pacquet 1999; Ratti et al. 1997; Debresson et al. 1996; Acs 2000). While these books take different approaches, rely on different methodologies, use different data, define the unit of analysis differently, they all suggest that there is something fundamental at work at the regional level. While these works are all interesting, illuminating pieces of the regional innovation puzzle, neither singularly, nor in concert, do they answer the bigger question of 'why some regions are more innovative than others and therefore grow faster.

2. Jaffe (1989), Acs, Audretsch and Feldman (1992, 1994b; Glaeser et al. (1992); Anselin, Varga and Acs (1997, 2000a; Varga (1998) and innovation systems (e.g. Saxenian 1994; Braczyk et al. 1998; Fischer and Varga 1999; Oinas and Malecki 1999; Sternberg 1999; Acs 2000).
3. This section draws heavily on Acs and Varga (forthcoming).
4. This is not a completed survey of an endogenous growth theory. For such surveys see for example Grossman and Helpman (1991); Helpman (1992); Romer (1994); Barro and Sala-I-Martin (1992); Nijkamp and Poot (1997); Aghion and Howitt (1998).
5. If we are concerned with the regional distribution of A then regional systems of innovation are the proper unit of analysis.

2. Knowledge, innovation and firm size

2.1 INTRODUCTION

Just as the economy has been besieged by a wave of technological change that has left virtually no sector of the economy untouched during the last decade, scientific understanding of the innovative process – that is, the manner by which firms innovate, and the impact such technological change has in turn on enterprises and markets – has also undergone a revolution, which, if somewhat quieter, has been no less fundamental. Well into the 1970s, a conventional wisdom about the nature of technological change generally pervaded the economics literature. This conventional wisdom had been shaped largely by scholars such as Joseph Schumpeter and John Kenneth Galbraith.

At the heart of this conventional wisdom was the belief that monolithic enterprises exploiting market power were the driving engine of innovative activity. Schumpeter had declared the debate closed, with his proclamation in 1950 [1942]) that, 'What we have got to accept is that (the large-scale establishment) has come to be the most powerful engine of progress'. Galbraith (1956: 86) echoed Schumpeter's sentiment, 'There is no more pleasant fiction than that technological change is the product of the matchless ingenuity of the small man forced by competition to employ his wits to better his neighbor. Unhappily, it is a fiction.'

While this conventional wisdom about the singular role played by large enterprises with market power prevailed in the economics literature during the first three decades subsequent to the close of the Second World War, more recently there has been a wave of new studies challenging this conventional wisdom (Acs and Audretsch 1987, 1988, 1990b, and 1991).[1] Most importantly, these studies have identified a much wider spectrum of enterprises contributing to innovative activity, and find that, in particular, small entrepreneurial firms as well as large established incumbents play an important role in the process of technological change. There are three major findings:

1. small firms tend to have the innovative advantage in those industries that are highly innovative, where skilled labor is relatively important, and large firms are present (Acs and Audretsch 1987);

2. the greater the extent to which an industry is composed of large firms the greater will be the innovative activity, but, ceteris paribus, the increased innovative activity will tend to emanate more from the small firms than from the large firms (Acs and Audretsch 1988);
3. there does not appear to be any evidence that increasing returns to R&D expenditures exist in producing innovative output. With just several exceptions, diminishing returns to R&D are the rule (Acs and Audretsch 1991).

Taken together, these studies comprise the new learning about innovative activity – both its sources and its consequences (Acs and Audretsch 1993b).

The new learning has raised a number of explanations why smaller enterprises may, in fact, tend to have an innovative advantage, at least in certain industries. Rothwell (1989) suggests that the factors giving small firms innovative advantage generally emanate from the difference in management structures between large and small firms. For example, Scherer (1991) argues that the bureaucratic organization of large firms is not conducive to undertaking risky R&D. The decision to innovate must survive layers of bureaucratic resistance, where an inertia regarding risk results in a bias against undertaking new projects. However, in the small firm the decision to innovate is made by relatively few people.

Second, innovative activity may flourish the most in environments free of bureaucratic constraints (Link and Bozeman 1991). That is, a number of small-firm ventures have benefited from the exodus of researchers who felt thwarted by the managerial restraints in a larger firm. Third, it has been argued that while the larger firms reward the best researchers by promoting them out of research to management positions, the smaller firms place innovative activity at the center of their competitive strategy (Scherer 1991).

Finally, research laboratories of universities provide a source of innovation-generating knowledge that is available to private enterprises for commercial exploitation. Jaffe (1989), for example, found that the knowledge created in university laboratories 'spills over' to contribute to the generation of commercial innovations by private enterprises. The purpose of this chapter is to identify the degree to which university and corporate R&D spills over to small firms at the state level. We find substantial evidence that spillovers are facilitated by the geographic coincidence of universities and research laboratories within the state. Moreover, we find that corporate R&D is a relatively more important source for generating innovation in large firms, while spillovers from university research laboratories are more important in producing innovative activity in small firms.

2.2   STATE PATTERNS OF INNOVATION

While previous research notes that innovative inputs are spatially concentrated, Peter Hall (1985: 11) concludes that the suspicion that product innovations are highly spatially concentrated remains unconfirmed in the literature. The Small Business Association (SBA) data[2] support the long-held notion that product innovations are concentrated in certain locations. Forty-six states plus the District of Columbia were the source of some innovative activity. However, there is significant concentration of activity as eleven states accounted for 81 percent of the 4200 innovations. The states which produced the greatest number of innovations were California (974), New York (456), New Jersey (426), Massachusetts (360), Pennsylvania (245), Illinois (231), Ohio (188), Texas (169), Connecticut (132), Michigan (112) and Minnesota (110).

To normalize for differences in state capacity, innovation can be measured on a per capita or per worker basis. Table 2.1 presents the number of innovations per 100 000 manufacturing employees in 1982, ranked from the most innovative to the least innovative. New Jersey had the highest rate of innovation, followed by Massachusetts and California. These states generated innovations at greater than twice the national rate of 20.34 innovation per 100 000 manufacturing workers. Seven other states, New Hampshire, New York, Minnesota, Connecticut, Arizona, Colorado and Delaware were also more innovative than the national average.

Table 2.2 provides a comparison of states for various measures of innovative activity. Although the alternative measures of innovative activity are highly correlated within states, the relative ranking of states between the categories is very different. Employment-based definitions of innovative industries rank states such as Arizona and Connecticut higher due to the prevalence of high-technology branch plants located there.[3] The patent measure ranks older, industrial states such as Illinois, Michigan and Ohio higher than the innovation measure.[4] This may be due to the fact that the state industrial mix reflects concentrations of industries which exhibit a higher propensity toward patenting. To the degree that innovation citations reflect new commercially viable innovations brought to the market, these other measures may misinterpret the success with which states are the sources of innovative activity.

The noted geographic concentration of innovations is more pronounced when greater industry detail is considered. Table 2.3 presents the distribution of the most innovative three-digit industries by state. For example, the state of California provided 365 innovations for SIC 357: on average, one innovation in the computing machinery industry in California for every day of the year. This was 38.3 percent of the innovations in the computing machinery industry as indicated by column 4. The state of California had a grand total of 974 inno-

Table 2.1   Which states are the most innovative?

State	Innovations	Innovations per 100 000 manufacturing workers
New Jersey	426	52.33
Massachusetts	360	51.87
California	974	46.94
New Hampshire	33	30.84
New York	456	29.48
Minnesota	110	28.65
Connecticut	132	28.51
Arizona	41	27.70
Colorado	42	22.46
Delaware	15	21.13
National	4 200	20.34
Rhode Island	24	18.46
Pennsylvania	245	18.28
Illinois	231	18.16
Texas	169	16.14
Wisconsin	86	15.61
Washington	48	15.38
Ohio	188	15.00
Florida	66	14.60
Oregon	32	14.48

Source: Number of innovations is from the SBA innovation data. Number of manufacturing workers is from the *1982 Census of Manufacturers*.

vations and column 5 reports that the computing machinery industry represented 37.6 percent of the state's innovations.

Location quotients, in the last column of Table 2.3, are used in the literature to assess the extent to which an activity is represented in a geographic area in comparison to its representation in the national economy.[5] An innovation location quotient of 100 indicates that the innovations are equally represented in the state and national economies. A location quotient greater than 100 indicates that the region can be regarded as relatively specialized in that activity. For the seven most innovative three-digit SIC code industries listed in Table 2.3 the average location quotient is 218.39, indicating that overall these areas have achieved some specialized advantage for the industry; indeed, on average, the technological knowledge which entrepreneurs in these areas capitalized on in starting new technology-intensive firms. The

Table 2.2   How do states compare on various measures of innovative activity?

State	Innovation per 100 000 workers	Rank	Patents per 100 000 workers	Rank	% High-tech workers	Rank
Arizona	27.70	8	70.20	19	41	1
California	46.94	3	925.50	1	37	4
Colorado	22.46	9	95.13	16	35	5
Connecticut	28.51	7	312.32	9	39	2
Florida	14.60	18	121.49	14	31	10
Georgia	10.10	27	55.01	22	10	42
Illinois	18.16	13	702.29	4	28	14
Indiana	7.49	34	224.46	10	21	26
Iowa	8.16	32	69.63	20	23	22
Kansas	7.77	33	41.55	24	37	3
Kentucky	3.33	42	59.89	21	17	33
Louisiana	2.39	44	46.70	23	29	13
Massachussetts	51.87	2	383.67	8	33	7
Michigan	11.02	25	494.27	7	15	36
Minnesota	28.65	6	179.94	12	27	16
Missouri	8.20	31	121.20	15	20	27
New Jersey	52.33	1	753.87	3	30	11
New York	29.48	5	818.62	2	22	24
Ohio	15.00	17	572.78	6	22	23
Oklahoma	10.15	26	129.80	13	33	6
Pennsylvania	18.28	12	667.34	5	23	20
Rhode Island	18.46	11	26.93	26	16	35
Utah	11.83	22	29.51	25	31	9
Virginia	9.09	29	85.10	18	26	17
Wisconsin	15.61	16	181.66	11	24	19

Source: Number of innovations is from the SBA Innovation Data.

effect of the location of industrial R&D and academic research on innovative activity will be explored in the next section.

2.3   REAL EFFECTS OF ACADEMIC RESEARCH

A fundamental issue which remains unresolved in the economics of technology is the identification and measurement of R&D spillovers, or the extent to which a firm is able to exploit economically the investment in R&D made by another company. In a 1989 paper in the *American Economic Review*, Adam

Table 2.3   Distribution of three-digit industries by state

Product	(2) State	(3) Count	(4) % of innovations	(5) % of state	(6) Location quotient
Computers SIC 357					n = 954
	California	365	38.3	37.6	167.84
	Massachusetts	82	8.6	22.8	100.44
Measuring and Controlling Instruments SIC 382					n = 668
	California	134	20.1	13.8	126.42
	Massachusetts	94	14.1	26.1	164.15
Communication Equipment SIC 366					n = 376
	California	116	30.9	11.9	132.22
	New York	45	12.0	9.9	110.00
Electrical Components SIC 367					n = 261
	California	128	49.0	13.2	211.29
	Massachusetts	26	10.0	7.2	116.13
Medical Instruments SIC 384					n = 228
	New Jersey	57	25.0	13.5	248.15
	New York	51	22.4	11.2	207.41
General Industrial Machinery and Equipment SIC 356					n = 164
	Pennsylvania	25	15.2	12.3	261.54
	New Jersey	18	11.0	4.0	107.69
Drugs SIC 283					n = 133
	New Jersey	52	39.1	12.3	381.25
	New York	18	13.5	4.0	121.88

Jaffe extended his pathbreaking 1986 study measuring the total R&D 'pool' available for spillovers to identify the contribution of spillovers from university research to 'commercial innovation' (Jaffe 1989: 957). Jaffe's findings were the first to identify the extent to which university research spills over into the generation of inventions and innovations by private firms.

To measure technological change, Jaffe relies upon the number of patented inventions registered at the US patent office, which he argues is 'a proxy for new economically useful knowledge' (Jaffe 1989). In order to relate the response of this measure to R&D spillovers from universities, Jaffe modifies the 'knowledge production function' introduced by Zvi Griliches (1979) for two inputs:

$$\log(K_{ik}) = \beta_{1k} \log(R_{ik}) + \beta_{2k} \log(U_{ik}) + \beta_{3k}[\log(U_{ik}) \times \log(C_{ik})] + e_{ik}$$
$$(2.1)$$

Where K is the number of patented inventions, R represents the private corporate expenditures on R&D, U represents the research expenditures undertaken at universities, C is a measure of the geographic coincidence of university and corporate research, and e represents stochastic disturbance. The unit of observation is at the level of the state, i, and what Jaffe terms the 'technological area', or the industrial sector, k. In addition, Jaffe includes the state population (Pop_{ik}) in his estimating equation in order to control for the size differential across the geographic units of observation.

Jaffe's (1989) statistical results provide evidence that corporate patent activity responds positively to commercial spillovers from university research. Not only does patent activity increase in the presence of high private corporate expenditures on R&D, but also as a result of research expenditures undertaken by universities within the state. The results concerning the role of geographic proximity in spillovers from university research are clouded, however, by the lack of evidence that geographic proximity *within the state* matters as well. According to Jaffe (1989: 968), 'There is only weak evidence that spillovers are facilitated by geographic coincidence of universities and research labs within the state'.

While Jaffe's (1989) model is constructed to identify the contribution of university research to generating 'new economically useful knowledge' (p. 958), F.M. Scherer (1983), Edwin Mansfield (1984) and Griliches (1990) have all warned that measuring the number of patented inventions is not the equivalent of a direct measure of innovative output. For example, Ariel Pakes and Griliches (1980: 378) argued that 'patents are a flawed measure (of innovative output); particularly since not all new innovations are patented and since patents differ greatly in their economic impact'. In addressing the question 'Patents as indicators of what?' Griliches (1990: 1669) concludes that 'Ideally, we might hope that patent statistics would provide a measure of the (innovative) output . . . The reality, however, is very far from it. The dream of getting hold of an output indicator of inventive activity is one of the strong motivating forces for economic research in this area.'

The use of patent counts to identify the effect of spillovers from university research might be expected to be particularly sensitive to what Scherer (1983: 108) has termed the 'propensity to patent'. Just as Albert N. Link and John Rees (1990) found that small new entrepreneurial firms tend to benefit more than their established larger counterparts from university research spillovers, Griliches (1990) and Scherer (1983) both concluded that the propensity to patent does not appear to be invariant across a wide range of firm sizes.

A different and more direct measure of innovative output was introduced in

Acs and Audretsch (1987), where the measure of innovative activity is the number of innovations recorded in 1982 by the US Small Business Administration from the leading technology, engineering and trade journals in each manufacturing industry. A detailed description and analysis of the data can be found in Acs and Audretsch (1988, 1990b). Because each innovation was recorded subsequent to its introduction in the market, the resulting database provides a more direct measure of innovative activity than do patent counts. That is, the innovation database includes inventions that were not patented but were ultimately introduced into the market and excludes inventions that were patented but never proved to be economically viable enough to appear in the market.

The extent to which university research spillovers serve as a catalyst for private-corporation innovative activity can be identified by using the direct measure of innovative activity in the model introduced by Jaffe in equation (2.1). This enables a direct comparison of the influence of university R&D spillovers on innovation with the results that Jaffe reported using the patent measure.

Table 2.4   Comparison among patent, university research, and innovation measures

Measure	Mean	Standard deviation	Minimum	Maximum	Number of innovations yielded per unit of input
University research expenditures (millions of dollars)	98.8	144.0	12.0	710.4	1.3
Drugs	28.5	35.3	2.2	142.3	3.3
Chemicals	5.7	9.7	0.5	46.7	1.9
Electronics	21.0	49.2	0.3	239.0	2.8
Mechanical	12.7	25.6	0.9	126.1	3.5
Corporate patents	879.4	975.7	39.0	3 230.0	0.148
Drugs	71.7	99.4	1.0	418.0	0.132
Chemicals	201.2	249.0	6.0	908.0	0.054
Electronics	225.0	295.3	7.0	1 142.0	0.263
Mechanical	300.8	319.9	20.0	993.0	0.146
Innovations	130.1	206.4	4.0	974.0	–
Drugs	9.5	16.0	0.0	75.0	–
Chemicals	10.9	17.7	0.0	80.0	–
Electronics	59.2	100.5	1.0	475.0	–
Mechanical	44.5	79.7	0.0	416.0	–

Notes: All dollar figures are millions of 1972 dollars. Data on university research funds by state are available for the four broad technical areas of drugs and medical technology; chemicals; electronics, optics and nuclear technology; and mechanical arts. These groups, along with the data for university research expenditures and corporate patents, are from Jaffe (1989).

Table 2.4 compares the mean measures of university research expenditures and corporate patents for all 29 states used by Jaffe with the mean number of innovations per state. It should be noted that, while Jaffe's university-research and patent measures are based upon an eight-year sample (1972–7, 1979 and 1981), the innovation measure is based upon a single year, 1982. Both the number of innovations per university research dollar (millions) and the number of innovations per patent vary considerably across the four industrial sectors included in Jaffe's sample. The number of innovations yielded per dollar of university research is apparently highest in the mechanical industries and lowest in the chemical industries. As in Acs and Audretsch (1988), the amount of innovative activity yielded per patent is highest in the electronics sector and lowest in chemicals.

While Jaffe (1989) was able to pool the different years across each state observation in estimating the production function for patented inventions, this is not possible using the innovation measure, due to data constraints. Thus, it is important first to establish that Jaffe's (1989) results do not differ greatly from estimates for a single year. This is done in equation (i) of Table 2.5, where Jaffe's (1989) patent measure for 1981 is used in the same estimating equation found in his table 4B, based on all (technological) areas. All of the data sources and a detailed description of the data and measures can be found in Jaffe (1989). Using the patent measure for a single year yields virtually identical results to those based on the pooled estimation reported in Jaffe's article. That is, both private corporate expenditures on R&D and expenditures by universities on research are found to exert a positive and significant influence on patent activity. Similarly, both the geographic coincidence effect and the population variables have positive coefficients. The estimated coefficient of 0.668 for $\log(I_i)$ in equation (i) of Table 2.5 is remarkably close to the coefficient of 0.713 estimated by Jaffe using the pooled sample. We conclude that using a single estimation year does not greatly alter the results obtained by Jaffe (1989) using several years to measure the extent of patent activity.

The number of 1982 innovations is substituted for the number of registered patents as the dependent variable in equation (ii) of Table 2.5, which estimates the impact of spillovers on all technological areas combined.[6] There are two important differences that emerge when the innovation measure is used instead of the patent measure. First, the elasticity of $\log(U_{ik})$ almost doubles, from 0.241 when the patent measure is used in equation (i) to 0.431 when the innovation measure is used in equation (ii). That is, the impact of university spillovers is apparently greater on innovations than on patented inventions. Second, the impact of the geographic coincidence effect also is much greater on innovation activity than on patents, suggesting that spillovers from geographic proximity may be more important than Jaffe (1989) concluded.

Table 2.5   A comparison between regression results using Jaffe's patent measure and the innovation measure

Independent variable	All areas		Electronics		Mechanical arts	
	Patents (i)	Innovations (ii)	Patents (iii)	Innovations (iv)	Patents (v)	Innovations (vi)
$Log(I_i)$	0.668	0.428	0.631	0.268	0.643	0.649
	(8.919)	(4.653)	(5.517)	(1.370)	(0.712)	(4.720)
$Log(U_{ik})$	0.241	0.431	0.265	0.520	0.059	0.329
	(3.650)	(6.024)	(2.598)	(2.977)	(0.490)	(1.999)
$Log(U_{ik}) \times Log(C_i)$	0.020	0.173	0.063	0.272	-0.046	0.224
	(0.244)	(1.914)	(0.531)	(1.331)	(-0.046)	(1.436)
$Log(Pop_i)$	0.159	-0.072	0.076	0.076	0.177	-0.143
	(1.297)	(-1.287)	(1.263)	(0.742)	(3.767)	(-0.051)
S:	0.444	0.451	0.203	0.348	0.181	0.247
R^2:	0.959	0.902	0.992	0.951	0.994	0.974
N:	145	125	29	29	27	27

Note: Numbers in parentheses are t statistics.

33

Jaffe (1989) also estimated knowledge production functions for what he calls specific technical areas.[7] Equations (iii) and (iv) in Table 2.5 compare the estimations based on the patent and innovation measures for the electronics area, and equations (v) and (vi) compare the estimations based on the two measures for the mechanical-arts area. The patent and innovation measures yield somewhat different results. For the electronics area, expenditures on R&D by private corporations are found to have a positive and significant influence on patents but not on innovative activity. By contrast, in the mechanical-arts area, both patent and innovative activity respond positively to private R&D spending. This may reflect the difference in what Sidney G. Winter (1984) termed the 'technological regime' between the electronics and mechanical-arts areas. That is, under the 'entrepreneurial regime', the underlying technological information required to produce an innovation is more likely to come from basic research and from outside of the industry. By contrast, under the 'routinized regime', an innovation is more likely to result from technological information from an R&D laboratory within the industry. Since the electronics area more closely corresponds to Winter's notion of the entrepreneurial regime, while the mechanical-arts area more closely resembles the routinized regime, it is not surprising that company R&D expenditures are relatively less important and university expenditures on research are relatively more important in producing innovations in electronics but not in the mechanical arts. Further, as Mansfield (1984: 462) noted, innovations may have a particular tendency not to result from patented inventions in industries such as electronics: 'The value and cost of individual patents vary enormously within and across industries ... Many inventions are not patented. And in some industries, like electronics, there is considerable speculation that the patent system is being bypassed to a greater extent than in the past.'

Substitution of the direct measure of innovative activity for the patent measure in the knowledge production function generally strengthens Jaffe's (1989) arguments and reinforces his findings. Most importantly, use of the innovation data provides even greater support than was found by Jaffe: as he predicted, spillovers are facilitated by the geographic coincidence of universities and research labs within the state. In addition, there is at least some evidence that, because the patent and innovation measures capture different aspects of the process of technological change, results for specific sectors may be, at least to some extent, influenced by the technological regime. Thus, we find that the importance of university spillovers relative to private-company R&D spending is considerably greater in the electronics sector when the direct measure of innovative activity is substituted for the patent measure.

2.4 R&D SPILLOVERS AND RECIPIENT FIRM SIZE

A recent series of studies for both the United States (Acs and Audretsch 1987, 1988 and 1990b) and Great Britain (Pavitt, Robson, and Townsend, 1987) found that while large corporations have the innovative advantage in certain industries, in other markets small firms are more innovative. This finding posed something of a paradox, because it is well known that the bulk of (R&D) is concentrated among the largest industrial corporations (Scherer, 1991). And, according to one of the most prevalent models of technological change (Griliches 1979), innovative output is the product of knowledge-generating inputs, most notably R&D. That small enterprises are the engine of innovative activity in certain industries despite an obvious lack of formal R&D activities,[8] raises the question, 'Where do small firms get the innovation producing inputs?'

One possible answer is from other firms and institutions investing in R&D (Link and Rees. 1990; and Dorfman 1983). An important finding of Jaffe (1986 and 1989) was that investment in R&D made by private corporations and universities 'spills over' for economic exploitation by third party firms. However, while Jaffe (1986 and 1989) identified the extent to which corporate and university research spills over onto the generation of inventions by other firms, he shed little light on which type of firm is the recipient of such spillovers. In other words we would like to explicitly identify the degree to which university and corporate R&D spills over to small firms, and the extent to which university R&D 'spills over' to large firms. By focusing on the recipients of the spillovers, rather than just upon the source, the manner by which large and small firms produce innovations can be more accurately identified.

Five factors favoring the innovative advantage of large enterprises have been identified in the literature. First is the argument that innovative activity requires a high fixed cost. As Comanor (1967) observes, R&D typically involves a 'lumpy' process that yields scale economies. Similarly, Galbraith (1956: 87) argues, 'Because development is costly, it follows that it can be carried on only by a firm that has the resources which are associated with considerable size'.

Second, only firms that are large enough to attain at least temporary market power will choose innovation as a means for maximization (Kamien and Schwartz 1975). This is because the ability of firms to appropriate the economic returns accruing from R&D and other knowledge-generating investments are directly related to the extent of that enterprise's market power (Cohen and Klepper 1991, 1992; Cohen et al. 1987).

Third, R&D is a risky investment; small firms engaging in R&D make themselves vulnerable by investing a large proportion of their resources in a single project. However, their larger counterparts can reduce the risk accompanying innovation through diversification into simultaneous research projects. The larger firm is also more likely to find an economic application of the uncertain outcomes resulting from innovative activity (Nelson 1959).

Fourth, scale economies in production may also provide scope economies for R&D. Scherer (1991) notes that economies of scale in promotion and in distribution facilitate the penetration of new products, thus enabling larger firms to enjoy a greater profit potential from innovation. Finally, an innovation yielding cost reductions of a given percentage results in higher profit margins for larger firms than for smaller firms.

Just as there are persuasive theories defending the original Schumpeterian Hypothesis that large corporations are a prerequisite for technological change, there are also substantial theories predicting that small enterprises should have the innovative advantage, at least in certain industries. First, Rothwell (1989) suggests that the factors giving small firms the innovative advantage generally emanate from the difference in management structures between large and small firms. Scherer (1991) argues that the bureaucratic organization of large firms is not conducive to undertaking risky R&D. The decision to innovate must survive layers of bureaucratic resistance, where an inertia regarding risk results in a bias against undertaking new projects. However, in the small firm the decision to innovate is made by relatively few people.

Second, innovative activity may flourish the most in environments free of bureaucratic constraints (Link and Bozeman 1991). That is, a number of small-firm ventures have benefited from the exodus of researchers who felt thwarted by the managerial restraints in a larger firm. Finally, it has been argued that while the larger firms reward the best researchers by promoting them out of research to management positions, the smaller firms place innovative activity at the center of their competitive strategy. Scherer (1988: 4–5) has summarized the advantages small firms may have in innovative activity:

> Smaller enterprises make their impressive contributions to innovation because of several advantages they possess compared to large-size corporations. One important strength is that they are less bureaucratic, without layers of 'abominable no-man' who block daring ventures in a more highly structured organization. Second, and something that is often overlooked, many advances in technology accumulate on a myriad of detailed inventions involving individual components, materials, and fabrication techniques. The sales possibilities for making such narrow, detailed advances are often too modest to interest giant corporations. An individual entrepreneur's juices will flow over a new product or process with sales prospects in the millions of dollars per year, whereas few large corporations can work up much excitement over such small fish, nor can they accommodate small ventures easily into their organizational structures. Third, it is easier to sustain a fever pitch of excitement in small organization, where the links between challenges, staff, and potential rewards are tight. 'All-nighters' through which tough technical problems are solved expeditiously are common.

The new learning about technological change has raised a number of questions about why smaller enterprises may, in fact, tend to have an innovative advantage over their larger counterparts, at least in certain industries. One answer was suggested by Link and Rees (1990), who surveyed 209 innovating firms to examine the relationship between firm size and university research. They found that, in fact, large firms are more active in university-based research. However, small- and medium-sized enterprises are apparently better able to exploit their university-based associations to generate innovations. Link and Rees (1990: 25) conclude that there are diseconomies of scale in the production of innovations, due to the 'inherent bureaucratization process which inhibits both innovative activity and the speed with which new inventions move through the corporate system towards the market'.

According to the model of technological change introduced by Griliches (1979), innovative output is the product of knowledge-generating inputs. Jaffe modified this production function approach for adoption to a model specified for spatial and product dimensions:

$$K_{si} = R_{si}^{\beta 1} * U_{si}^{\beta 2} * (UR_{si} * GC_{si})^{\beta 3} * e_{si} \qquad (2.2)$$

where K is innovative output, R is private corporate expenditures on R&D, U the research expenditures undertaken at universities, and e represents a stochastic error term. The unit of observation is at the spatial level, s, and product level, i.[9] To overcome the conceptual problem of using state-level data to measure geographic spillovers, Jaffe constructs an index of the geographic coincidence of university and industrial research labs, GC.[10] Jaffe argued that the proximity of university research to corporate laboratories should raise the potency of spillovers from the universities.

As we saw in the previous section, using the number of patented inventions to proxy innovative activity, Jaffe (1989) estimated equation (2.1) and found that university research does, in fact, spill over to promote corporate patent activity. That is, not only does patent activity increase in the presence of high private corporate expenditures on R&D, but also from research expenditures undertaken by universities within the state.

Jaffe's results made it clear that spillovers play an important role as an input in generating innovations in third-party firms,[11] but they shed little light on the recipients of the spillovers. By estimating equation (2.2) for the innovative activity contributed by large firms separately from the innovative activity contributed by small firms, and directly comparing the magnitude of the coefficients of R, UR and $U * GC$, the relative importance of R&D spillovers from universities and corporate laboratories for large and small firms can be explicitly ascertained.

Although Jaffe (1989) used patent counts to proxy innovative activity, we use a direct measure – the number of innovations in 1982. Griliches (1990), Scherer (1983) and Mansfield (1984) have all observed that patent counts measure an intermediate output in the entire process of producing an innovation.

In contrast to patent data, which mark the certification of an invention, innovation citations announce the market introduction of a commercially viable product.[12] Thus, the resulting database provides a more direct measure of innovative activity than does the number of patented inventions. Not only are inventions which were not patented but ultimately introduced into the market included in the database, but those inventions which were patented but never developed into innovations are excluded.

The innovation data are classified according to the size of the innovating firm. Large firms are defined as having at least 500 employees, and small firms are defined as having fewer than 500 employees. Innovations are attributed to the state in which the establishment responsible for the commercial development of the innovation is located. The database distinguishes between the location of the innovating establishment and the location of the parent firm. In the case of a multi-establishment firm, the innovation would be classified by size on the basis of the employment of the entire parent firm, but would be located at the innovating establishment and not at the headquarters of the parent firm.

Table 2.6 ranks the states according to innovative activity and shows the distribution of innovations across large and small firms, along with the corresponding industry R&D expenditures and expenditures on research by universities. The two innovative inputs included in Table 2.6 are taken from Jaffe (1989). The industry and university expenditures are based upon the average value measured (in constant 1972 million dollars) over the eight-year period. 1972–7, 1979 and 1981. We follow Jaffe (1989) by including the population of each state to control for size differentials across the geographic unit of observation. We also include the geographic coincidence index to control for within-state variation. The geographic coincidence index is explained and documented by Jaffe (1989: 959) and our note 10. While Jaffe rescaled the index 'for estimation purposes' so that its log had a mean of zero, we see no advantage in doing so and leave the geographic coincidence index unscaled.

The dependent variable is the number of innovations (alternatively by all firms, by large firms and by small firms) in a specific technological area and within a particular state. Since data are available for five technological areas over 29 states, the entire sample size is 145 observations.[13] There are no innovations registered for certain technological areas within particular states. Thus, equation (I) is estimated using the Tobit model. The results for the innovative output for all firms and separately for large and small firms are shown in Table 2.7.[14]

The first equation estimates the innovative activity of all firms, the second

Table 2.6 *Innovative output in large and small firms and R&D inputs by state[a]*

State	Total innovations	Large firm innovations	Small firm innovations	Industry R&D expenditures	University research
California	974	315	659	3 883	710.4
New York	456	180	276	1 859	371.0
New Jersey	426	162	264	1 361	70.8
Massachusetts	360	148	212	954	245.3
Pennsylvania	245	104	141	1 293	139.2
Illinois	231	100	131	894	254.9
Ohio	188	76	112	926	76.2
Connecticut	132	77	55	650	54.7
Michigan	112	61	51	1 815	103.2
Minnesota	110	64	46	399	55.7
Wisconsin	86	33	53	224	65.0
Florida	66	21	45	375	70.1
Georgia	53	20	33	78	57.8
Indiana	49	20	29	398	51.3
Colorado	42	13	29	167	77.2
Arizona	41	23	18	201	37.4
Virginia	38	19	19	207	45.9
North Carolina	38	16	22	193	64.6
Rhode Island	24	4	20	32	14.9
Oklahoma	20	12	8	93	19.9
Iowa	20	12	8	135	46.4
Kansas	15	3	12	66	26.6
Utah	11	2	9	72	32.5
Nebraska	9	1	8	9	20.4
Kentucky	9	6	3	72	17.5
Louisiana	5	0	5	65	33.4
Arkansas	5	5	0	9	12.0
Alabama	5	0	5	54	28.3
Mississippi	4	1	3	420	61.4

Note: [a] Industry R&D and university research expenditures are in millions of 1972 dollars and are taken from Jaffe (1989). Data are available for 29 states.

equation estimates the innovative activity of large firms and the third equation estimates the innovative activity of small firms. Regardless of firm size, the knowledge production function for innovative output holds. Additional inputs in knowledge-generating R&D, both by private corporations and by universities, lead to increases in innovative output.

However, the relative importance of industry R&D and university research as inputs in generating innovative output clearly varies between large and small firms. That is, for large firms, not only is the elasticity of innovative activity with respect to industry R&D expenditures more than two times

Table 2.7   Tobit regressions of innovative activity by state and technological area

	(1) All firms	(2) Large firms	(3) Small firms
Log Industry (R)	0.615	0.950	0.550
	(5.457)[b]	(7.133)[b]	(4.184)[b]
Log (U)	0.550	0.446	0.661
	(5.635)[b]	(4.569)[b]	(5.848)[b]
Log Geographic Coincidence	0.089	0.033	0.111
× University Research	(1 .802)[a]	(0.687)	(1.965)[b]
Log *Pop*	−0.246	−0.554	−0.314
	(−3.653)[b]	(−6.558)[b]	(−3.9 14)[b]
Log-likelihood	−233.21	−202.19	−225.86
Sample size	145	145	145

Note: t-statistics listed in parentheses.
[a] Statistically significant at the 90 percent level of confidence for a two-tailed test.
[b] Statistically significant at the 95 percent level of confidence for a two-tailed test.

greater than the elasticity with respect to expenditures on research by universities, but it is nearly twice as large as the elasticity of small-firm innovative activity with respect to industry R&D. By contrast, for small firms the elasticity of innovative output with respect to expenditures on research by universities is about one-fifth greater than the elasticity with respect to industry R&D. And the elasticity of innovative activity with respect to university research is about 50 percent greater for small enterprises than for large corporations.[15]

These results support the hypothesis that private corporation R&D plays a relatively more important role in generating innovative activity in large corporations than in small firms.[16] By contrast, spillovers from the research activities of universities play a more decisive role in the innovative activity of small firms.

Geographic proximity between university and corporate laboratories within a state clearly serves as a catalyst to innovative activity for firms of all sizes. However, the impact is apparently greater on small firms than on large firms. The elasticity of innovative activity with respect to the geographic coincidence index multiplied by university research is nearly four times greater for small firms than for their larger counterparts.

A particular concern with the estimates in Table 2.7 is multicollinearity between the log of industrial R&D expenditures and the log of university research expenditures. The simple correlation coefficient between the two variables is 0.61. When the log of industry R&D is omitted from the regressions, the coefficient of the log of university research rises somewhat to 0.592 (*t*-ratio of 8.733) in estimating large-firm innovative activity and to 0.828 (*t*-ratio of 8.036) in estimating small-firm innovative activity. Similarly, when the log of university research is omitted from the regressions, the coefficient of the log of industry R&D rises to 1.289 (*t*-ratio of 9.541) in estimating large-firm innovative activity and to 0.790 (*t*-ratio of 10.465) in estimating small-firm innovative activity. Thus, even when only one source of knowledge-generating R&D is included in the regression equation, the results hold. The innovative activity of small enterprises responds more to university research, while the innovative activity of large corporations responds more to industry R&D.[17]

2.5   EXPANDING THE KNOWLEDGE PRODUCTION FUNCTION

Griliches (1979) introduced a model of technological innovation which views innovative output as the product of knowledge-generating inputs. Jaffe (1989) modified this production function approach to consider spatial and technical area dimensions. However, Jaffe's model only considers what were previously defined as the elements of the formal knowledge base. Such a formulation does not consider other types of knowledge inputs which contribute to the realization of innovative output. This is important since innovation requires both technical and business knowledge if profitability is to be the guide for making investments in research and development. Following the innovation knowledge base conceptual model, a more complete specification of innovative inputs would include

$$\log(K_{ik}) = \beta_{1k} \log(R_{ik}) + \beta_{2k} \log(U_{ik}) + \beta_{3k}(BUS_k) + \beta \log(VA_{ik}) + e_{ik}$$
(2.3)

where i indexes industry and k indexes the spatial unit of observation. K_{ik} is the number of patents or innovations for industry i, in a state, k. VA_k is the tacit knowledge embodied by the industry's presence in an area. BUS_k represents the presence of business services that represent a link to commercialization.

The last input in the knowledge base model is the most evasive. There is a variety of producer services that provide knowledge to the market and the commercialization process. For example, the services of patent attorneys are a critical input to the innovation process. Similarly, marketing information plays an important role in the commercialization process.

2.6   CONCLUSIONS

The findings in this chapter provide some insight into the puzzle posed by the recent wave of studies identifying vigorous innovative activity emanating from small firms in certain industries. How are these small, and frequently new, firms able to generate innovative output while undertaking generally negligible amounts of investment in knowledge-generating inputs, such as R&D? At least one answer, implied by the findings in this chapter, is that small firms innovate through exploiting knowledge created by expenditures on research in universities and on R&D in large corporations.

The empirical results suggest that the innovative output of all firms rises along with an increase in the amount of R&D inputs, both in private corporations as well as in university laboratories. However, R&D expenditures made by private companies play a particularly important role in providing inputs to the innovative activity of large firms, while expenditures on research made by universities serve as an especially key input for generating innovative activity in small enterprises. Apparently large firms are more adept at exploiting knowledge created in their own laboratories, while their smaller counterparts have a comparative advantage at exploiting spillovers from university laboratories.

NOTES

1. The state of knowledge regarding technological change has generally been shaped by the nature of the data, which were available to scholars for analysis. Such data have always been incomplete and, at best, represented only a proxy measure reflecting some aspect of the process of technological change. Measures of technological change have typically involved one of the three major aspects of the innovation process: (1) a measure of inputs into the innovation process, such as R&D expenditures, or else the share of the labor force accounted for by employees involved in R&D activity; (2) an intermediate output, such as the number of inventions which have been patented; or (3) a direct measure of innovative output.
2. For a discussion of the SBA data at the state level, see Feldman (1994).
3. Estimates of employment in high technology industry are for the year 1977 from Amy Glasmeier (1985). This measure has a correlation coefficient of 0.4474 with innovations and 0.3201 with patents.
4. Patent counts are from Jaffe (1989) and represent the average annual corporate patenting activity for a state for the years 1972–7, 1979 and 1981. Jaffe only provides data for 29 states and ranking here reflects the relative position out of the 29 listed cases.
5   The innovation location quotation, listed in column 6, is calculated as the percentage of innovation in a state accounted for by an industry, divided by the percentage of national innovations accounted for by that industry:

$$LQ_{is} = \frac{\lambda_{is}}{\displaystyle\sum_{s=1}^{50} \lambda_{is}} * 100$$

where λ_{is}, the numerator, is the percentage of the innovations in a state, s accounted for by the industry, i. The denominator is the percentage of national innovations accounted for by that industry. The ratio is then multiplied by 100.

6. The sample sizes differ between the patent and innovation estimations because the observations with the value of zero had to be omitted.

7. The technological areas are based on a technological classification and not on an industrial classification. For further explanation see appendix A in Jaffe (1989).

8. Kleinknecht (1987 and 1989) has found that informal R&D activity plays a larger role in small firms than in large enterprises.

9. Jaffe (1989) used 'technological areas' for the product dimension.

10. The geographic coincidence index is calculated as

$$GC_s = \frac{\sum UNIV_{ci} TP_{ci}}{\left[\sum_c UNIV_{ci}^2 \right]^{1/2} \left[\sum_c TP_{ci}^2 \right]^{1/2}}$$

where TP_{ci} is the total number of industrial R&D lab workers in a city or SMSA. The geographic coincidence index is calculated as the uncentered correlation of the vectors U_i and TP_i across SMSAs within a state. Jaffe's (1989) hypothesis is that research will yield more innovative activity if university and industrial labs are geographically concentrated. For example, more patents would be expected in Illinois, where industrial and research labs are concentrated around Chicago, than in Indiana where university labs are located in different SMSAs from industrial labs.

11. Acs, Audretsch and Feldman (1992) confirm that Jaffe's results for R&D spillovers onto patenting activity hold using the direct measure of innovative activity used in this chapter.

12. Another distinction is that an innovating firm did not necessarily make the invention.

13. For a detailed description of these technological areas as well as the manner by which they were selected, see Jaffe (1989, appendix A).

14. The logarithmic transformation of the left-hand side of equation (I) uses a linear transformation of $((I_{si} + 1) * 10)$. The Tobit censoring boundary is set to correspond to a zero observation.

15. There may be greater measurement error for the small-firm equation because large firms generate most of the state R&D expenditures. The size of any resulting bias is difficult to predict.

16. There is a statistically discernible difference in the coefficients of industry R&D for small and large firms at the 95 percent level of confidence using a two-tailed test.

17. For a study comparing patents and innovations at the MSA level see Acs, Anselin and Varga (2002).

3. Local geographic spillovers

3.1 INTRODUCTION

The accumulation of knowledge and its spillover into productive capacity through technological change is a central theme in the new theory of endogenous economic growth (Romer 1986, 1990, 1994; Grossman and Helpman 1991, 1994). An interesting aspect of this perspective has been the renewed attention to the geographic scope of the spillovers between knowledge creation and production, or, the extent of Marshallian spatial externalities as exemplified in the new economic geography of David and Rosenbloom (1990), Krugman (1991), Glaeser et al. (1992), and others. In urban and regional economics, a large number of empirical studies have focused on the creation of knowledge, on research and development activities (R&D), and on technological innovation as determinants of various aspects of local and regional economies. Examples are analyses of the location of R&D facilities and high-technology production, and the effect of universities and technology parks on characteristics of the labor market and regional growth (e.g. Malecki 1981, 1986, 1991); Markusen et al. 1986; Andersson et al. 1990; Goldstein and Luger 1990; Luger and Goldstein 1991; Glasmeier 1991; Florax 1992).

An important aspect of studies of technological innovation at the regional scale is the role of spatial interaction and spatial structure, as expressed in the form of organizational networks of innovators, regional innovation complexes and regional knowledge infrastructure (e.g. Stohr 1986; Von Hippel 1988; Storper and Walker 1989; DeBresson and Amesse 1992; Feldman 1994; Saxenian 1994). Universities play a central role in this process, not only as producers of basic research, but also by creating human capital in the form of higher skilled labor. Both of these aspects have received considerable attention in the literature, from a theoretical as well as from an empirical perspective. The importance of basic (university) research in the stimulation of technological innovation (and higher productivity) is derived from the public-good nature of the research, and the resulting positive externalities to the private sector in the form of knowledge spillovers. The initial conceptualization of this process was provided by Arrow (1962) and Nelson (1959) and further refined by Griliches (1979), Nelson (1982), Von Hippel (1988), Cohen and

Levinthal (1989), among others (for recent reviews, see e.g. Dosi 1988; Acs and Audretsch 1990b; Griliches 1990, 1992; Mansfield 1991; Florax 1992; Feldman 1994). The role of universities in the development of human capital that is more likely to create technological innovations is highlighted in the work of Bartel and Lichtenberg (1987) and Lucas (1988), among others. Both the knowledge spillovers and the human capital development constitute important locational attractors for private sector R&D and for high-technology production (Malecki 1991).

While conceptually clear, the role of universities as 'engines of growth' or 'regional boosters' (Florax 1992), is not uniformly confirmed by empirical studies. A significant and positive effect of the presence of universities is found on the location of high technology production, new start-ups and R&D facilities in, among others, Malecki (1986), Nelson (1986), Lund (1986), Rees and Stafford (1986), Harding (1989), Bania, Calkins and Dalenberg (1992), Parker and Zilberman (1993), but others have either qualified these findings or did not discover such a relationship. For example, Link and Rees (1990), Rees (1991), and Malecki and Bradbury (1992) point out that the locational attraction may show little relationship to the research activities of universities, but instead may be determined by their teaching and training roles. Others, such as Howells (1987), Markusen, Hall and Glasmeier (1986), Glasmeier (1991), Florax and Folmer (1992), Bania, Eberts and Fogarty (1993) and Beeson and Montgomery (1993), find a weak, inconsistent (across sectors) or no relationship at all between the university research activities and high-technology (or R&D) location, or other regional variables such as manufacturing investment, local labor market conditions and high technology start-ups. A number of explanations have been offered for this lack of uniform evidence, such as the difficulty of quantifying the inputs and outputs in a 'knowledge production function' (Griliches 1990) and various sectoral and spatial aggregation problems (e.g. as argued in Markusen et al. 1986: 156).

The goal of our chapter is to shed further light on this issue by focusing on the spatial extent of the 'local' geographic effects that university research (at both private and public universities) may have on the innovative capacity in a region, both directly and indirectly through its interaction with private sector R&D efforts. Our conceptual framework is based on the knowledge production function of Griliches (1979) and is implemented at an aggregate level, as in other recent studies of this phenomenon by Jaffe (1989), Acs, Audretsch and Feldman (1992, 1994a, 1994b), and Feldman and Florida (1994). This chapter extends the empirical evidence in two important respects:

1. We broaden the cross-sectional basis for empirical analysis by utilizing data for 43 states (compared to 29 in the above-mentioned studies) and for 125 metropolitan statistical areas (MSAs). This is the first time

MSA-level data are used in this type of analysis, which avoids many problems associated with the inappropriate spatial scale of a state as the areal unit of analysis. MSA-level results are obtained by using R&D laboratory employment as a proxy for R&D activity, based on a specially compiled data set.

2. We focus on more precise measures of local geographic spillovers. At the state level, we introduce several alternatives to Jaffe's (1989) 'geographic coincidence index' that are more tightly integrated with the existing body of spatial interaction theory, and are able to significantly improve on his results. At the MSA scale, we formalize the spatial extent of the geographic spillovers by means of so-called spatial lag variables that capture the research activities in concentric rings around the MSA as well as in the MSA itself.

In the remainder of the chapter, we first introduce the formal model of the knowledge production function and briefly review current empirical evidence on geographic knowledge spillovers of universities. We next elaborate on the data set used in the study. Subsequently, we present the results of our analysis at the state level and at the MSA level, focusing in particular on our alternative definitions of spatial interaction. We conclude with a summary and evaluation of our findings.

3.2   THE KNOWLEDGE PRODUCTION FUNCTION

3.2.1   Model

The conceptual framework for analyzing geographic spillovers of university research on regional innovative capacity is based on the knowledge production function of Griliches (1979) (see also Jaffe 1986, 1989). In essence, this is a two-factor Cobb-Douglas production function that relates an output measure for 'knowledge' to two input measures: research and development performed by industry; and research performed by universities. Formally, this is expressed as:

$$\log(K) = \beta_k \log(R) + \beta_k \log(U) + \varepsilon_k \tag{3.1}$$

where K is a proxy for knowledge output (either patents or innovation counts), R is industry R&D and U is university research, with ε_k as a stochastic error term. The analysis is typically carried out for aggregate cross-sectional units (e.g. states), possibly for several points in time and/or disaggregated by sector.

Following Jaffe (1989), the potential interaction between university and industry research is captured by extending the model with two additional equations that allow for simultaneity between these two variables:

$$\log(K) = \beta_{R1} \log(R) + \beta_{R2}Z_1 + \varepsilon_R \qquad (3.2)$$

and

$$\log(K) = \beta_{U1} \log(U) + \beta_{R2}Z_2 + \varepsilon_U \qquad (3.3)$$

where U and R are as before, Z_1 and Z_2 are sets of exogenous local characteristics, and ε_U and ε_R are stochastic error terms.

Jaffe (1989) introduced an additional term in (3.1) to compensate for the inappropriateness of using states as the units of observation. This acknowledges that states are too large to accurately capture the local spatial interaction between universities and firms. The additional term consists of the product of the logarithms of a 'geographic coincidence index' *(C)* and university research. This term therefore adjusts the magnitude of university research in the state by a measure of the extent to which private and university research coincide in space (we return to a more detailed specification of this term below). The extended 'geographic' knowledge production function then becomes:

$$\log(K) = \beta_{K1} \log(R) + \beta_{K2} \log(U) + \beta_{K3}[\log(U).\log(C)] + \varepsilon_K \qquad (3.4)$$

in the same notation as before.

The framework expressed in equations (3.2) to (3.4) has become the basis of several empirical investigations, which we will briefly review in the next section. Before proceeding, however, note that the geographic interaction term in (3.4) is an artifact of using states as the unit of analysis and is not needed when the spatial units of observation correspond more closely to the spatial scale of interaction between firms and universities. For example, this may be the case when the analysis is carried out at the MSA or county scale.

3.2.2 Previous Empirical Evidence

Almost all empirical investigations of geographic knowledge spillovers of universities in the United States have been aggregate in nature and based on the Griliches–Jaffe knowledge production function framework applied at the state level. A few notable exceptions are studies that use micro-data derived from surveys or patent information, for example, Mansfield (1995), Jaffe, Trajtenberg and Henderson (1993) and Almeida and Kogut (1995). These studies all provide strong evidence of the importance of spatial interaction at the *local* level. However, this does not find uniform confirmation in the aggregate studies. As noted above, this may be somewhat due to the fact that the unit of analysis – the state – only partially captures this interaction. We argue in this chapter that it is also due to the formal specification of local spatial interaction in the form of a geographic coincidence index.

The empirical studies in the literature vary somewhat in terms of research design, but they all find a strong and positive relationship between innovative activity and both industry R&D and university research at the state level. However, the situation is different in terms of the significance of a *local* geographic spillover effect. Overall, the evidence is non-existent, weak or mixed, only pertaining to a few individual sectors (e.g. in Jaffe (1989) for only two out of four sectors considered).

We suggest that, in part, this lack in the evidence for local geographic spillovers (which contradicts the strong findings in micro-level studies) is due to the specification of the geographic effects in the model. All studies use the idea initially suggested in Jaffe (1989: 959) where the product of the logarithm of state-level university expenditures with the logarithm of a geographic coincidence index is used. The latter is obtained as the uncentered correlation coefficient (i.e. without subtracting the mean) between university research and professional employees in R&D labs for the SMSAs in the state (i.e. R&D and university research outside SMSAs are not included in the computation of the index). The resulting index is rescaled such that its mean is zero. While the coincidence index may make intuitive sense, it is unrelated to the existing large body of research on spatial interaction and measures of spatial accessibility (for a recent review, see e.g. Frost and Spence 1995; Talen and Anselin 1997). We will therefore consider the extent to which alternative indices provide a clarification of this issue.

3.3   DATA AND VARIABLE DEFINITIONS

We extend previous empirical evidence by using a detailed data set on innovation counts and R&D employment at both the state and MSA scale of geographic aggregation. We use a count of innovations as the dependent variable in the geographic knowledge production function (K in (3.4)), constructed from the US Small Business Administration Innovation Database.

At the sectoral scale, the innovation data were aggregated to the two-digit SIC code level. Our interest focused on innovations in the 'high technology' sector as an aggregate. Clearly, this is not an unambiguous determination and a number of different classifications have been suggested in the literature (e.g. Premus 1982; Herzog et al. 1986); Malecki 1986; Glasmeier 1991). In general, the objective is to identify sectors dominated by the importance of non-routine functions, in contrast to standardized mass production. A number of criteria to identify such sectors have been suggested in the literature, such as the percentage of scientists and engineers employed, and the number of innovations per employee. At the two-digit SIC level, it is virtually impossible to designate sectors as 'pure' high technology, although the SIC codes 28 and SIC 35–8 contain most of the commonly identified high-technology sectors at the more appropriate three- and four-digit level (see e.g. Herzog et al. 1986). We consequently proceeded to use the aggregate of these five SIC codes as 'high technology'. To the extent that the sectoral mix in these sectors shows systematic variation over space in terms of its 'pure' high-tech content, our results on the relationship between innovation and research could be affected. However, we are confident that we will be able to detect such systematic variations by means of careful specification tests for spatial effects (Anselin 1988; Anselin and Bera 1997).

Earlier studies of the aggregate knowledge production function were limited to data for 29 US states as shown in Table 3.1 and Table 3.2. This was not due to the lack of data on innovations or patents (for which actual addresses are available), but to data limitations for the explanatory variables in the model, in particular for the variable on private R&D expenditures (R in equations (3.2) and (3.4)). Instead, we constructed a proxy for industrial R&D activity on the basis of data on professional employment in high-technology

Table 3.1   Research design characteristics in recent studies

Characteristic	Jaffe	AAF-92	AAF-94	FF
Space	29 US states	29 US states	29 US states	29 US states
Time	8 years (1972–7, 1979, 1981)	1982	1982	1982
Sectors	pooled + 4	pooled + 2	pooled	pooled
Coincidence index	$\log U \times \log C$ (C centered)	$\log U \times \log C$ (C centered)	$\log U \times \log C$ (C uncentered)	C (share of state manufacturing shipments by largest MSA)
Auxiliary variables	population	population	population	related industry
				industry sales business
Estimation	OLS/3SLS	OLS	tobit	3SLS
Zeros	$\log(y) = -1$	dropped	included	$\log (10(y+1))$
Spatial diagnostics	none	none	none	Durbin-Watson

Table 3.2   Significance of local geographic spillovers in recent studies

Study	Dependent variable	*t*-statistic for local geographic spillover
Jaffe	patents	3.18
AAF-92	patents	0.244
AAF-92	innovations	1.914
AAF-94	innovations (all firms)	1.802
AAF-94	innovations (large firms)	0.687
AAF-94	innovations (small firms)	1.965
FF	innovations	5.40

Note: *t*-statistics computed from listed standard errors when not given in original study.

research laboratories in the Bowker directories (Jaques Cattell Press 1982). While imperfect, this approach allowed us to construct a private R&D variable for 43 US states and for 125 MSAs (see also Bania et al. 1992: 218–19, for a similar approach). As it turns out, our proxy variable is remarkably similar to the R&D expenditure variable used in Jaffe (1989), yielding a correlation of 0.91 for the 29 states common to both studies (the data on innovations, private R&D employment and university research expenditures for 43 US states in 1982 are listed in Appendix B). Clearly, the use of lab employment as a proxy for expenditures assumes a constancy of the labor intensity and capital/labor ratio of R&D across the units of observation. Again, to the extent that this is not the case, it will tend to yield misspecifications in the form of heteroskedastic and/or spatially autocorrelated error terms, which will merit special attention in our analysis.

Our data for university research expenditures (U in equations (3.3) and (3.4)) follow the common approach in the literature and are compiled from the NSF Survey of Scientific and Engineering Expenditures at Universities and Colleges for the year 1982 (National Science Foundation 1982). In addition, this data set also provides the source for exogenous variables used in the estimation of equation (3.3) at the MSA level: a proxy for the overall academic quality of high-technology departments at universities, *RANK;* and a proxy for size, the total enrollment at universities, *ENRL.* We also consider data for total educational expenditures, *EDEXP,* from the *County and City Data Book.* We match the sectoral aggregation of the two-digit SIC industries to university departments using the same approach as in Feldman (1994: 58).

In addition, we also included a number of variables compiled from County Business Pattern data for 1982: high-technology employment, *HTEMP;* a location quotient for high-technology employment, *LQ;* employment in business services (SIC 73), *BUS;* and the percentage of 'large' firms (i.e. firms with employment exceeding 500), *LARGE.* Following general practice in the literature, the first three variables are included to capture agglomeration economies (see also Feldman and Florida 1994), the last one to assess the effect of firm scale (see also Acs et al. 1994a). A proxy for the coincidence of R&D and headquarter locations is a dummy variable for the presence of at least ten headquarters of Fortune 500 companies in an MSA, *FORTUNE,* compiled from the 2 May 1982 listing in *Fortune Magazine.*

Our final data set only included those MSAs for which there were innovations in the high-technology sector as well as both private industry R&D and university research expenditures (see Appendix C for a listing of the MSAs, innovation counts and research data). This results in 125 MSAs being considered that meet the three criteria, an almost complete match of university MSAs (125 out of 130), and a better than 70 per cent portion of both the innovative MSAs (169) and the R&D MSAs (159). This selection leaves out a number of important non-MSA university locations, such as Ithaca, New York, and State College, Pennsylvania, but it covers more than 80 per cent of the relevant interaction (92 per cent of all university research is in the 130 university MSAs). This limitation also excludes from consideration the joint determination of 'location' and 'magnitude' of high-technology innovation and research. On the other hand, it avoids the problem of 'zeros', and is motivated by a focus on the strength of interaction between the two forms of research and the generation of innovations where these are present. In other words, we address the strength and spatial extent of local geographic spillovers for metropolitan areas where an innovative complex is already in place. We leave the explanation of the more complex issue of the establishment and absence of these links for future research.

3.4 LOCAL GEOGRAPHIC SPILLOVERS AT THE STATE LEVEL

3.4.1 Alternative State-Level Geographic Coincidence Indicators

In addition to the familiar Jaffe indicator of geographic coincidence, we considered four alternative measures of local spatial interaction between university and industry research for states. One is constructed similarly to Jaffe's approach, in that the log of a coincidence index is multiplied by the log of university research expenditures at the state level. However, rather than the uncentered correlation coefficient between university research and total professional employees in R&D laboratories for the MSAs in the state, we used the proportion of counties where industry research (proxied by R&D lab employment) and university research are co-located (out of all counties with university research). Formally, for state *s:*

$$CUR = \Sigma_i \, \delta R_i \delta U_i \, / \, \Sigma_i \, \delta U_i \qquad (3.5)$$

where the summation is over counties, and δR_i and δU_i are Kronecker deltas that take on a value of 1 when respectively $RI > 0$ and $UI > 0$, and a value of zero otherwise. In contrast to the Jaffe index, CUR also includes information on counties that do not belong to an MSA in the state.

The other three measures are more closely related to traditional accessibility indices from spatial interaction theory (see e.g. Weibull 1976). The first is a gravity or potential measure with distance decay parameter 2 (see also Sivitanidou and Sivitanides 1995 for a slightly different approach) for each industry R&D county in a state with respect to all university counties:

$$GRAV_i = \Sigma_j \, U_j \, / \, (d_{ij})^2 \qquad (3.6)$$

where i is an index for each industry R&D county in the state, j an index for each university county, U is as before and d_{ij} is the distance between the two counties. When an industry and university county coincide, no distance decay is applied to the U_i variable to avoid the familiar self-potential problem (e.g. Frost and Spence 1995). To obtain an index for each state, an average is taken over all counties in the state for which $GRAV_I > 0$.

The other two indices are based on the notion of 'covering', that is, a measure of how much university research is carried out in counties within a given distance band of an industry R&D county (note that the university counties do not need to be within the same state):

$$COV_i = \Sigma_j \, \delta_{ij} U_j \qquad (3.7)$$

where δ_{ij} takes on a value of 1 when d_{ij} is less than or equal to a critical 'covering' distance, respectively 50 and 75 miles in our application. Again, to obtain an index for a state, an average is taken over all industry R&D counties in the state.

The computation of the indices was carried out by means of the access functions in the SpaceStat software (Anselin 1995) from data on boundary files for US counties.

3.42 Empirical Results

In Table 3.3, we present the results of the estimation of a cross-sectional regression of the geographic knowledge production function (3.4) for 43 US

Table 3.3   Regression results for log(innovations) at the state level (N = 43, 1982)

Model	Jaffe (OLS)	Jaffe (ML-SER)	*CUR* (OLS)	*GRAV* (OLS)	*COV*(50) (OLS)	*COV*(75) (OLS)
Constant	−7.079	−7.084	−7.117	−10.181	−7.205	−8.386
	(0.100)	(0.093)	(1.032)	(1.574)	(1.001)	(1.103)
Log(R)	0.508	0.549	0.396	0.350	0.451	0.375
	(0.100)	(0.098)	(0.110)	(0.110)	(0.095)	(0.104)
Log(U)	0.574	0.544	0.676	0.633	0.402	0.549
	(0.142)	(0.129)	(0.144)	(0.133)	(0.153)	(0.133)
Log(Local	0.0266	0.0164	0.0463	0.301	0.268	0.255
Spillover	(0.030)	(0.027)	(0.026)	(0.121)	(0.109)	(0.100)
λ		0.507				
		(0.218)				
R^2-adj	0.820		0.831	0.841	0.841	0.843
Log-Lik	−41.99	−39.91	−40.62	−39.28	−39.31	−39.08
White	6.29		9.09	5.42	6.91	5.38
LM-Err	5.40		1.01	0.84	0.60	0.52
	(IDIS2)		(D500)	(IDIS2)	(D500)	(D500)
LM-Lag	0.91	0.48	0.56	1.90	0.02	0.48
	(CONT)	(IDIS2)	(CONT)	(D500)	(D500)	(D500)

Notes: Estimated standard errors are in parentheses; critical value for the White statistic with nine degrees of freedom is 16.92 (p = 0.05); critical value for LM-Err and LM-Lag statistics is 3.84 (p = 0.05); spatial weights matrices are row-standardized: CONT is first-order contiguity; D500 is distance-based contiguity for 500 miles; and IDIS2 is inverse distance squared; only the highest values for a spatial diagnostic are reported.

states in 1982. All variables are in logarithms. In addition to a replication of the standard Jaffe approach (but using innovation counts as the dependent variable, as in Acs, Audretsch and Feldman (1992: 365), reported in the first column of the table), we also estimated the model with the four new indices of local geographic interaction (reported in columns 3 to 6).

All regressions yield highly significant and positive coefficients for both private R&D and university research (at p < 0.01), confirming the consensus result in the literature. The new gravity and covering indices are positive and significant as well (at p < 0.05), whereas the co-location index (3.5) is only marginally significant (at p < 0.10). Jaffe's geographic coincidence index does not turn out to be significant, confirming earlier findings of Acs, Audretsch and Feldman (1991, 1994a). For all models, diagnostic tests were carried out for heteroskedasticity, using the White (1980) test. In addition, specification tests for spatial autocorrelation were carried out, using the Lagrange Multiplier tests for spatial error and spatial lag dependence implemented in the SpaceStat software (for technical details, see Anselin 1988, 1992, 1995); Anselin and Hudak 1992; Anselin and Bera 1997). The tests for spatial autocorrelation were computed for three different spatial weights matrices which reflect different prior notions on the spatial structure of dependence. The weights matrices have non-zero elements for each observation pair (an observation – row – and its potential neighbor – column) that is assumed to interact. The magnitude of the non-zero elements is either a function of contiguity (the presence of a common border), or some function of the distance between the two observations (for further details, see Anselin 1988; Anselin and Bera 1997). The three weights used for the 43 states are based on simple contiguity (common border between states), on distance-based contiguity with a 500 mile cut-off (states are neighbors if their geographic centers are within 500 miles of each other); and on inverse distance squared (the magnitude of the interaction is proxied by the squared inverse distance between the geographic centers of states). Only the results for the most significant diagnostics are reported in Table 3.3. No evidence of heteroskedasticity was found, but the Jaffe model showed significant spatial error autocorrelation. Maximum likelihood estimation of the Jaffe model with spatial error autocorrelation (reported in column 2) did not alter the substantive interpretation of the model: both private R&D and university research remained strongly significant, but the geographic coincidence index was not (the spatial autoregressive coefficient was significant and positive; no evidence was found of any remaining higher-order spatial dependence).

Interestingly, relative to the results of the Jaffe model, the effect of the introduction of the gravity and covering interaction indices seems to be to lower the coefficient of private R&D, whereas the coefficient of university research remains virtually unchanged. This may suggest that the original results overestimated the 'pure' effect of private R&D on innovation, in the sense that some of it may be due to local geographic interaction with university research. The new indices seem to capture this interaction, while the original Jaffe index does not. Also, the introduction of the new indices removes any misspecification in the form of spatial autocorrelation, which is present in the original Jaffe formulation.

In sum, these results suggest that the spatial range of interaction between private R&D and university research reaches beyond the county (or MSA) where the R&D is carried out. Even the crude averages at the state level provide consistent evidence of this. Parenthetically, our results also demonstrate the usefulness of high-technology lab employment as a proxy for private R&D activity, since no significantly different relationship was found compared to earlier results in the literature that used a 'purer' measure of R&D expenditures.

3.5 LOCAL GEOGRAPHIC SPILLOVERS AT THE MSA LEVEL

3.5.1 Spatially Lagged Variables

The use of R&D lab employment as a proxy for private R&D activity allows us to carry out an analysis of the geographic knowledge production function at a smaller spatial scale than the state level. We constructed a database for 125 MSAs in the United States for which some innovative and research activity was present (see Appendix C for a listing). Given the indication of a wider range of spatial interaction than purely within-county between university and private R&D from the results at the state level, we constructed two new variables that we refer to as *spatial lags*. These variables are designed to capture the effect of university research and private R&D respectively in counties surrounding the MSA, within a given distance band from the geographic center of the MSA. Specifically, for any MSA i, the spatial lags $U50_i$ and $R50_i$ are the sums of respectively the university research and private R&D in those counties surrounding the MSA (and not part of the MSA) whose geographic centers are within 50 miles of the geographic center of the core MSA county. Similar measures were computed for a 75 mile range as well ($U75$, $R75$). These measures correspond to our notion of covering used in the state-level analysis.

Since the analysis is carried out at the scale at which we assume that the spatial interaction takes place (MSA and possibly its surrounding counties), there is no need to create an artificial index of geographic coincidence, as is the case at the state level. In fact, by explicitly including both the research magnitude at the MSA as well as for surrounding counties, we are able to get a much more precise insight into the spatial extent of 'local' geographic spillovers.

3.5.2 Estimation Issues

Our model consists of three equations, the knowledge production function for K (3.1), an industry research equation, R (3.2), and a university research equation, U (3.3). The knowledge production function contains both R and U as explanatory variables and will be extended with the two spatial lag variables, $U50$ (or $U75$) and $R50$ (or $R75$). Both R and U equations contain the other as explanatory variable, as well as the spatial lags. The form of this system of equations raises a number of issues with respect to estimation and identification.

First, while the system is recursive between K and R and U, the exogeneity of the latter two in the knowledge production function should not be taken on faith. In fact, misspecifications (e.g. errors in variables) could easily lead to endogeneity and must be checked. We address this by means of the Durbin-Wu-Hausman (DWH) test for exogeneity (e.g. Davidson and MacKinnon (1993: 237–42). We also take this approach to test the extent to which R and U are endogenous to each other in equations (3.2) and (3.3).

Second, even in a purely recursive system, ordinary least squares (OLS) estimation of the knowledge production function would only be legitimate in the absence of interequation correlation, that is, correlation between the error terms of the equations (e.g. Greene (1993: 600). We check this by means of a Lagrange Multiplier test on the diagonality of the error covariance matrix for the least squares residuals (Breusch and Pagan 1980).

Third, the spatially lagged variables $R50$ (or $R75$) in the R equation, and $U50$ (or $U75$) in the U equation could be endogenous as well. In spatial econometric models, such variables are often referred to as spatially lagged dependent variables and it is well known that their presence causes OLS to be biased and inconsistent (Anselin 1988). In our model, however, the locations to which these lags pertain (counties surrounding the MSA, but not part of the MSA) are not part of the observation set (the MSAs) and hence exogenous, unless they belong to the MSA counties of a neighboring MSA. There is some degree of overlap for 71 out of the 125 MSAs and we assess the extent to which this may cause endogeneity by means of a DWH test.

Finally, the use of a cross-sectional sample potentially leads to spatial autocorrelation in the regression equations. We assess this by means of a Lagrange Multiplier test for spatial error dependence using three spatial weights based on distance: the same 50 and 75 mile cut-offs as used in the construction of the lag variables, and a squared inverse distance weights matrix. These tests are only valid when the explanatory variables in the regression are exogenous and should be interpreted with caution when this is not the case. They are used here to assess the extent to which remaining unspecified spatial spillover may be present, even after the inclusion of the spatial lags (provided that the latter are exogenous, which turns out to be the case in our study).

3.5.3   Empirical Results

We first focus on the knowledge production function in equation (3.1), that is, without a geographic coincidence index. The estimation results for a cross-sectional regression on 125 MSAs in 1982 are reported in Table 3.4. Three models are presented: a bare-bones Jaffe model; a spatial model which also includes the spatial lags for university and private R&D (only the most significant of respectively $U50$ and $U75$ and $R50$ and $R75$ are reported), and an extended spatial model, which includes local economic characteristics as explanatory variables as well.

Table 3.4   OLS regression results for log(innovations) at the MSA level (N = 125, 1982)

Model	Jaffe	Extended Jaffe	Spatial
Constant	−1.045	−1.500	−1.523
	(0.146)	(0.172)	(0.206)
Log(R)	0.540	0.316	0.294
	(0.054)	(0.056)	(0.057)
Log($R75$)			−0.025
			(0.038)
Log(U)	0.112	0.097	0.113
	(0.036)	(0.033)	(0.033)
Log($U50$)			0.036
			(0.015)
Log(LQ)		0.674	0.655
		(0.155)	(0.165)
Log(BUS)		0.334	0.333
		(0.058)	(0.057)
Log($LARGE$)		-0.350	−0.336
		(0.093)	(0.095)
R^2-adj	0.599	0.708	0.718
White	1.18	20.39	31.24
LM-Err	2.69	0.28	0.77
	(D75)	(IDIS2)	(D50)
LM-Lag	5.62	3.40	1.41
	(D50)	(D50)	(D75)

Notes: Estimated standard errors are in parentheses; critical values for the White statistic with respectively five, 20 and 35 degrees of freedom are 11.07, 31.41 and 49.52 (p = 0.05); critical values for LM-Err and LM-Lag statistics are 3.84 (p = 0.05) and 2.71 (p = 0.10); spatial weights matrices are row-standardized: D50 is distance-based contiguity for 50 miles; D75 is distance-based contiguity for 75 miles; and IDIS2 is inverse distance squared; only the highest values for a spatial diagnostic are reported.

The standard Jaffe model (in column 1 of Table 3.4) confirms the strong significance (at p < 0.01) of both private R&D and university research on the level of innovative activity in an MSA. However, compared to the analysis at the state level, there is a clear dominance of the coefficient of private R&D over university research, indicating an elasticity that is almost five times higher (compared to roughly equal elasticities at the state level in Table 3.3). There is no evidence of heteroskedasticity, but there is a strong indication of misspecification in the form of a spatial lag (at $p < 0.05$). When the spatial variables *U50* and *R75* are added to the Jaffe specification (instead of a coincidence index at the state level), the model fit improves slightly, with a positive and significant effect for *U50,* but an insignificant effect for the research spatial lag. Neither heteroskedasticity nor spatial dependence remains. In the full model (in column 3), the spatial lag for university research, with a 50 mile range (*U50*), remains positive and significant ($p < 0.05$). However, there is no evidence that the effect of private R&D on MSA innovative activity spills over from outside the MSA (the coefficient of *R75* is negative, but not significant). The addition of the local economic variables causes the elasticity with respect to private R&D to drop substantially, while the one for university research stays roughly the same. All three local economic variables are highly significant (with $p < 0.001$) and have the expected sign: positive for specialization in high technology (*LQ*) and the importance of business services (*BUS*), and negative for the presence of large firms (*LARGE*). Note that the negative sign for the presence of large companies confirms earlier evidence in Acs, Audretsch and Feldman (1994: 338) that smaller firms tend to be more innovative. In other words, ceteris paribus, MSAs dominated by the presence of larger firms tend to show less innovative activity. A fourth variable is added to correct for potential unmeasured 'quality' effects that may cause inter-equation correlation. Following Jaffe (1989), we use the rank of the universities as a proxy for quality. This variable turns out to be positive and significant ($p < 0.05$).

For the full specification, we further tested the exogeneity of each of the four variables *R, U, R75* and *U50,* using the DWH test for a two-stage least squares (2SLS) estimation with *Log(HTEMP), Log(ENRL), Log(EDEXP)* and *FORTUNE* as instruments. We failed to reject the null hypothesis for each (none achieved a p value less than 0.20). In other words, there was no evidence *against* exogeneity of these variables. In addition, the LM tests on diagonality of the error covariance between *K* and *R* and *K* and *U* were, respectively 1.17 ($p = 0.28$) and 1.73 ($p = 0.19$), which did not provide evidence against the null hypothesis of no inter-equation error correlation.

The OLS estimation results in column 3 can thus be reliably interpreted to indicate the strong influence of university research on innovative activity in an MSA, not only of university research in the MSA itself, but also in the surrounding counties. By contrast, the effect of private R&D seems to be contained within the MSA itself. Of course, private and university R&D are not independent, and we turn to their interaction/simultaneity in Tables 3.5 and 3.6.

Following Jaffe (1989), we estimated two additional models that explicitly incorporate the potential simultaneity between private R&D and university research. The results in Table 3.5 show the estimation of the private R&D equation (3.2) in which, in addition to university research, the spatial lags of

Table 3.5   Regression results for log(private R&D) at the MSA level
           (N = 125, 1982)

Model	OLS	OLS-Robust	2SLS	2SLS-Robust
Constant	−0.312	−0.312	−0.374	−0.382
	(0.323)	(0.802)	(0.337)	(0.496)
Log(*R50*)	0.093	0.093	0.100	0.103
	(0.035)	(0.036)	(0.037)	(0.035)
Log(*U*)	0.181	0.181	0.336	0.346
	(0.049)	(0.095)	(0.070)	(0.099)
Log(*U75*)	0.041	0.041	0.033	0.032
	(0.043)	(0.048)	(0.045)	(0.042)
Log(*LQ*)	0.353	0.353	0.432	0.414
	(0.190)	(0.218)	(0.199)	(0.207)
Log(*BUS*)	0.515	0.515	0.388	0.380
	(0.078)	(0.272)	(0.091)	(0.183)
R^2	0.510	0.510	0.662	0.670

Notes: Estimated standard errors are in parentheses; instruments in 2SLS estimation are log(*ENRL*) and *RANK*.

both university research and private R&D are included, as well as the log of high-technology employment (*FITEMP*), the *FORTUNE* dummy and the *RANK* measure as exogenous variables (the latter to control for potential quality effects). Given the strong indication of heteroskedasticity (the White test in the OLS regression of the model yielded 42.54, which is significant at $p < 0.02$), both standard and robust results are reported. University enrollment (*ENRL*) and education expenditures (*EDEX*) were used as instruments in the 2SLS estimation reported in columns 3 and 4 of Table 3.5, with *U* as the endogenous variable.

The estimates and their significance vary considerably between the standard and robust results on the one hand and the OLS and 2SLS approaches on the other hand, indicating the strong effect of both heteroskedasticity and simultaneity bias. A DurbinWu-Hausman test on the exogeneity of university research is clearly rejected at $p < 0.05$ (the statistic was 5.27). The OLS results are therefore only reported for comparison purposes and should not be the basis of any substantive interpretation.

Focusing on the results in column 4, we find a strong positive and significant effect of university research on private R&D ($p < 0.001$), but only within the MSA itself (the coefficient of *U75* is not significant). On the other hand, there is an indication of spatial spillover in private R&D, supported by a

Table 3.6   Regression results for log(university research) at the MSA level (N = 125, 1982)

Model	OLS	OLS-Robust	2SLS	2SLS-Robust
Constant	–4.346	–4.346	–4.168	–4.173
	(0.722)	(0.811)	(0.793)	(0.803)
Log($U75$)	0.093	0.093	0.085	0.090
	(0.057)	(0.073)	(0.059)	(0.066)
Log(R)	0.050	0.050	0.157	0.133
	(0.109)	(0.146)	(0.221)	(0.156)
Log($R50$)	0.076	0.076	0.087	0.080
	(0.046)	(0.043)	(0.050)	(0.041)
Log($ENRL$)	1.785	1.785	1.690	1.701
	(0.179)	(0.219)	(0.248)	(0.230)
$RANK$	0.546	0.546	0.507	0.487
	(0.207)	(0.151)	(0.219)	(0.151)
R^2	0.631	0.631	0.651	0.636

Notes: Estimated standard errors are in parentheses; instruments in 2SLS estimation are log(LQ) and *log(BUS)*.

significant (at $p < 0.05$) and positive coefficient of *R50*. Both specialization in high technology and the presence of Fortune 500 companies also contribute significantly to the magnitude of private R&D. Note that the latter has a positive sign, in contrast to the effect of larger firms on innovations. A DWH test on the exogeneity of the spatial lag variable *R50* cannot be rejected ($F(1, 117) = 0.078$, $p = 0.78$), hence the results in the last column of Table 3.3 yield a valid interpretation.

The effect of private R&D on university research is quite different, as borne out by the results for equation (3.3) reported in Table 3.6, in the same format as in Table 3.5. There is no evidence of a significant influence of private R&D in the MSA itself on university research, nor of spatial spillovers. The only strongly significant coefficients are for internal characteristics of the universities, that is, their size (enrollment) and quality, both with the expected positive sign. In contrast to the R&D equation, there is no significant evidence of heteroskedasticity (White test yields 34.03, with 38.89 as the critical level for 26 degrees of freedom at $p = 0.05$), nor of spatial autocorrelation. More importantly, there is no indication of simultaneity bias (a Durbin-Wu-Hausman test on the exogeneity of R yields 0.21, which is clearly non-significant at $p = 0.65$). The correct interpretation should therefore be based on column 1 and the other results are only reported for completeness' sake.

In sum, the estimates in Tables 3.5 and 3.6 support the earlier finding of Jaffe (1989: 968) about the direction of 'causality' in the relation between private R&D and university research, but now at a much finer level of spatial detail and with an explicit measure of spatial spillovers. There is no evidence that private R&D in the MSA or its surrounding counties is endogenous to the university research equation. By contrast, there is a strong indication that university research in an MSA is endogenous in the private R&D equation.

3.6 CONCLUSIONS

In this chapter, we have been able to shed additional light on the issue of *local* geographic spillovers between university research and high-technology innovations. Our point of departure was Jaffe's (1989: 968), often cited as finding that 'there is only weak evidence that spillovers are facilitated by geographic coincidence of universities and research labs within the state'. We approached this issue from an explicit spatial econometric perspective and implemented the classic Griliches–Jaffe knowledge production framework for high-technology innovations in 43 US states as well as in 125 MSAs. The latter became possible by using a specially compiled set of data on R&D laboratory employment. This yielded more precise insight into the range of spatial externalities between innovation and R&D in the MSA and university research, both within the MSA and in surrounding counties.

We also refined Jaffe's geographic coincidence index for analysis of local spillover based on data for states. We suggested four alternative measures, three of which were derived from established principles in spatial interaction theory, that is, the gravity potential and covering index. We showed that the inclusion of the alternative indices in the geographic knowledge production function provided strong and unequivocal evidence of local spatial externalities. In addition, the evidence suggested that these externalities transcended the boundaries of counties.

Overall, we confirmed the positive and significant relationship between university research and innovative activity, both directly, as well as indirectly through its impact on private sector R&D. We found that the spillovers of university research on innovation extended over a range of 50 miles from the innovating MSA, but not with respect to private R&D. We also confirmed earlier findings on the direction of 'causality' between university and private research, the former being endogenous to the latter, but not vice versa.

Our findings are important in that they highlight the relevance of a precise consideration of the spatial range of interaction in the analysis of spatial externalities. However, some cautionary remarks are in order as well. Our analysis is limited by the use of a single cross-section. Unfortunately, there is currently no update of the 1982 US SBA innovation database for later points in time, precluding a more extensive analysis of the space–time dynamics. Also, we have elected to focus on studying the relations between research and innovations in those locations for which both were observed. This leaves aside the issue of why certain locations have research and innovative activity and others do not, especially when one of the two is present, but the other is not. We leave this aspect of the study for a separate paper.

4. Sectoral characteristics

4.1 INTRODUCTION

In the last chapter we started to shed some light on the issue of local geographical spillovers between university research and high-technology innovations, taking an aggregate perspective. Our point of departure was Jaffe's (1989: 968) often-cited finding that 'there is only weak evidence that spillovers are facilitated by geographic coincidence of universities and research labs within the state'. We approached this issue from an explicit spatial econometric perspective and implemented the classic Griliches–Jaffe knowledge production framework for high-technology innovations in 43 US states as well as in 125 MSAs. This yielded more precise insight into the range of spatial externalities between innovation and R&D in the MSA and university research both within the MSA and in surrounding counties.

In the current chapter we extend the empirical evidence in three important respects:

1. We broaden the cross-sectional basis for empirical analysis by utilizing data for four high-technology sectors. Whereas the analysis in the last chapter studied local geographic spillovers based on an aggregate of high-technology industries, the disaggregated approach followed in this chapter opens up the possibility to study likely variations across industries. As before, the data are measured at the geographic scale of the MSA.
2. Specific measures of local geographic spillovers are developed. These measures are based on a modification of the spatial lag variable previously used. They are intended to capture research activities in concentric rings around the MSA as well as in the MSA itself.
3. In the analysis of the sectorally disaggregated data we explicitly consider the potential for spatial effects such as spatial autocorrelation and spatial heterogeneity that may invalidate the interpretation of econometric analyses based on contiguous cross-sectional data. In the existing literature, these effects are typically ignored or treated inappropriately (e.g. by the application of time series techniques). We implement a spatial econometric approach by both testing for the presence of

spatial effects and, when needed, by implementing models that incorporate them explicitly (Anselin 1988; Anselin and Bera 1997).

The chapter is organized into four remaining sections. We first introduce the analytical framework applied to model local geographic research spillovers. We next outline the data set and briefly highlight the distinctive characteristics of a spatial econometric approach. Subsequently, we present the results of our disaggregated analysis at the MSA level and conclude with a summary and policy evaluation.

4.2   THE KNOWLEDGE PRODUCTION FUNCTION

The conceptual framework for analyzing the geographic spillovers of university research on regional innovative capacity is based on the knowledge production function of Griliches (1979). In essence, this is a two-factor Cobb-Douglas production function that relates an output measure for 'knowledge' to two input measures: research and development performed by industry; and research performed by universities. Formally, this is expressed as:

$$\log(K) = \beta_{K1} \log(R) + \beta_{K2} \log(U) + \varepsilon_K \qquad (4.1)$$

where K is a proxy for knowledge (either patents or innovation counts), R is industry R&D and U is university research, with ε_K as a stochastic error term. The analysis is typically carried out for aggregate cross-sectional units (e.g. states), possibly for several points in time and/or disaggregated by sector.

Following Jaffe (1989), the potential interaction between university and industry research is captured by extending the model with two additional equations that allow for simultaneity between these two variables:

$$\log(R) = \beta_{R1} \log(U) + \beta_{R2} Z_2 + \varepsilon_R \qquad (4.2)$$

and

$$\log(U) = \beta_{U1} \log(R) + \beta_{U2} Z_1 + \varepsilon_U \qquad (4.3)$$

where U and R are as before, Z_1 and Z_2 are sets of exogenous local characteristics, and ε_R and ε_U are stochastic error terms. Since our interest is in university effects only, the third equation is not estimated.

4.3 DATA AND SPATIAL ECONOMETRIC METHODOLOGY

4.3.1 Data and Variable Definitions

We use the innovation data at the county level, and aggregate the original data to the MSA level. We consider innovations in four 'high-technology' sectors. We defined this (broadly) as drugs and chemicals (SIC 28), machinery (SIC 35), electronics (SIC 36) and instruments (SIC 38). These four two-digit categories contain most of the three- and four-digit high-technology sectors.[1] At the two-digit SIC level, it is virtually impossible to designate sectors as 'pure' high technology. To the extent that the sectoral mix in these sectors shows systematic variation over space in terms of its 'pure' high-tech content, our results in the relationship between innovation and research could be affected. However, we are confident that we will be able to detect such systematic variations by means of careful specification tests for spatial effects (Anselin 1988; Anselin and Bera 1997).

We constructed a proxy for industrial R&D activity on the basis of data on professional employment in high-technology research laboratories in the Bowker directories (Jaques Cattell Press 1982). While imperfect, this approach allowed us to construct a private R&D variable for 43 US states and for 125 MSAs (see also Bania et al. (1992: 218–19), for a similar approach). As it turns out, our proxy variable is remarkably similar to the R&D expenditure variable used in Jaffe (1989), yielding a correlation of 0.91 for the 29 states common to both studies. Clearly, the use of lab employment as a proxy for expenditures assumes a constancy of the labor intensity and capital/labor ratio of R&D across the units of observation. To the extent that this is not the case, it will tend to yield heteroskedastic and/or spatially autocorrelated error terms, which will merit special attention in our analysis and will be addressed by means of a spatial econometric approach.

Our data for university research expenditures (U in (4.1) and (4.2)) follow the common approach in the literature and are compiled from the NSF Survey of Scientific and Engineering Expenditures at Universities and Colleges for the year 1982. In addition, this data set also provides the source for two exogenous variables used in the estimation of equation (4.1) at the MSA level: total educational expenditure *EDUEX* from the City and County Data Book; a dummy variable for the overall academic quality of high technology departments at universities, *RANK*; and a proxy for size, the total enrollment at universities, *ENRL*. Note that these variables will be used as instruments in the 2SLS estimation of equation (4.2). We match the sectoral aggregation of the two-digit SIC industries to university departments using the same approach as in Feldman (1994: 58).

In addition we also included a number of variables compiled from County Business Pattern data for 1982: high-technology employment, *HTEMP*; a location quotient for high-technology employment, *LQ*; employment in business services (SIC 73), *BUS*; and the percentage 'large' firms (i.e. firms with employment exceeding 500), *LARGE*. An alternative proxy for firm size is a dummy variable for the presence of at least ten headquarters of Fortune 500 companies in an MSA, *FORTU*, compiled from the 2 May 1982 listing in *Fortune Magazine*. *FORTU* is included to test for the importance of headquarters in the location of R&D companies. Following general practice in the literature the first three variables are included to capture agglomeration economies (see Feldman and Florida 1994 and Anselin et al. 1997).

Our final data set only included those MSAs for which there were innovations in the high-technology sector as well as both private industry R&D and university research expenditures. Admittedly, this excludes from consideration the joint determination of 'location' and 'magnitude' of high-technology innovation and research. On the other hand, it avoids the problem of 'zeros', and is motivated by a focus on the strength of interaction between the two forms of research and the generation of innovations where these are present. We leave the more complex issue for future research.

4.3.2 Spatial Econometric Methodology

When models are estimated for cross-sectional data on neighboring spatial units, the lack of independence across these units (or, the presence of spatial autocorrelation) can cause serious problems of model misspecification when ignored (Anselin 1988). The methodology of spatial econometrics consists of testing for the potential presence of these misspecifications and of using the proper estimators for models that incorporate the spatial dependence explicitly (for a recent review, see Anselin and Florax 1995).

The two forms of spatial autocorrelation that are most relevant in applied empirical work are so-called substantive dependence, or dependence in the form of a spatially lagged dependent variable, and nuisance dependence, or dependence in the regression error term. The former can be expressed as:

$$y = \rho Wy + Xb + \varepsilon \qquad (4.4)$$

where y is a vector of observations on a dependent variable, Wy is a spatially lagged dependent variable for spatial weights matrix W, ρ is a spatial autoregressive coefficient, X is a matrix with observations on the explanatory variables with coefficients b, and ε is an error term. The weights matrix W is typically constructed from information on contiguity between two spatial units, but more general definitions are used as well, leading to a large range of potential specifications. The resulting spatial lag Wy can be considered as a (spatial) weighted average of the observations at 'neighboring' locations. Ignoring a spatially lagged dependent variable yields inconsistent and biased estimates for the β coefficients in the model. The second form of spatial dependence is often expressed as a spatial autoregressive process for the error term in a regression model, or:

$$y = Xb + \varepsilon \tag{4.5}$$

with

$$\varepsilon = \lambda W\varepsilon + i \tag{4.6}$$

where λ is a spatial autoregressive coefficient and i is a standard spherical error term. Ignoring spatial dependence in the error term does not lead to biased least squares estimates, but the estimate of their variance will be biased, yielding misleading inference (for further discussion, see, among others, Anselin 1988, 1990).

In this chapter the procedure is to estimate b by regressing y on X, and then to test separately for $\rho = 0$ and $\lambda = 0$ using LM tests. We will test each estimated model for potential spatial autocorrelation by means of Lagrange Multiplier (LM) or score tests.

4.4   LOCAL DISAGGREGATED GEOGRAPHIC SPILLOVERS AT THE MSA LEVEL

4.4.1   Spatially Lagged Variables

We constructed a database for 125 MSAs in the United States for which some innovative and research activity was present (see Appendix D for a listing). Given the indication of a wider range of spatial interaction than purely within-county between university and private R&D, we constructed two new variables that we refer to as *spatial lags* (see previous chapter). These variables are designed to capture the effect of university research and private R&D respectively in counties surrounding the MSA, within a given distance band from the geographic center of the MSA. Specifically, for any MSA *i*, the spatial lags $UCOV50_i$ and $RCOV50_i$ are the sums of respectively university research and private R&D in the MSA and those counties surrounding the MSA whose geographic centers are within 50 miles of the geographic center of the core MSA county. Similar measures were computed for a 75 mile range as well (*UCOV75*, *RCOV75*).

Note that since the analysis is carried out at the scale at which we assume that the spatial interaction takes place (MSA and possibly its surrounding counties), there is no need to create an artificial index of geographic coincidence, as is the case at the state level. In fact, by explicitly including both the research magnitudes at the MSA as well as for surrounding counties, we are able to get a much more precise insight into the degree of 'local' geographic spillovers.

4.4.2 Estimation Issues

Our model consists of two equations, the knowledge production function for K (4.1), and an industry research equation, R (4.2). The knowledge production function contains both R and U as explanatory variables and will be extended with the two spatial lag variables, *RCOV50* (or *RCOV75*) and *UCOV50* (or *UCOV75*). Both R and U equations contain the other as explanatory variable, as well as the spatial lags. The form of this system of equations raises a number of issues with respect to estimation and identification, that were discussed in Section 3.5.

4.4.3 Empirical Results

Table 4.1 presents the results of the estimation of an OLS cross-section regressions for the four high-technology sectors at the MSA level in 1982. All variables are in logarithms. We estimate a standard Jaffe knowledge production function with spatial lags for university and industrial R&D, and local economic characteristics as explanatory variables as well.

Most regressions yield significant and positive coefficients for both private R&D and university research (at $p < 0.05$), confirming the consensus result in the literature (only the most significant of respectively R, *RCOV50*, *RCOV75*, U, *UCOV50* and *UCOV75* are reported). However, there are variations across industries. Industrial R&D was significant for all four sectors. However, lagged industrial R&D was insignificant, indicating that industrial R&D spills over only within the MSA. University research was positive and significant for only electronics and instruments.

In most of the regressions the three local economic variables are highly significant (with $p < 0.01$) and have the expected sign. Concentration of business activity (measured by *LQ*) has a significant effect on innovation in the instruments and electronics industries. Innovative activity depends on the presence of business services (*BUS*) in all sectors but the chemical industry and is negative for the presence of large firms (*LARGE*). However, in three out of four cases (chemicals, electronics and instruments) the coefficient was insignificant. Note that the negative sign for the presence of large companies

Table 4.1   Industry detailed regression results for log(innovations) at the MSA Level (1982) – OLS results

Model	Log(INN28)	Log(INN35)	Log(INN36)	Log(INN38)
CONSTANT	−1.796	−2.041	−2.620	−1.850
	(0.438)	(0.275)	(0.437)	(0.600)
Log(R)	0.322	0.081	0.133	0.190
	(0.126)	(0.047)	(0.064)	(0.071)
Log(U)		−0.013		
		(0.035)		
Log(UCOV50)	0.0361			
	(0.028)			
Log(UCOV75)			0.165	0.256
			(0.063)	(0.112)
Log(LQ)	0.275	0.591	0.400	0.157
	(0.157)	(0.156)	(0.153)	(0.134)
Log(BUS)	0.191	0.632	0.545	0.212
	(0.126)	(0.080)	(0.097)	(0.065)
Log(LARGE)	0.077	−0.254	−0.087	0.008
	(0.114)	(0.097)	(0.097)	(0.080)
RANK		0.337		0.237
		(0.104)		(0.125)
R2-adj	0.423	0.673	0.654	0.538
N	48	89	70	63
White	16.193	28.130	21.150	41.388
LM-Err	0.583	2.338	5.908	0.425
	(IDIS2)	(IDIS2)	(D50)	(IDIS2)
LM-Lag	1.553	10.459	2.620	1.105
	(IDIS2)	(D50)	(IDIS2)	(D50)

Notes: Estimated standard errors are in parentheses; critical values for the White statistic with respectively five, 20 and 35 degrees of freedom are 11.07, 31.41 and 49.52 (p = 0.05); critical values for LM-Lag and LM-Err statistics are 3.84 (p = 0.05) and 2.71 (p = 0.10); spatial weights matrices are row-standardized: D50 is a distance-based contiguity for 50 miles; D75 is a distance-based contiguity for 75 miles; IDIS2 is inverse distance squared; only the highest values for a spatial diagnostic are reported.

confirms earlier evidence in Acs, Audretsch and Feldman (1994a: 338) that smaller firms tend to be more innovative in only the machinery industry. In other words, ceteris paribus, MSAs dominated by the presence of large firms tend to show less innovative activity.

Following Jaffe (1989), a fourth variable rank (RANK) is added to equations 4.2 and 4.4 to correct for potential unmeasured 'quality' effects that may cause inter-equation correlation. There is evidence of heteroskedasticity in only one sector (instruments), but there is strong evidence of misspecification in the form of a spatial lag (at $p < 0.01$) in machinery and of spatial error (at $p < 0.05$) in electronics.

We further tested the exogeneity of each of the four variables *R*, *U*, *UCOV50* and *UCOV75*, using the Durbin-Wu-Hausman test for a two-stage least squares estimation with log(*EMP*), log(*ENRL*), log(*EDEXP*), and *FORTUNE* as instruments. We failed to reject the null hypothesis for each (none achieved a p value less than 0.12). In other words, there was no evidence against exogeneity of these variables. By and large these results are consistent with aggregate results at the MSA level found in the previous chapter.

Table 4.2 presents revised regression results for all four sectors corrected for spatial dependence and heteroskedasticity. Regression (1) shows OLS regression results for the chemical sector. While industrial R&D spills over only within the MSA, the positive coefficient for lagged university research (*UCOV50*) is insignificant. Local spillovers from university research were not significant. Column (2) shows the regression results of a spatial lag model for machinery. While the spatial lag has been eliminated, the coefficients for industrial R&D and university research remain positive although insignificant. These results are broadly consistent with Jaffe (1989, chapter 2) that there are no local spillovers in the mechanical-arts sector.

The spatial error model in column (3) shows regression results for the electronics industry. With the exception of log(*Large*) all signs are as expected and significant at least at the ($p < 0.05$) level. The coefficient for industrial R&D and lagged university research (*UCOV75*) are both of about the same magnitude. This is consistent with Acs, Audretsch and Feldman (1994) and inconsistent with Jaffe (1989) who found the elasticity of industrial research to be about twice as large as university research. While we find strong research spillovers in electronics from both within the MSA and from up to 75 miles around the MSA, Jaffe (1989) and Acs, Audretsch and Feldman (1992) found no such spillovers. This might be due to significant spatial error autocorrelation at the state level.

The results in Table 4.2 can thus be reliably interpreted to indicate the strong influence of university research in the electronics and instruments industries in an MSA, not only of university research in the MSA itself, but in the surrounding counties. By contrast, the effect of private R&D seems to be contained within the MSA itself. Of course, private and university R&D are not independent, and we turn to their interaction/simultaneity in Table 4.3.

Following Jaffe (1989), we estimate one additional model that explicitly incorporates the potential simultaneity between the private R&D equation (4.2) in which, in addition to university research, the spatial lag for university research is included, as well as the log of the high-technology employment (*HTEMP*), the *FORTUNE* dummy and the *RANK* measure as exogenous variables (the latter to control for potential quality effects). Strong significance of

Table 4.2 *Industry detailed regression results for log(innovations) at the MSA Level (1982)*

Model	Log(INN28) OLS	Log(INN35) IV Spatial Lag	Log(INN36) ML Spatial Error	Log(INN38) OLS Robust
CONSTANT	−1.796	−2.12	−2.55	−1.850
	(0.438)	(0.261)	(0.414)	(1.883)
Log(R)	0.322	0.029	0.132	0.190
	(0.126)	(0.048)	(0.058)	(0.095)
Log(U)		0.002		
		(0.034)		
Log($UCOV50$)	0.0361			
	(0.028)			
Log($UCOV75$)			0.164	0.256
			(0.065)	(0.122)
Log(LQ)	0.275	0.612	0.420	0.157
	(0.157)	(0.147)	(0.136)	(0.132)
Log(BUS)	0.191	0.649	0.534	0.212
	(0.126)	(0.075)	(0.087)	(0.410)
Log($LARGE$)	0.077	−0.239	−0.086	0.008
	(0.114)	(0.091)	(0.085)	(0.097)
RANK		0.255		0.237
		(0.102)		(0.181)
W_Log(*INN*)		0.199		
		(0.073)		
		(D50)		
λ			0.303	
			(0.13)	
			(D50)	
R2-adj	0.423	0.720	0.670	0.538
N	48	89	70	63
White	16.193			
LM-Err			5.190	
			(D50)	
LM-Err	0.583			5.190
	(IDIS2)		(D50)	
LM-Lag	1.553		2.197	
	(IDIS2)		(IDIS2)	

Notes: Estimated standard errors are in parentheses; critical values for the White statistic with respectively five, 20 and 35 degrees of freedom are 11.07, 31.41 and 49.52 (p = 0.05); critical values for LM-Lag and LM-Err statistics are 3.84 (p = 0.05) and 2.71 (p = 0.10); critical value for LM-Err statistic with one degree of freedom is 3.84 (p = 0.05); spatial weights matrices are row-standardized: D50 is a distance-based contiguity for 50 miles; IDIS2 is inverse distance squared; only the highest values for a spatial diagnostic are reported.

Innovation and the growth of cities

Table 4.3 *Industry detailed regression results for log(private research) at the MSA Level (1982)*

Model	Log(RD28) 2LS	Log(RD35) OLS	Log(RD36) OLS	Log(RD38) 2SLS
Constant	1.197	–1.930	–1.677	–0.173
	(0.506)	(0.621)	(0.682)	(0.891)
Log(*U*)	0.240			0.283
	(0.068)			(0.151)
Log(*UCOV50*)		0.440	0.280	
		(0.091)	(0.105)	
Log(*EMP*)	0.233	0.617	0.732	0.310
	(0.129)	(0.152)	(0.156)	(0.172)
FORTU	0.387	0.520	0.358	0.372
	(0.161)	(0.254)	(0.210)	(0.254)
RANK		–0.128		–0.059
		(0.227)		(0.267)
R2-adj	0.637	0.491	0.453	0.394
N	48	89	70	63
White		8.674	7.597	
LM-Err		0.960	0.735	
		(D75)	(D75)	
LM-Lag		0.731	0.664	
		(IDIS2)	(IDIS2)	

Notes: Estimated standard errors are in parentheses; critical values for the White statistic with respectively five, 20 and 35 degrees of freedom are 11.07, 31.41 and 49.52 (p = 0.05); critical values for LM-Lag and LM-Err statistics are 3.84 (p = 0.05) and 2.71 (p = 0.10); spatial weights matrices are row-standardized: D50 is a distance-based contiguity for 50 miles; D75 is a distance-based contiguity for 75 miles; IDIS2 is inverse distance squared; only the highest values for a spatial diagnostic are reported. Log(URD) is considered endogenous in the chemicals and instruments research equations. Instruments in 2SLS estimations are log(*ENRL*) and log(*EDEX*).

the Durbin-Wu-Hausman test for chemicals (p = 0.01), and its marginal significance for instruments (p = 0.16) suggest that 2SLS is the appropriate estimation method for these two equations. University enrollment (*ENRL*) and education expenditures (*EDEX*) were used as instruments in the specifications reported in columns 1 and 2 of Table 4.3.

4.5 CONCLUSIONS

In this chapter, using sectorally disaggregated data, we have been able to shed additional light on the issue of local geographic spillovers between university research and high-technology innovations. We approached this issue from an explicit spatial econometric perspective and implemented the classic Griliches–Jaffe knowledge production framework for high-technology innovations in 125 MSAs and four technical areas. The latter became possible by using a specially compiled set of data on R&D laboratory employment. This yielded more precise insight into the range of spatial externalities between innovation and R&D in the MSA and university research both within the MSA and in surrounding counties.

We found apparent differences across sectors with respect to the 'mix' of applied local knowledge inputs in general, and the extent to which university research plays a role in innovation in particular. Our main conclusion is that local university spillovers seem to be very much specific to certain industries. Specifically, as evidenced at the two-digit SIC level, no university spillover effects are at work in the drugs and chemicals (SIC 28) and in the machinery (SIC 35) sectors. On the contrary, very strong and significant university research spillovers are evidenced in the electronics (SIC 36) and the instruments (SIC 38) industries. These spillovers extend the boundary of the MSA within a 75-mile range from the central city.

How do these findings help us formulate endogenous growth policies within the context of a regional growth policy? As Stough, Lall and Trice (1999) point out, a fundamental concern of regional policy is to maintain local competitiveness in a global economy. Regions are increasingly becoming basic units of interaction in a more borderless economy and regional fortunes are shaped by the demands of the global economy, rather than higher political entities. The findings in this chapter suggest that regional institutions – universities, research laboratories, specialized business services, related industries and entrepreneurship – are key ingredients in promoting regional growth.

These results are further reinforced by the findings of Jacobs, Nihuis and Tang (1999) who find that regional R&D spillovers are much more important than international R&D spillovers in productivity growth. In fact regional R&D speeds up the absorption of foreign technologies. Therefore, regions that want to stay competitive internationally should invest in those aspects of the region's knowledge infrastructure that promote regional knowledge spillovers.

NOTE

1. For details on the construction of the set of high-technology industries applied in this study see Varga (1998).

5.   Innovation of entrepreneurial firms

5.1   INTRODUCTION

The growing interest in the behavior of small entrepreneurial firms refocuses attention on the role that the entrepreneur plays in the firm and the economy (Brock and Evans 1989; Acs and Audretsch 1990a and 1990b). This chapter describes recent theoretical research into the function of the entrepreneur and provides an empirical test of the implications of the limited attention which must be allocated between maintaining current operations and innovating new products.

One of the implications of the optimal allocation is that innovation depends on firm size and monopoly profits only if the ability to maintain current operations is high relative to the ability to innovate new products. In this case, some attention is allocated to trying to improve current products through product improvement or process innovation and away from new product innovation. This diverts attention away from efforts to innovate new products. The inability to maintain the profitability of current operations is defined as obsolescence.

As the firm grows, more attention is diverted away from new product innovation in order to maintain the profitability of a growing number of current product lines. However, greater profits decrease the frequency with which each product must be improved and so increase the amount of attention allocated to new product innovation. Therefore, if the firm conducts product improvement as well as new product innovation, then new product innovation decreases with firm size and increases with monopoly profits. Product improvement is optimal only if the degree of obsolescence of current product lines is not too great. However, if obsolescence is severe, then the firm conducts no product improvement and allocates all attention to new product innovation. In this case, new product innovation is at a constant rate independent of firm size and monopoly profits.

The emphasis of this analysis is on the limits of entrepreneurial attention in carrying out the entrepreneurial role in the economy. The function of the entrepreneur has in the past been defined as risk bearer, manager, innovator and arbitrageur. However, the entrepreneur by necessity plays all these roles and while wearing the hat of innovator or arbitrageur, the entrepreneur is not undertaking managerial activities.

This opportunity cost of innovation embodied in the neglect of current operations has significant implications for the innovativeness and growth of the entrepreneurial firm. Because of the opportunity costs of innovation and growth, the entrepreneurial firm is limited in size but may not be limited in innovativeness. Whether an entrepreneurial firm remains innovative as it grows depends on what might be called the degree of obsolescence of its current products. The degree of obsolescence is the degree to which entry of competing products makes current products economically obsolete. The difficulty with testing this determinant of innovation is that the degree of obsolescence has not been measured before.

The limits of the growth of the firm due to this fixed input of entrepreneurial attention has been recognized before. Kaldor (1934) attributes the limits on firm size to the fixed input of the entrepreneur in his role as coordinator.[1] Among the various roles of the entrepreneur, he dismisses the role of risk-bearing as the cause of a limit on firm size since the emergence of joint-stock companies makes it possible to spread risk over many individual stockholders. Kaldor also dismisses the managerial, or supervisory, role of the entrepreneur as the source of diseconomies of scale, since an army of supervisors of equal ability may be as efficient as a single supervisor. This leaves the role of 'coordinator'. Kaldor describes the role of coordinator as 'that part of the managerial function which determines what sort of contracts should be entered into' (p. 68). This function limits the size of the firm since, even if this responsibility falls to a board of directors, in all important strategic decisions each member of the board will have to keep all alternatives in his or her mind, which is limited.[2] Thus, it is the boundedness of the entrepreneurial function of 'coordination' which limits the span of control and thus firm size.

If the entrepreneur has coordinating activities which lead to new product lines and supervisory responsibilities of overseeing the production processes of these products, then one would expect that the number of products the entrepreneur can enter into is limited by the number of products which the entrepreneur can supervise. This is the problem addressed in the model developed in Gifford and Wilson (1995) and Gifford (1992a). This model suggests that if the degree of obsolescence is sufficiently low, then the entrepreneur both conducts new product innovation and supervises product improvement. In this case new product innovation decreases with firm size and increases with monopoly profits. However, if the degree of obsolescence is sufficiently high then the entrepreneur conducts only new product innovation and new product innovation is independent of both firm size and monopoly profits.

Thus the degree of obsolescence has significant implications for the Schumpeterian Hypotheses (Schumpeter 1934) of the relationship between innovation, on the one hand, and firm size and monopoly profits on the other. In addition, the bound on firm size implies that Gibrat's law (Gibrat 1931) of proportionate effect does not apply to the entrepreneurial firm. Finally, if the degree of obsolescence is sufficiently low, then the size of the firm is bounded away from a larger firm size which would be more profitable if the optimal firm size were derived without modeling the growth process itself.

The purpose of this chapter is to test the effect of the degree of obsolescence on the rate of new product innovation and its significance for tests of the Schumpeterian Hypotheses. The task of carrying out this test is made difficult by the fact that the degree of obsolescence is difficult to measure. However, since the firm conducts product improvement only if the degree of obsolescence is low, we test the effect of product improvement on the dependence of new product innovation on firm size and monopoly profits. Although these preliminary results are weak, they suggest that product improvement reduces the positive effect of firm size on new product innovation and at least partially offsets the negative effect of monopoly profits on new product innovations. This suggests that the degree of obsolescence may be an important determinant of the validity of the Schumpeterian Hypotheses. In addition, product improvement decreases the effect of technological opportunity on new product innovation, which may explain previous mixed results on this relationship.

The main focus here is the decision to attempt new product innovation at all, considering the opportunity cost embodied in the neglect of current operations. By focusing on the implications of limited attention, the model ignores other aspects of the innovation production process, such as patent races, optimal timing of innovation and other decision problems which must be addressed once the firm has decided to try to innovate a new product. The analysis proceeds as follows. Section 5.2 briefly outlines the model of the entrepreneurial firm and describes the optimal innovation, firm size and growth rate of the firm. Section 5.3 interprets the implications of the model for new product innovation and relates them to the empirical literature. Because of the significance of the degree of obsolescence for the results of the model, Section 5.4 describes various possible sources of measures of the degree of obsolescence. Section 5.5 presents a preliminary and indirect empirical test of the significance of obsolescence for the Schumpeterian Hypothesis.

5.2   THE ENTREPRENEURIAL FIRM

Following Kaldor, a firm is defined as a 'production combination possessing a given unit of coordinating ability'.[3] A firm may be composed of any number of current projects. A current project is denoted by the number of periods since it was last inspected by the entrepreneur. Call this the 'age' of the project. Let the sequence a $\{a_i\}_{i \in Z+}$ denote the projects currently held by a firm, where a_i denotes the number of current projects of age i. Let a be an element of **A**, the set of all such sequences. Current projects are either functioning or failed. A project of age i is functioning with probability $p_i = \gamma^i$, where $(1\,\gamma\,() = \phi$ is the one-period probability of failure. The current returns to a project of age i are $r_i \equiv p_i g - (1\,p_i)b$ where, $g > 0$ and $b > 0$. Denote the number of current projects by $N(a) = \Sigma_{i=1}^{\infty} a_i$. The current state of the firm is completely described by a.

During any period, the entrepreneur may inspect a new project for possible adoption or inspect a current project to determine whether it has failed. If a current project has failed, it can be restored to a profitable state with probability ρ. Thus, if a current project is evaluated, it is good in the next period with probability $\rho_i = \gamma^i + (1 - \gamma^i)\rho$. If a new project is evaluated, it is good with probability ρ_0 and adopted. Let $u \in Z+$ denote the evaluation decision, where $u = 0$ if a new project is evaluated and $u = i > 0$ if current project i is evaluated. Note that $u = i$ implies $a_i = 1$. The entrepreneur may also freely discard any number of current projects. Let $q \equiv \{q_i\}_{i \in Z+}$ denote the retained projects, where q $\ni$ A, $q_i \leq a_i$ and $q_u = 1$ for $u > 0$. The current returns to the firm in state q after discard is $R(q) = \Sigma_{i \in Z+} r_i q_i$.

The transition of the state takes place after current projects have been discarded, a project, new or current, has been evaluated and adopted or restored, or not, and all current projects fail with probability í. To denote the adoption or restoration of a project, define $y + a = \{\max(y_i, a_i)\}_{i \in Z+}$, for y, $a \in A$. Let e1 denote the sequence with a one in the first position and zeros elsewhere. Then e1+ a is the addition of a project of age one to the sequence a of projects. This project of age one may be a newly adopted project or a newly restored current project. To denote the discard of a current project, let q_{-j} denote the sequence q' with $q'_i = q$, $i \neq j$, and $q_j = 0$. Thus q_{-j} denotes the deletion of project j. To denote the aging of projects, define the operator $S:A \rightarrow A$ such that $(Sq)_i = q_{i-1}$ and $(Sq)_1 = 0$. That is, the age of each retained unevaluated current project increases by one unit each period. Then the state in the next period is $e_1 + Sq_{-u}$ with probability ρ_u and is Sq_{-u} with probability $1-\rho_u$.

If $R(q)$ is bounded and returns are discounted by $\beta < 1$, then there exists a stationary optimal policy (a) which prescribes the decision rules $\{u_\lambda(a), q_\lambda(a)\}$. The optimality equation for the entrepreneur is

$$F(a) = \max_{q,u}\{R(q) + \beta[\rho_u F(e_1 + Sq_{-u}) + (1-\rho_u)F(Sq_{-u})]\}.$$

The optimal policy takes two forms:[4] (1) an age-inspection rule which prescribes that each current project is evaluated periodically and a new project is evaluated if no current project requires evaluation; and (2) an innovate-and-discard rule which prescribes that current projects are discarded, unevaluated, upon reaching a critical age and a new project is evaluated every period.

To describe the optimal policy λ, let V_i denote the discounted expected returns to a project of age one which is discarded at age i. Then $V_{i\cdot} = \Sigma_v \Sigma^{v-1} r_v$. Let d denote the i which maximizes V_i. Then $r_d \geq 0$ and $r_{d+1} < 0$. Let W_i denote the incremental returns from a current project of age one which is evaluated every i periods instead of evaluating a new project. Then $W_i = \Sigma_{s=0}^{\infty} \beta^{si}(\rho_{i-}\rho_0)V_i = V_i / [1 - \beta^i(\rho_{i-}\rho_0)]$. Let c denote the value of i which maximizes W_i. Let $\mathbf{A}^s$ denote the set of all sequences $\{a_i\}_{i \in Z+}$ such that $a_j = 0$ for $j > s$. The optimal policy is as follows:

(i) If $V_d > W_c$, then, for all $a \in = \mathbf{A}^d$, $\lambda = \delta$, where $u_\delta(a) = 0$ and $q_\delta(a) = a_{-(d+1)}$.
(ii) If $V_d \leq W_c$, then, for all $a \in \mathbf{A}^c$, $\lambda = \psi$, where

$$u_\psi(a) = \begin{cases} c & \text{if } a_c = 1 \\ 0 & \text{otherwise} \end{cases}$$

and $q_\psi(a) = a$.

The following statements characterize the implications of the optimal policy.

1. Firm size is bounded by c if $V_d \leq W_c$, and by d if $V_d > W_c$ and $c \leq d$. That is, if the innovate-and-discard rule is optimal then the bound on firm size is greater than if the age-inspection rule is optimal.

2. If $V_d \leq W_c$, then $\rho_c \geq \rho_0$. This implies that, if effort to maintain current projects is optimal then the probability of restoring a current project is greater than the probability of adopting a new project.

3. If $V_d \leq W_c$, then c (i) is non-decreasing in ρ_0, (ii) is non-decreasing in $(1 - \rho)$, and (iii) is non-decreasing in g/b. When the optimal rule is to evaluate current projects then the bound on firm size is increasing in the level of technological opportunity, the degree of obsolescence, and monopoly profits.

4. If $V_d \leq W_c$, then for any $a \in \mathbf{A}^c$, there are unattainable states $a' \in \mathbf{A}^d$ for which $N(a') > N(a)$ and $F(a') > F(a)$. If the age-inspection rule is optimal, then there are larger, more valuable, firm sizes which are unattainable under this rule.

5. If $\rho = 1$, then $V_d \leq W_c$ and firm size approaches the steady state $a_c \in \mathbf{A}^c$, in which there are c projects of ages 1 to c, and $u(a_c) = c$. If maintenance of current operations is certain, then current projects will be evaluated and a steady state is reached in which a current project is evaluated every period and new product innovation ceases.

6. If $V_d \leq W_c$, then the rate of innovation decreases with firm size and increases with monopoly power.

7. If $V_d > W_c$, then the rate of innovation is constant and equal to ρ_0, the level of technological opportunity.

8. The rate of growth decreases with age for young firms.
9. For any $\rho_0 < 1$, there is a ρ large enough such that $V_d \leq W_c$. For any level of technological opportunity less than certainty, there is a level of endurance for which evaluating current projects is optimal.
10. For any $\rho < 1$, there is a ρ_0 large enough such that $V_d > W_c$. For any level of endurance less than certainty, there is a level of technological opportunity for which the innovate-and-discard rule is optimal.

Both rules imply bounds on firm size which depend positively on the level of technological opportunity. The age-inspection rule ψ implies a smaller bound on firm size than does the innovate-and-discard rule δ, even though current projects may never become obsolete. The age-inspection rule also implies a rate of innovation that is decreasing in firm size and increasing in monopoly profits, while the innovate-and-discard rule implies a constant rate of innovation. Thus, the validity of the Schumpeterian Hypotheses depends upon which rule is optimal. Since this depends upon the degree of obsolescence, the most significant result is the effect of the degree of obsolescence on the innovative ability of the firm and its dependence on firm size and monopoly profits.

To make this clear, call ρ the endurance of current projects; that is, the probability that a failed current project can be restored through product improvement upon evaluation. Then $(1 - \rho)$ is the degree of obsolescence. The age-inspection rule holds if endurance is sufficiently high (the degree of obsolescence is low) relative to the level of technological opportunity, ρ_0. For any level of technological opportunity, there is a level of the degree of obsolescence low enough that the age-inspection rule holds. If the degree of obsolescence is sufficiently low, then innovation decreases with firm size and increases with monopoly profits and new product innovation is negatively related to product improvement. Otherwise, innovation is constant and equal to the level of technological opportunity and there is no product improvement. Thus, even though two firms may face the same technological opportunity for innovation, the same monopoly profits and the same frequency of failure, if the degree of obsolescence of its products is sufficiently greater for one firm than the other, the first firm may have a constant rate of innovation independent of firm size and monopoly profit while the rate of innovation of the other firm may increase with monopoly profits and decrease with firm size.

The intuition of this result is that current projects less subject to obsolescence represent a higher opportunity cost to the innovation of new products. If endurance is high relative to the level of technological opportunity, then this opportunity cost is high enough to distract the entrepreneur from evaluating new projects. On the other hand, innovation represents an opportunity cost to maintaining current projects. If the level of technological opportunity is sufficiently high relative to endurance, then this opportunity cost is high enough to distract the entrepreneur's attention from maintaining current projects. A firm with a sufficiently high endurance of its products, relative to the level of technological opportunity, eventually reaches a level of operation at which maintaining valuable current operations distracts the entrepreneur from efforts to innovate and grow. A low endurance reduces this opportunity cost of innovation and results in a high level of innovative effort and output, although firm size remains bounded.

5.3   INTERPRETATION OF THE MODEL

To relate the results of the model to the empirical literature, it is necessary to interpret the model and indicate how the values of the parameters and variables may be estimated. The endogenous variables of the model include the number of current projects, which represents firm size and may be proportional to employment or sales, and changes in firm size, which reflect firm growth. The crucial aspect of firm size in the model is that increases in firm size may increase the demands on the entrepreneur's attention and that firm size can reach a critical maximum level at which innovation ceases. This should be kept in mind when choosing a measure of firm size.

Also among the endogenous variables are the two forms of innovation, new product innovation and current product improvement. New product innovation is the adoption of an evaluated new project. Current product improvement or process innovation restores current projects that have failed. Process innovation and product improvement affect current projects while product innovation occurs only with new projects. Note that in the model, the rate of process innovation is negatively related to the rate of product innovation. That is, they are alternative activities. The rate of evaluation of new projects reflects innovative effort, usually measured by R&D expenditures. The rate of adoption of new projects is the innovative output, usually measured by patents numbers.[5] The ratio of the rate of evaluation to the rate of adoptions reflects the productivity of R&D expenditures. This is a common measure of technological opportunity.

The distinction made here between product innovation and process innovation is not uncommon. For example, Scherer (1982) states that 'A new process in the sense used here is a technical improvement in one's own production methods, whereas a new product is an improvement sold to others, either to other business enterprises or to consumers' (p. 227). However, in the analysis above, the significance of the distinction is that process innovations increase productivity while product innovation changes the total mix of goods and services available. This has significant implications for the measurement of real growth (Scherer 1978). However, as pointed out by Gomulka (1990), this distinction is not always clear cut. A new product innovation requires new combinations of inputs that constitute process innovations. And process innovations often result in modifications of the product characteristics to such an extent as to imply new product innovation. In addition, a product innovation for one firm may result in process innovation by a firm downstream.

The distinction between product and process innovation made in the analysis of this paper avoids these issues by emphasizing the implications for the demands on the entrepreneur's attention. Product innovation adds to the number of subunits of the firm which would require the entrepreneur's attention to maintain their profitability, if those efforts were justified. On the other hand, process innovation, though it may increase the production of a current product, does not increase the demands on the entrepreneur's time, even if maintenance efforts are justified.

The composition of innovative effort and inter-firm differences have been empirically tested only recently. However, most of these investigations do not distinguish between product and process innovation. The first empirical investigation of the determinants of the composition of R&D expenditure was provided in Mansfield (1981). Mansfield found that inter-firm differences in the composition of R&D increased with the concentration of the industry. However, Mansfield distinguished between basic, applied and new product or process innovation but not between product and process innovation. Scott (1984) found significant firm-specific influences on the level of R&D spending, but did not consider its composition. Link (1982) tests the effects of profits, diversification, concentration, federal R&D spending and ownership control on the mix of innovative effort between basic research, applied research and development.

Other empirical studies of process innovation or product improvement have been conducted in Kraft (1990) and Lunn (1986, 1987). However, these studies compare the determinants of process innovation which occurs in the development of new products. That is, process and product innovation are complementary activities. Mansfield (1981) considers the effects of size and concentration on the composition of R&D but lumps new product and new process innovations in the same category. Link (1982, 1985) distinguishes between basic R&D, applied R&D and development. Link (1985) estimates separate regression models for new product innovation and for process innovation. The coefficients of the various determinants have opposite signs in the two regressions, although these coefficients are insignificant. To capture the results described above for the negative relationship between product innovation and product improvement, measures of R&D activity must be separated by whether it is related to new products or the improvement of established products of the firm.

There are, however, two empirical investigations of the composition of innovative activities between product and process innovation and the dependence of this composition on firm characteristics. Not surprisingly, neither specifically tests the results of the above analysis. Pavitt (1984) explores sectoral influences on the level and composition of firms' innovative activity. He finds that the mix of product and process innovation depends on the source of technical change and the scale of production. For example, in traditional manufacturing, such as textiles, technical change comes predominantly from the suppliers of equipment. These firms conduct mostly process innovation using the product innovations of other firms. Large-scale production-intensive firms, such as motor vehicles, tend to produce their own process innovations, and few product innovations. However, small-scale mechanical and instrument engineering firms tend to concentrate on product innovations for use in other sectors, such as large-scale production-intensive firms. Science-based firms, such as chemicals and electronics, produce a mixture of process and product innovations. Therefore, large-scale intensive producers emphasized process innovation, either produced in house or provided by suppliers. However, small-scale high-tech firms emphasize new product innovation and are not concerned with producing the innovations in large-scale operations themselves.

Link (1985) also considers the determinants of changes in the mix of product and process innovation, as well as basic and long-term R&D from 1970 to the early 1980s. Among the determinants investigated are changes in company strategy from defensive to offensive, and vice versa, the existence of a central lab, and changes in diversification. Only the classification of the firm's product is significant for the mix of product and process innovation. Firms in producer goods industries are found to increase their process innovation over time while those in consumer goods industries increase their product innovation over time. In addition, the coefficients for all the variables for new product innovation have the opposite sign from the coefficients for process innovation.

The adoption of new projects can also be interpreted as the acquisition of other firms or as expansion of products into new markets and/or through new plants, as long as projects are acquired one at a time. These alternative interpretations are possible because the R&D process itself is not modeled explicitly. Thus the model can be used to explain growth (or lack thereof) through any activity which requires the entrepreneur's attention.[6]

The parameters of the model also require interpretation. The model of the allocation of entrepreneurial attention contains three dimensions of competition: (1) monopoly profits from current projects, (2) the frequency of failure from the entry of competition and (3) the degree of obsolescence. Because of these three measures of competition, the vagueness of the term 'monopoly power' is avoided. Monopoly power can be reflected in high current profits, entry barriers or a low degree of obsolescence. Monopoly profits reflect the degree of price competition from current competitors. This is usually captured by concentration ratios. The frequency of entry of competition is the per-period probability of failure of a current project. Failure can be due to the introduction of an innovation or the imitation of the current product by another firm, either within the industry or not. Measures of firm entry are not sufficient. Measures of innovations themselves are the best way of capturing this form of entry (Acs and Audretsch 1990b).

The third dimension of competition is the degree of obsolescence which is the probability of failing to restore the profits of a current project through product improvement or process innovation. The degree of obsolescence reflects the extent to which efforts at product improvement or process innovation fail. Firms with a lower degree of obsolescence conduct product improvement. For example, Link (1985) shows that firms in producer goods industries have increased their process-related R&D while firms in consumer goods industries have been increasing their new product R&D. The implication of the analysis above is that producer goods industries have a lower degree of obsolescence than consumer goods. Measures of the degree of obsolescence are discussed in the next section.

The probability of adopting an evaluated current project represents the level of technological opportunity for innovation and so is an indication of R&D effectiveness in producing new products. It can be increased by scientific breakthroughs that have applications in the industry and by spiller effects from the R&D of other firms and from government expenditures on R&D. Questions concerning the productivity of R&D expenditures and the relative value of basic research, versus other research, have been tested empirically (Griliches 1986).

It should be noted that the degree of obsolescence and the level of technological opportunity may be correlated. The success of product improvement or process innovation may increase or decrease with the level of technological opportunity. This depends on whether new technological opportunities can be adapted to current products. If new technologies can be adapted, then the degree of obsolescence may decrease and product improvement may increase with technological opportunities. However, if these technological improvements cannot be adopted, then the degree of obsolescence may increase and product improvement cease. This interaction between technological opportunity and the degree of obsolescence is not analyzed in the current chapter but should be considered in future research, since this interaction may affect the evolution of the industry.

5.4   THE SCHUMPETERIAN HYPOTHESIS AND THE DEGREE OF OBSOLESCENCE

The model of Section 5.2 has significant implications for the role of obsolescence in testing the Schumpeterian Hypotheses of the relationship between innovation, on the one hand, and firm size and monopoly profits on the other. Therefore, this section describes this literature and the implications of the model for future research.

The empirical literature on the Schumpeterian Hypothesis can be divided into two groups: that investigating the effects of monopoly profit and that investigating the effects of firm size on innovation.[7] The results on the effect of monopoly profit on innovative effort are inconclusive. Monopoly profit appears to be necessary but not sufficient to induce R&D expenditure. The results appear to depend on some measure of technological opportunity. The effect of monopoly profit on innovative output is even less satisfactory. Kamien and Schwartz (1982: 93) conclude that 'even "technological opportunity class" may not be enough to sort out the underlying relationship sought; a deeper study of components of industrial structure may be required'. The implication of the allocation of attention is that it is not just the absolute level of technological opportunity that matters, but its size relative to the endurance of current projects.

Recent empirical investigations of the relationship between innovation and monopoly profit have found that this relationship is more complex than previous tests have assumed. For example, Levin, Cohen and Mowery (1985) offer stylized facts concerning the effects of concentration on R&D and innovation. They show that these effects are mitigated by the inclusion of the effects of technological opportunity, appropriability and imitation. They conclude that 'R&D spending appears to be encouraged in youthful industries where a strong science base is present and where the government makes substantial contributions to technological knowledge' (p. 23).

In tests of the effect of firm size on innovative activity, there is little support found for the hypothesis that large firms exhibit greater innovative effort or produce more innovative output. Kamien and Schwartz (1982: 103) conclude that 'R&D activity measured either by input or output activity, appears to increase with firm size up to a point, then level off or decline'. There is no accounting for inter-industry differences. It appears that the hypothesis may be true up to some firm size and then fail. Until now, there was, however, no explanation for this result in the theoretical literature.

This result is seen again in Cohen, Levin and Mowery (1987). They find that firm and business unit size explain only a 'negligible fraction' of the variance in R&D while industry characteristics, such as technological opportunity, appropriability and demand conditions, are significant in explaining R&D

intensity. Their results do suggest, however, that business unit size does affect the probability of conducting R&D and they conclude that, if firm size matters at all, it matters only in industries with low technological opportunity.

Acs and Audretsch (1988) interpret their results on the effect of firm size on innovation to imply that 'the greater extent to which an industry is composed of large firms, the greater will be the innovative activity, but that increased innovative activity will tend to emanate more from the small firms than from the large firms' (p. 687).

The lack of a conclusive test of the Schumpeterian Hypotheses may be due to the fact that the hypotheses themselves are insufficiently well formulated. Acs and Audretsch (1990b) suggest that '[t]heory should perhaps develop further how firms of varied size may have disparate innovative responses to different economic environments, rather than focusing on which firm size is uniquely endowed to best promote technological progress' (p. 59). One of the difficulties with formulating a coherent model of innovation is the ambiguity of the arguments behind the Schumpeterian Hypotheses of the effects of firm size and monopoly profits on innovation.

The motivations to innovate from monopoly profit in the market for the innovated good are unambiguous. However, the effect of monopoly profit in the current product markets is ambiguous. The motivations come from the financial advantages stemming from current monopoly profits. These profits allow the firm to internally finance its R&D projects which may be advantageous for two reasons. First, it may be very difficult to convince an external source of financing of the probability of success of the project because of the vast amount of knowledge required to properly evaluate its prospects. The second reason external financing may be difficult is in the development stage. If the invention cannot be patented then the information required to obtain external financing may expose the invention to imitation. However, there are also disincentives to innovate stemming from monopoly profits in the current market. Current monopoly profit is an opportunity cost if innovation requires resources to be diverted from current production or if the innovation is a substitute in use for the current product.

Firm size is also a source of both motivations and hindrances to innovation. Motivations stem from several aspects of firm size. A large operating staff (non-research) may be better able to market a new product and/or to perceive market demand for innovations. A large research staff may have the advantages of a greater specialization of its members and greater ability to engage in parallel projects and to exploit specialized equipment. Product diversification of large firms provides greater incentive to undertake R&D projects which have a large number of expected applications. Diversification also allows a large firm to better exploit the unforeseen outcomes of R&D. This reduces the risk involved in R&D. High sales volume may imply a large distribution system for the innovation. Large assets may provide the ability to undertake the high risk involved in R&D.

Large firm size can also result in hindrances to innovation. The effectiveness of communication between operating staff and research staff can diminish with firm size. A large research staff may have difficulty viewing the research project as a whole (with proper gestalt) and may have problems coordinating the activities of its members. Also, large operating and research staffs may result in costs due to monitoring their activities. Extensive assets of a firm represent opportunity costs if the innovation causes resources to be diverted from these assets.

To resolve these ambiguities, the conditions affecting innovation can be separated into two types: demand-pull and technology-push. Demand-pull manifests itself in greater expected revenues from innovation. Some examples of demand-pull effects are a large market and competitive bidders for the innovation. Technology-push manifests itself in the increased ability to innovate successfully. The only motivation or disincentive mentioned above which is of the demand-pull type is monopoly profit in the market for the innovated good. This is a demand-pull effect because it affects the market value of innovations, not the ability of a firm to produce innovations. The demand-pull effect has an unambiguous effect on innovation. Greater monopoly profit in the market for the innovation has an unambiguously positive effect on the expected revenues from innovation.

However, most of the technology-push conditions have ambiguous effects on innovation. Monopoly profit in current markets can imply financial advantage or opportunity costs. There may or may not be economies of scale in research staff. A large operating staff may better perceive market demand and be better able to market the innovation but be unable to communicate well with the research staff. Diversification can result in a greater ability to exploit the results of R&D but may also result in obsolescence of current products. Assets can allow greater risk-taking or represent opportunity costs. Because of these ambiguities, generalizations, such as that monopoly profit and large firm size promote innovations, are unjustified. The effects of these conditions depend on the particular circumstances of the firm and a more detailed model of the determinants of innovative ability is needed.

The model presented above is an attempt to address these problems by modeling the effect of the scarce resource of attention on the innovative ability of the firm. The results offer an explanation of the empirical observations above. One implication of the model is that it is not the absolute level of technological opportunity which affects innovation, but the relationship between technological opportunity and the degree of obsolescence. In youthful industries with a strong science base, the level of technological opportunity may be sufficiently larger than the degree of obsolescence to promote innovation. In addition, innovation does decrease with firm size, but only if the degree of obsolescence is sufficiently low or technological opportunity is sufficiently low. The observation that greater innovation takes place in markets with large firms but is performed by small firms is consistent with the result that industries with high technological opportunity will grow large firms but with low obsolescence, while smaller firms in those industries will be more innovative.

The model above implies that the effects of firm size and monopoly profits on product innovation depend on the degree of obsolescence. However, one must be careful how the term obsolescence is used. It is clear that the electronic calculator made the slide rule obsolete. In this case, slide rules were discarded from the producers' product lines. The technology of electronic calculators could not be adopted to the design of slide rules. One might also legitimately say that the IBM-PCXT made the IBM-PC obsolete. However, the IBM-PC continued to be produced by IBM and cloned by other companies. Therefore, it was not discarded from firms' current product lines. In everyday usage, the term obsolete often means only that the product is no longer on the cutting edge of technology. This is technological obsolescence. However, in the analysis above, a product is not economically obsolete as long as it is produced. Obsolescence in this analysis refers to economic obsolescence, not technological obsolescence.[8]

The measure of the degree of obsolescence may depend on the scale of the analysis. Obsolescence can result from business cycles or such technological phenomena as the industrial revolution and the current information revolution. In some cases obsolescence may be an economy-wide, or world-wide, characteristic. Alternatively, obsolescence may be limited to a single industry which exhibits product innovations that make previous products obsolete. The degree of obsolescence is the inability to improve current products or processes after the entry of new products of other firms cause the product to fail. However, this concept is not a common one in economic literature. It is probably most closely related to Schumpeter's 'creative destruction'. However, in Kirchhoff (1989), creative destruction is measured by small firm entry. Clearly, entry is one source of obsolescence, but only if the entry makes successful product improvement, or leap-frogging, unlikely. Also, new firm entry is not necessary for new product entry which causes the failure of a current product. Expenditure on process innovation or product improvement would indicate the level of effort towards restoring the profits of current products. What is needed is an indication of the effectiveness of these efforts.

A related concept is the appropriability of profits. If failure of a current product is due to another firm's innovated product which cannot be imitated and adapted to the failed current product, then the degree of obsolescence is high. Therefore, the degree of obsolescence depends positively on the appropriability of the returns to the entrant's innovation; that is, the ability of the competitor to capture the value of its R&D output. This is increased by the protection offered by patents and also the degree of brand loyalty.[9] The adoption of new technologies would indicate the extent to which current products can incorporate new technologies and remain viable.[10]

Since the concept of obsolescence has not been explicitly modeled before, empirical studies containing measures of it are not available. However, the issue of the degree of obsolescence has been addressed in other contexts. One source of obsolescence is from competition from within an industry which exhibits product innovations that make previous models of the product obsolete. A possible measure of inter-industry differences in the degree of obsolescence is offered by the taxonomy of Abernathy and Clark (1985). They distinguish among innovations along two scales. The first scale, a measure of 'market transilience', indicates the degree to which an innovation affects current markets. The second scale, the 'technology transilience' indicates the degree to which the innovation makes current products obsolete, what Abernathy and Clark call Schumpeterian creative destruction. In the model above, a market susceptible to obsolescence must face entering innovations, and so must exhibit market transilience. The degree of obsolescence would be reflected in the technology transilience, and thus the inability of the firm to adopt the new technology. New products which result in the obsolescence of current products are what Abernathy and Clark call revolutionary innovations. These are innovations which are introduced into established markets. Regular innovation involves applying established technologies to existing markets and is represented by process and product improvements. Examples from the auto industry are described to illustrate these concepts.

Another indication of the degree of obsolescence is provided by the literature on Schumpeterian business cycle theory. One concern of this literature is whether innovations appear in bunches during depressions, which then bring an end to the depression. For example, Kleinknecht (1987) points out that during depressions, the values of current products decline and firms are motivated to taking on more risky R&D, even though funds are drastically reduced. This is evident in the foundation of new research labs from 1929–36. In this case, firms shift their concern from process innovation to product innovation. As Kleinknecht points out: 'Why should an enterprise deal with the uncertainties and costs of introducing radically new products on the market as long as its established products can easily be sold? Is it not more attractive to restrict R&D activity to the gradual improvement of existing products?' (p. 63). The model above implies that innovations should appear in bunches during depressions because the degree of obsolescence is sufficiently high. Firms cease improving current products (process innovation) and concentrate on innovating new products.

Another source of obsolescence is the user-specific nature of the products of the firm. For example, Pavitt (1984) provides a taxonomy which compares the relative importance of product versus process innovation as a proportion of all innovations produced by firms in different sectors. He finds that product innovation is high in small mechanical and instrument engineering firms while process innovations are more important in large, more scale-intensive enterprises. This suggests an interpretation of the degree of obsolescence as the degree of idiosyncratic trade. These two sectors might be described in terms of the above model as follows. The specialized suppliers produce custom instruments for specific tasks for their customers which are not mass produced and so are discarded and new projects (new customers) are frequently evaluated. Because of a high degree of obsolescence (idiosyncratic trade), in that instruments developed for one use are not suitable for another, the firm uses an innovate-and-discard rule and the bound on firm size is small. Scale-intensive firms face a low degree of obsolescence resulting in the firm using the age-inspection rule with a large bound on firm size. The firm eventually grows large and concentrates on process improvement.

These various sources of measures of obsolescence are offered in the hope that useful data may be available in some of these areas. Since the model is not specific about the source of the obsolescence, it provides no guidance for specific measurements of obsolescence. This is also true for the nature of the 'projects', which here are interpreted as product lines but may also be interpreted as other activities.[11] The lack of characterization of these projects, the innovation process and the source of obsolescence is by design and makes the model broadly applicable.

5.5   EMPIRICAL RESULTS

Perhaps the greatest challenge facing researchers who undertake to measure innovation and its determinants has been the lack of data. The database used in this study was constructed by combining two sources of data: the US Small Business Administration database, and the *Business Week* Survey of company-financed R&D expenditures. While the first data source provides one of the most important and unique direct measures of innovative activity (Acs and Audretsch 1988 and 1993b) the second source provides company data on R&D expenditures, sales and profits. The *Business Week* data, which incorporates 95 percent of the total company-financed R&D expenditures in the United States, have been used in previous studies (Soete 1979; Acs and Audretsch 1991). In particular we were able to match these data for 634 firms.

The measure of a firm's innovative activity is the number of innovations recorded by the US Small Business Administration in 1982 which were attributed to that firm. This prevents the problems associated with using R&D

expenditures or patents as the measure of innovation. The database was created by recording product innovations and product improvements in new product sections of technology, engineering and trade journals in 1982. Although these data are described in detail in the Acs and Audretsch (1990b) study, several points should be emphasized. First, the database consists of 8 074 innovations and includes service firms as well as manufacturing firms. Second, based on a sub-sample of innovations from the entire database, it was determined that the innovations recorded in 1982 were the results of inventions made, on average, 4.2 years earlier. Third, each innovation was classified by Edwards and Gordon (1984) according to the following levels of significance: (1) the innovation established an entirely new category of product, (2) the innovation is the first of its type on the market in a product category already in existence, (3) the innovation represents a significant improvement in existing technology, and (4) the innovation is a modest improvement designed to update an existing product.

While none of the innovations in the sample was in the first level of significance, 80 were in the second level and 576 in the third level, and 4 282 were classified in the fourth level. To provide a test for any biases that might arise in the assignment of the innovation significance classification, The Futures Group undertook telephone interviews based on a subset of 600 innovating companies that were randomly selected. The respondents of the interviews tended to rate their innovation as being more important than the rating assigned by The Futures Group. Then the innovation data were classified into two groups. Significance level two and three were combined as new product innovations, and significance group four was identified as product improvements.

Table 5.1 lists the 32 firms ranked by the most innovation in the product improvement category. Hewlett-Packard had 51 innovations in the product improvement category. Column one is the rate of new product innovation dividing significant innovations by total innovations. We can see that the rate of new product innovation varies across firms. For example, General Electric has a much higher new product innovation rate (28.6) than General Motors (7.1).

Since the firm conducts product improvement only if the degree of obsolescence is low, we test the implications of the degree of obsolescence for the Schumpeterian Hypotheses by testing the effect of product improvement on the dependence of new product innovation on firm size and monopoly profits. The effect of product improvement on new product innovation can be expressed by the following function and the signs of its second derivatives:

$$y = f(i, s, m, t) \tag{5.1}$$
$$\text{where } f_{si} < 0, f_{mi} > 0.$$

Table 5.1 The rate of new product innovation

OBS	Firms	Rate of new product innovation	Significant innovation	Product improvement
		(1)	(2)	(3)
		(2)/[(2)+(3)]		
1	Hewlett-Packard	7.3	4	51
2	Minnesota Mining & Manufacturing	28.2	11	28
3	General Electric	28.6	10	25
4	General Signal	17.2	5	24
5	National Semiconductor	0.0	0	26
6	Texas Instruments	16.7	4	20
7	RCA	14.3	3	18
8	Gould	19.0	4	17
9	International Business Machines	23.8	5	16
10	Digital Equipment	33.3	7	14
11	Motorola	15.0	3	17
12	Honeywell	11.1	2	16
13	United Technologies	22.2	4	14
14	Whee Labrator Frye	27.8	5	13
15	Johnson & Johnson	5.9	1	16
16	Eastman Kodak	11.8	2	15
17	Pitney Bowes	17.6	3	14
18	Data General	23.5	4	13
19	Exxon	6.3	1	15
20	Rockwell International	18.8	3	13
21	Du Pont	18.8	3	13
22	Pennwalt	0.0	0	15
23	Sperry Rand	6.7	1	14
24	Stanley Works	13.3	2	13
25	General Motors	7.1	1	13
26	Harris	14.3	2	12
27	ITT	14.3	2	12
28	Becston, Dickison	35.7	5	9
29	Squibb	15.4	2	11
30	Sybron	23.1	3	10
31	North American Philips	23.1	3	10
32	Sterling Drug	38.5	5	8

The left-hand-side variable, y, is the rate of new product innovation, i is the rate of product improvement, s is firm size, m is monopoly profit, and t is technological opportunity. The signs of the cross partial derivatives, f_{si} and f_{mi}, reflect the hypothesis that for firms facing a sufficiently low degree of obsolescence to warrant conducting product improvement, new product innovation is decreasing in firm size and increasing in monopoly profits. As described above, the 1982 innovations are the result of inventions made, on average, in 1977. Following the example of Scherer (1965), we assume a seven-year lag exists between the implementation of a firm's strategy, such as expenditures on R&D, and the subsequent innovation. Thus, the 1982 innovations correspond roughly to 1975 firm profits, R&D and technological opportunity.

To test the hypotheses, we estimate the following reduced form model:

$$NP_i = B_0 + B_1 PI_i + B_2 FS_i + B_3 MP_i + B_4 TO_i + B_5 FS*PI_i$$
$$+ B_6 MP*PI_i + B_7 TO*PI_i + u_i. \tag{5.2}$$

The dependent variable NP is the new product innovation rate in 1982, defined as new product innovations of firm i divided by total firm innovations (new product innovations and new product improvements for firm i). Since NP is a limited dependent variable that takes values between zero and one, the model will be estimated using a Tobit model.

PI is the number of new product improvements in 1982. FS is firm size, employment, defined as firm size for firm i in industry j divided by the employment of the largest firm in industry j in 1975.[12]

MP is defined as monopoly profit and is measured as net income in 1975 divided by total company sales in 1975. TO is technological opportunity measured as company research and development expenditures in 1975 divided by total company sales in 1975.

Three interactive terms are also included in the model to capture the effect of obsolescence on new product innovation indirectly through the effect of product improvement. $FS*PI$ measures the interaction of new product improvement and firm size on innovation and is expected to be negatively related to innovation. This captures the effect of an increasing number of activities competing for the entrepreneur's attention as firm size approaches the maximum if the firm conducts product improvement as well as new product innovation. Product improvement should further reduce the negative effect of firm size on new product innovation.

$MP*PI$ is the interaction of product improvement and monopoly profits and is expected to be positively related to innovation. The larger are monopoly profits, the less frequent are efforts to improve current products and the larger is the number of activities which the entrepreneur can undertake. If the firm conducts product improvement as well as new product innovation, product improvement should add a positive component to the effect of monopoly profits on new product innovation.

TO*PI is the interaction of new product improvement and technological opportunity. Greater technological opportunity increases the number of successful innovations, increases the number of product lines which can be maintained with product improvement and can eliminate product improvement altogether. The first effect implies that, given the amount of attention allocated to evaluating new projects, greater technological opportunity increases the number of successful innovations. The second effect implies that, for firms conducting product improvement, greater technological opportunity increases the amount of attention available for new product innovation. The third effect implies that all attention is allocated to new product innovation. All of these effects imply that the total effect of technological opportunity on new product innovation is positive.

However, for a firm which conducts product improvement, less attention is allocated to new product innovation, and so the first effect on successful innovations is that there are fewer attempted innovations to operate through. In addition, this firm does not benefit from the third effect, since it continues to improve products. Therefore, the theoretical prediction is for a negative sign for B_7.

Using the ratio of new product innovation to total firm innovation, including product improvement, in 1982 as the dependent variable, the Tobit regression model is estimated for 632 firms.[13] Our data include the universe of all firms which do R&D, and therefore have the potential to innovate. Some firms innovate and others do not. Therefore, we assign a zero value to non-innovating firms and a positive value to innovating firms. The large number of non-innovating firms calls for a Tobit analysis. For the Tobit model, the regression results are[14]

$$NP_i = -88.433 + 8.543\ PI_i + 28.259\ FS_i - 3.983\ MP_i + 8.275\ TO_i$$
$$(-8.705)^{**}\quad (5.618)^{**}\quad (1.860)^*\quad (-2.388)\ ^{**}\ (4.421)^{**}$$
$$-\ 2.504\ FS^*PI_i + 1.292\ MP^*PI_i - 0.839\ TO^*PI_i. \qquad (5.3)$$
$$(-1.430)\qquad\quad (2.108)^{**}\qquad\ (-4.168)^{**}$$

The positive and statistically significant coefficient of *PI* suggests that product improvement is an important determinant of innovation even after controlling for other major influences. However, the total effect of *PI* is actually measured by

$$\partial NP/\partial PI = 8.543 - 2.504\ FS + 1.292\ MP - 0.839\ TO. \qquad (5.4)$$

Note that firm size decreases the positive effect of product improvement on new product innovation and that monopoly profits increase the effect of product improvement on new product innovation. This is consistent with the theory above. However, the coefficient on *FS* is not significant. Note that the right-hand side of (5.4) cannot be negative since firm size and technological opportunity are both less than one.

The coefficient of *FS* is positive and statistically significant, indicating that larger firms are more innovative even after controlling for product improvements. However, the total effect of firm size on new product innovation is

$$\partial NP/\partial FS = 28.259 - 2.504\ PI. \tag{5.5}$$

Therefore, current product improvement reduces the positive effect of firm size on new product innovation, as the theory suggests, although not significantly. The effect of firm size on new product innovation would be negative for $PI > 11.28$. This is consistent with the theory above.

The negative and statistically significant coefficient of *MP* indicates that higher levels of monopoly profits are associated with less and not more innovation. This is consistent with Acs and Audretsch (1988) and Connally and Hirschey (1984). However, the total effect of monopoly profits on new product innovation is

$$\partial NP/\partial MP = -3.983 + 1.292\ PI \tag{5.6}$$

which is positive for $PI > 3.08$. That is, current product improvement increases the effect of monopoly profits on new product innovation, making it positive for a relatively low value of *PI*. This is consistent with the theory which suggests that increased monopoly profits increase the upper bound on firm size only when the firm conducts product improvement, allowing the firm to innovate more new product lines.

The coefficient for technological opportunity is positive and statistically significant, indicating that even after controlling for firm size, higher levels of technological opportunity lead to greater innovative output. However, note that the total effect of technological opportunity on new product innovation is

$$\partial NP/\partial TO = 8.275 - 0.839\ PI. \tag{5.7}$$

The negative coefficient on $TO*PI$ implies that the fact that the firm is conducting current product improvement reduces the positive effect of technological opportunity. This supports the argument that product improvement reduces the number of attempted new product innovations, and so reduces the effect of technological opportunity on the success of innovative effort. These results are robust for different specifications of the model.

The weakness of these results may be due to the fact that in the theory, new product innovation refers to products which are new to the firm in question, and so increase the demands on the entrepreneur's attention, while product improvement refers to products which the firm currently markets. However, in the data, it was not possible to determine whether an innovation in classification (3), which is a significant improvement on current technology, is new to the firm or is an improvement on one of the firm's current products. If it is the latter, this would tend to generate the positive effect of product improvement on new product innovation because these 'new product innovations' are actually improvements of the firm's current products and so do not increase the number of activities of the firm.

In addition, innovations in classification (4), modest improvements in design of a current product, which were used to measure product improvement, may actually be new products for the firm. If an innovation in classification (4) is actually new to the firm, then this would tend to bias the results towards a negative effect of product improvement on new product innovation. This is because these 'product improvements' actually increase the number of activities of the firm.

5.6   CONCLUSION

The most significant implication of the theoretical model of Section 5.2 is that firm size and monopoly profits matter for new product innovation only if the endurance of current products is sufficiently large relative to the level of technological opportunity so that the firm conducts current product improvement as well as new product innovation. In this case, as firm size increases, the entrepreneur is required to allocate more time to maintaining current operations through current product improvement and less time to new product innovation. However, higher monopoly profits imply a higher upper bound on the size of the firm, allowing the firm to innovate a greater number of new products. If the endurance of current products is sufficiently low relative to the level of technological opportunity, then the firm conducts no current product improvement and allocates all attention to innovating new products. Therefore, in this case, the rate of new product innovation is independent of firm size and monopoly profits.

The empirical results suggest an interaction between the degree of obsolescence and the validity of the Schumpeterian Hypotheses of the effect of firm size and monopoly profits on new product innovation. The positive effect of firm size on new product innovation is reduced by current product improvement, implying that for firms which conduct product improvement, and thus face low obsolescence, innovation may be decreasing in firm size while for firms facing high obsolescence, innovation increases with firm size. The effect of monopoly profits may be reversed by current product improvement, suggesting that, for firms which face low obsolescence, innovation may be increasing in monopoly profits, while for firms facing high obsolescence, innovation is decreasing in monopoly profits.

The allocation of entrepreneurial attention thus models a crucial aspect of the innovation production process: the effect of the limitations of attention on the ability of a firm to innovate. The optimal allocation of attention implies that the endogenous opportunity cost of product innovation embodied in the neglect of current operations affects the dependence of new product innovation on firm size and monopoly profits. In addition, it is not the absolute level of technological opportunity that determines innovation, but the level of technological opportunity relative to the level of endurance.

NOTES

1. See Gifford (1993) and the references there for a more in-depth discussion of the various roles of the entrepreneur.
2. See Gifford (1992b) for a more extensive discussion of limited entrepreneurial ability. Although the current analysis addresses the problems of the 'entrepreneurial' firm, Kaldor's remark suggests that the implications of limited attention apply to large bureaucratic firms as well.
3. A helpful analogy of the model is to imagine a juggler who spins plates on sticks on a table. Only a fraction of the plates are balanced. As more plates are set spinning, the first one starts to slow and requires respinning. The issue is whether to continue setting up new plates or go back and respin old plates. This decision depends on the probability that the old plate, which was originally balanced, falls and breaks and the probability that a new plate is balanced. The probability that a new plate is balanced can be interpreted as the level of technological opportunity and the breakage rate can be interpreted as the degree of obsolescence.
4. See Gifford and Wilson (1995).
5. Shankerman and Pakes (1986) provide an alternative measure of R&D output and productivity using data on patent renewals and renewal fee schedules.
6. If expansion implies the acquisition of more than one project at a time, then this changes the analysis significantly.
7. More extensive reviews of this literature are contained in Schmookler (1966), Jewkes, Sawers and Stillerman (1969), Kamien and Schwartz (1982), Freeman (1982), Stoneman (1983), Scherer (1984) and Baldwin and Scott (1987).
8. Also, one might consider the IBM-PCXT to be an improved version of a more generically defined product, the personal computer. Thus, the production status of the product may depend on how narrowly the product is defined.
9. Cockburn and Griliches (1988) use survey data to create a measure of patent protection. Estimates of the rate of decay of returns to patents in Shankerman and Pakes (1986) indicate the degree to which these patents are either imitated or displaced by innovations.
10. The adoption and diffusion of new technologies for various industries have been investigated by Pavitt (1984).
11. In Gifford (1994a, 1994b and 1994c) the projects are interpreted as ventures in a venture capital portfolio and contracts, either internal or market.
12. This captures the fact that it is firm size as a fraction of the upper bound on firm size which affects new product innovation.

13. The results for the OLS model were similar to the Tobit.
14. (*t*-statistics in parentheses)
    Maximum Likelihood Estimate −793.92.
      * Significant at the 90% level, two-tail test.
    ** Significant at the 95% level, two-tail test.

6. Capital structure, innovation and firm size

6.1 INTRODUCTION

The role of finance in promoting entrepreneurship and innovation is the subject of a large literature. One of the main questions in this literature is whether or not the financial markets are biased against entrepreneurs and small firms in the sense that small firms suffer from lack of information about and/or lack of access to financial markets. A rich theoretical literature has emerged in the last decade, flowing from the early papers of Jaffee and Russell (1976) and Stiglitz and Weiss (1981).[1] Whilst the underpinnings of the notions of a 'debt gap' and 'asymmetric information' thesis have been questioned (de Meza and Webb 1987), its broad implications seem to have been accepted by policy-makers around the world. The belief that capital markets do not provide adequate funds for new business is one of the rationales for government-assisted programs for small business (ENSR 1993; SBA 1996; Besley and Levenson 1996).

In support of the debt–gap thesis are the findings of Evans and Jovanovic (1989), Blanchflower and Oswald (1996) and more recently Holtz-Eakin, Joulfaian and Rosen (1994), and Black, de Meza and Jeffreys (1996). They show that the probability of survival is a function of the individual's assets. For example, Holtz-Eakin et al. (1994) show that a $150,000 inheritance in 1985 increases the probability that an individual will continue as a sole proprietor by 1.3 percentage points. Also, an inheritance has a substantial impact on firm growth: receipt of any surviving enterprise increases by almost 20 percent.

Although pioneering works, these studies include only a relatively small set of human and financial capital variables in the survival function, thus excluding the 'people' factors that are often regarded by practitioners as critical to small business success. If, as some recent studies have suggested (Cressy 1996a), assets are in fact explained by human capital, an observed correlation of financial capital and survival may instead indicate the human deficiencies of the business. This alternative view, presented in Cressy (1996b), argues from United Kingdom start-up data that funds, and the assets that underpin them, are determined entirely by the human capital engaged in the business:

the bank selects businesses, or businesses self-select for finance to yield maximum returns. Thus, in this view credit rationing does not necessarily play a role in small business start-ups.

A growing body of empirical research suggests that new firms, especially technology-intensive ones, may receive insufficient capital. This literature on capital constraints documents that an inability to obtain external financing limits many forms of business investment. Particularly relevant are works by Hall (1992), Hao and Jaffe (1993), Himmelberg and Petersen (1994) and Lerner (1999). These show that capital constraints appear to limit research and development expenditures, especially in smaller firms.

Why firms choose a particular capital structure has eluded financial economists for quite some time. Current thinking on capital structure theory has evolved over the past three decades since Modigliani and Miller (1958) applied the standard tools of economic analysis to corporate finance and revolutionized the field. The main Modigliani and Miller insight is that, 'the average cost of capital to any firm is completely independent of its capital structure and is equal to the capitalization rate of a pure equity stream of its class' (1958: 269). Expansion of the model to allow for taxes (Miller 1977) leads to the conclusion that, due to the subsidy created by deductibility of interest payments, the optimal capital structure for a firm is exclusively composed of debt. The difference between this and observed reality is further explained by the existence of positive bankruptcy and liquidation costs associated with debt, and asset specificity (Altman 1984; Titman 1984; Titman and Wessels 1988).

Recently, the 'capital structure puzzle' has been examined through the lens of Transaction Cost Economics (TCE), where debt and equity are viewed as alternative forms of corporate governance. While many agree that firms prefer internal to external financing, and debt to equity, these recent theories suggest that capital structure choice is dictated by the firm's asset specificity. For example, Williamson (1988) posits that the firm's debt/equity ratio is determined by the optimal governance structure given the redeployability of the firm's assets. If assets are easily redeployed between production alternatives, debt, a rules-based governance structure, is optimal. If assets are not easily redeployed, a more flexible governance structure, is appropriate. Hall (1990) analyzed the effect of several forms of corporate restructuring on R&D investment, found that restructuring involving substantial *increases* in leverage did result in subsequent *declines* in R&D intensity.

Previous empirical studies, mostly by financial economists, have tended to focus on tax-shelter effects and business risk in the presence of bankruptcy cost, as explanations for cross-section variations in leverage. Balakrishnan and Fox (1993) show that firm-specific effects contribute most to the variance in leverage, suggesting a strong link between strategy and capital structure. The purpose of this chapter is to add to the empirical literature examining capital structure by introducing a new measure of asset specificity – innovation. By employing innovation as a measure of uniqueness, this study measures both input and output specificity. Innovation is important because it represents the manifestation of a firm's commitment to invest in the production of unique products that have not been previously introduced in the market. A clear limitation in using only R&D activity as a proxy measure for asset specificity is that R&D reflects only the resources devoted to producing innovation inputs, and advertising does not necessarily measure asset or product uniqueness.[2] We present a model that investigates the degree to which capital structure is conditioned by asset specificity, and the extent to which large and small firms respond to different stimuli.[3] The econometric analysis enables the testing of two hypotheses: (1) innovation is negatively related to capital structure; and (2) that innovation will have a disparate effect on small- and large-firm capital structure choice.

This chapter extends research on capital structure in an important way. By introducing the innovation measure we broaden the concept of asset specificity to include both input and output measures, and simultaneously investigate the importance of innovation on the capital structure choice of small and large firms, across a broad spectrum of publicly traded companies. The only study to examine the determinants of capital structure on small firms was by Wijst and Thurik (1993). They found that most of the traditional determinants of financial structure appear to be relevant for small firms. However, their sample was limited to retail establishments and they were unable to examine issues of asset specificity. In the second section of this chapter the data is introduced, while in the third section the empirical model is presented. The econometric results of the study are presented in the fourth section, followed by conclusions in Section 6.5. We find that innovation is an important determinant of capital structure choice. For large firms, asset specificity is consistent with discretionary governance. However, for small firms innovation is associated with a rules-based governance structure.

6.2   THE DATA

The data base for this study is constructed by combining three previously uncombined sources of data – the US Small Business Administration Innovation Data Base (SBIDB), the *Business Week* Survey of Company Financed R&D expenditures, and the Standards and Poor's Compustat Annual Industrial File. The Compustat files provide all relevant balance sheet and income statement data. The *Business Week* data provide company data on R&D expenditures, which incorporates 95 percent of the company-financed R&D in the United States and has been used in other previous studies (Soete

1979).[4] The SBIDB provides one of the most important and unique direct measures of innovative activity.

As systematic data measuring the number of inventions *patented* were introduced in the mid-1960s, many scholars interpreted this new measure not only as being superior to R&D but also as reflecting innovative output. In fact, the use of patented inventions is not a measure of innovative output, but is rather a type of intermediate output measure. A patent reflects new technical knowledge, but it does not indicate whether this knowledge has a positive economic value. Only those inventions which have been successfully introduced in the market can claim that they are innovations as well. While innovations and inventions are related, *they are not identical*. This distinction is that an innovation is 'a process that begins with an invention, proceeds with the development of the invention, and results in the introduction of a new product, process or service to the marketplace' (Edwards and Gordon 1984: 1).

The development and application of this new direct measure of output specificity has led to a new learning about the sources of innovative activity (Acs and Audretsch 1993a, 1993b). Central to the new learning is that small firms, as well as large enterprises, play an important role in innovative activity. Small firms tend to have the innovative advantage in those industries that are highly innovative, where skilled labor is relatively important, and large firms are present. 'This suggests that, ceteris paribus, the greater the extent to which an industry is composed of large firms the greater will be the innovative activity, but the increased innovative activity will tend to emanate more from the small firms than from the large firms' (Acs and Audretsch 1988: 687).

Previous studies have used different measures of capital structure. In this study, three measures of capital structure are tested in an attempt to capture the effect of asset specificity on short-term, long-term and total indebtedness. The measures are obtained by taking the book values of short-term debt, long-term debt and total debt divided by the total market value of common equity.[5] While data availability precludes the use of market value data for debt, its book and market values are found to be highly correlated (Bowman, 1980). In addition, there is no reason to assume that differences between market and book values of debt are related cross-sectionally to variables used to explain capital structure (Titman and Wessels 1988).

Table 6.1 introduces these data and compares long-term debt to common equity, the innovation rate and total assets for the 30 least leveraged firms. Although data for only the least leveraged firms are reported here, the debt-to-equity ratios are broadly distributed. The mean long-term debt to equity ratio for 1982 is 46.37, with a standard deviation of 56.14. Innovations are normalized by dividing by the log of total assets, converting the variable into a measure of the concentration of a firm's investment in innovative assets. The

Table 6.1 Long-term debt to common equity, innovation rate, and total asset size ($ m.) for the 30 least leveraged firms in the sample, 1982

Name	LTD/CE	In./Ln (TA)	(Rank)	Tot. Assets	(Rank)
Norton Simon	0.000	1.215	(41)	26.93	(381)
Reeves Brothers	0.000	0.185	(173)	222.51	(267)
Winnebago Industries	0.000	0.214	(163)	108.07	(330)
Hazeltine	0.254	0.658	(92)	95.32	(337)
Hewlett-Packard	0.502	6.747	(1)	3470.00	(50)
Kellog	0.578	0.279	(147)	1297.40	(124)
Lilly	1.132	0.248	(154)	3155.13	(56)
General Dynamics	1.320	0.508	(110)	2639.50	(69)
EG&G	1.457	2.143	(16)	270.39	(247)
NALCO Chemical	1.458	0.326	(136)	464.87	(194)
Johnson & Johnson	1.515	2.037	(18)	4209.57	(40)
Raytheon	1.799	0.490	(111)	3510.19	(49)
United Industrial	1.980	0.201	(165)	144.69	(302)
AMP	2.168	0.143	(193)	1076.32	(139)
Diebold	2.255	1.076	(48)	264.74	(249)
Digital Equipment	2.395	2.530	(9)	4024.01	(42)
Eastman Kodak	2.459	1.834	(26)	10622.00	(13)
Bristol-Myers	2.496	0.631	(96)	2756.20	(65)
Binks Mfg.	2.811	0.225	(161)	85.55	(342)
Syntex	2.947	0.148	(189)	859.15	(161)
Petrolite	3.065	0.189	(172)	200.32	(273)
Nashua	3.146	0.178	(176)	274.29	(245)
SmithKline	3.415	0.880	(64)	2857.52	(61)
CTS	3.468	0.199	(166)	151.32	(298)
Minnesota Mining & Mfg.	3.844	4.643	(3)	5514.00	(30)
Scientific-Atlanta	3.996	0.363	(132)	247.55	(254)
Abbott Laboratories	4.037	0.382	(128)	2566.91	(73)
Marion Laboratories	4.138	0.623	(98)	123.39	(320)
Pittway	4.184	0.177	(178)	287.07	(241)
Millipore	4.265	0.721	(88)	256.80	(251)

distribution of innovations is apparently skewed, with a small number of firms making numerous innovations, and most firms contributing fewer than three innovations. In fact, of 315 firms included in our sample, the mean number of innovations was 3.22 (un-normalized), with about one-third of the firms contributing zero innovations.

For each of the three debt measures reported in Table 6.2, there exists a monotonic, inverse relationship between the debt/equity (D/E) ratio and the average innovation rate. A *t*-test indicates that the differences in mean D/E ratios between the least and most innovative firms (i.e. categories 0 and 2) are significant in the cases of long-term and total debt. While no evidence regarding a potential size effect is provided, it is interesting to note that innovation and asset size do appear to be positively correlated.

6.3 THE HYPOTHESIS

Once corporate finance views individual investment projects in terms of their asset specificity, a departure is made from Agency Theory, where the unit of analysis is the individual, and a move is made toward TCE, with emphasis on the transaction. According to Williamson (1988: 571–2):

> Of the several dimensions with respect to which transactions differ, the most important is the condition of asset specificity. This has a relation to the notion of sunk cost, but the organizational ramifications become evident only in an intertemporal,

Table 6.2 *Mean short-term, long-term and total debt to common equity, innovations and total assets ($ m.) by innovation class for 1982 (standard deviation in parentheses)*

Variable	*INNOV* = 0	*INNOV* = 1	*INNOV* = 2	*t*-test*
LTD/CE	51.582	47.604	38.484	2.059
	(62.469)	(52.437)	(48.188)	
STD/CE	13.718	12.515	11.742	0.675
	(27.301)	(30.429)	(22.735)	
TD/CE	68.426	60.722	50.227	2.206
	(75.582)	(65.328)	(65.427)	
Innov. rate	0.000	0.210	1.225	
	(0.000)	(0.073)	(0.998)	
Total assets	955.60	1,803.31	3,541.49	
	(2,463.34)	(2,558.71)	(7,880.21)	

Note: *H_0: Mean D/CE$_{innov=0}$ = Mean D/CE$_{innov=2}$

incomplete contracting context . . . A condition of bilateral dependency arises when incomplete contracting and asset specificity are joined. The joining of incomplete contracting with asset specificity is distinctively associated with Transaction Cost Economics. This joiner has contractual ramifications both in general and specifically with reference to corporate financing.

The ramifications for corporate finance are that each investment project has to be analyzed on its attributes. Previous work has treated investments as undifferentiated capital.

In contrast with the earlier literature on capital structure, which began with an equity-financed firm, and sought a special rationale for debt, the TCE approach postulates that debt is the natural financial instrument. Equity, the administrative form, appears as the financial instrument of last resort. The discriminating use of debt and equity is thus predicted by the foregoing.

Along the lines of Williamson we suggest a very simple model. There are only two kinds of finance, debt and equity. Projects are ranked according to their degree of specificity. Suppose that a firm is seeking to finance a project with a low level of specificity completely out of debt. Suppose further that debt is a governance structure that works almost entirely out of rules. In the event of bankruptcy, the debt holders will exercise pre-emptive claims against the assets in question. If all goes well interest and principal will be paid. However, failure to make scheduled payments will result in liquidation. The various debt holders will then realize differential recovery in the degree to which the assets in question are redeployable.

Since the value of pre-emptive claims declines as the degree of asset specificity deepens, the terms of debt financing will be adjusted adversely. Confronted with the prospect that specialized investments will be financed on adverse terms, the firms might respond by sacrificing some of the specialized investment features in favor of greater redeployability.[6] In response equity becomes the preferred financing instrument. The board of directors becomes a mechanism by which the cost of capital for projects that involve limited redeployability is reduced. Not only do the added controls to which equity has access have better assurance properties, but equity is more forgiving than debt. Efforts are therefore made to preserve the value of a going concern. Thus, whereas the governance structure associated with debt is based on a set of predetermined, non-discretionary rules, 'that associated with equity is much more intrusive and is akin to [discretionary] administration' (Williamson 1988: 580).

Let S_i be an index of asset specificity and let the cost of debt and equity capital, expressed as a function of asset specificity be $k_d(S_i)$ and $k_e(S_i)$, respectively. Firms will switch between debt and equity as asset specificity increases if $k_d(0) < k_e(0)$ but $k_d' > k_e' > 0$.

That $k_d(0) < k_e(0)$ is because debt is a comparatively simple governance structure. Being a rules-governed relation, the set-up costs of debt are relatively low. By contrast, equity finance, which is a much more complex governance relation that contemplates intrusive involvement in the oversight of a project, has higher set-up costs. Allowing as it does greater discretion, it compromises incentives intensity and invites politicking.

Although the cost of both debt and equity finance increases as asset specificity deepens, debt financing rises more rapidly. This is because a rules-governance regime will sometimes force liquidation or otherwise cause the firm to compromise value-enhancing decisions that a more adaptable regime, of which equity governance is one, could implement. Accordingly, whereas highly redeployable assets will be financed with debt, equity is favored as assets become non-redeployable. Let S_i^* be the value of S_i for which $k_d'(S) = k_e'(S)$.[7] The optimal choice of all-or-no finance is to use debt finance for all projects for which $S < S^*$, and equity finance for all $S > S^*$. 'Equity finance is thus reserved for projects where the needs for nuanced governance are great' (Williamson 1988: 581). To test the hypothesis that input and output specificity is negatively related to debt in a firm's capital structure we estimate the following model:

$$DICE_{it} = \alpha_0 + \beta_1(INNOV)_{it} + \beta_2(R/S)_{it} + \beta_3(ASSETS)_{it} + \beta_4(OPM)_{it} + \beta_5(DICE)_{it-5} + e_{it} \qquad (6.1)$$

where the dependent variable, *DICE* is alternatively defined as the ratio of total debt to common equity, long-term debt to common equity and short-term debt to common equity in 1982.

Innovation (*INNOV*) is the innovation rate defined as the ratio of total innovations divided by total assets in 1982. Innovation as a measure of output specificity is the exercise of the growth option represented by R&D. In many cases, investment in specific capital assets is necessary to implement production of an R&D result. Regardless of whether new assets are purchased, however, once assets are dedicated to the production of an innovation (which on average takes almost five years), they cannot be redeployed without incurring the opportunity cost of lost profits from the innovation, and thus, the assets are specific. Hence, the expected relationship between innovation and debt is negative.

(*R/S*) is the ratio of research and development expenditures divided by 1982 sales. *R/D* can be considered a measure of input uniqueness (Titman and Wessels 1988) and agency costs (Myers 1977). In the context of asset specificity, R&D measures investment in the process of identifying and developing unique products. Since R&D generally requires specialized labor, it is directly associated with asset uniqueness. In terms of agency costs, R&D can be viewed as a risky option on future investment, whereby its findings lead to a decision regarding capital investment. If this point precedes the maturity of associated debt financing, an agency cost is created (Myers 1977). In each of these interpretations, the predicted relationship between R&D and debt is negative.

Assets are a proxy for diversification measured by the log of total assets in 1982. Agency costs can be offset by diversification on the part of the firm (Warner 1977). Diversification reduces volatility in expected cash flows, and hence, increases debt capacity. As such, it would be expected that larger firms face lower debt costs due to their greater diversification opportunities. Hence, the log of asset size is included in the model as a measure of debt capacity, and its sign is predicted to be positive.

Operating profit margin (OPM) is employed as a measure of internal cash availability. This is included in the model as a measure for the firm's position in relation to the pecking order theory of capital structure. If firms prefer to finance with internal, rather than external funds, the sign on OPM should be negative (Jensen 1986). The long payback period, and the intangible nature of the asset that is created, all combine to make it difficult to finance R&D using external sources of capital (Leland and Pyle 1977). Therefore, firms with ample sources of internal financing are thought to be better able to invest in R&D, ceteris paribus.

Capital structure is viewed by most firms as a long-term strategic decision. Lagged debt to common equity (D/CE_{it-5}) is included as a measure of the firm's long-term capital structure choice. Fischer et al. (1989) argue, however, that despite the long-term nature of the capital structure decision, capital market friction may cause temporary deviations from the optimal debt/equity ratio. Lagged debt is expected to be positively related to capital structure.

Williamson (1975: 201) has emphasized the inherent tension between hierarchical bureaucratic organizations and entrepreneurial activity,

> Were it that large firms could compensate internal entrepreneurial activity in ways approximating that of the market, the large firm need experience no disadvantage in entrepreneurial respects. Violating the congruency between hierarchical position and compensation appears to generate bureaucratic strains, however, and is greatly complicated by the problem of accurately imputing causality.

This leads Williamson (1975: 205–6) to conclude that,

> I am inclined to regard the early stage innovative disabilities of large size as serious and propose the following hypothesis: An efficient procedure by which to introduce new products is for the initial development and market testing to be performed by independent inventors and small firms (perhaps new entrants) in an industry, the successful development then to be acquired, possibly through licensing or merger, for subsequent marketing by a large multinational enterprise. Put differently, a division of effort between the new product innovation process on the one hand, and management of proven resources on the other may well be efficient.

However, theory offers no insight into the effect of this division of labor on the firm's capital structure choice.

By estimating the model separately for large and small firms the hypothesis that asset specificity will have a disparate effect on small- and large-firm capital structure choice is examined. The model is estimated both with and without the lagged capital structure variable. There are two estimation issues. First, since the error terms may be related to the size of the dependent variable, the estimates of the variance of the OLS coefficients may be biased downward. The equations are re-estimated and corrected for heteroskedasticity. Second, to measure the interactive impact of firm size on capital structure, a seemingly unrelated regression (SUR) technique similar to that used in Acs and Isberg (1991) is estimated. The medium and large firms are combined to form one sample, while the small firms form the second group.[8] The model in equation (6.1) is reestimated in SUR form as follows:

$$DICE = \alpha + \Sigma \, \beta_{1i}(INNOV * D_i) + \Sigma \, \beta_{2i}(R/S * D_i) + \Sigma \, \beta_{3i} \, (SIZE * D_i)$$
$$+ \Sigma \, \beta_{4i}(OPM * D_i) + \Sigma \, \beta_{5i}(D/CE_5 * D_i) + e \qquad (6.2)$$

where:

D_i = a dummy variable for small firms ($i = s$: D_s = 1 if small firm,
0 otherwise) and combined medium/large firms
($i = ml$: D_{ml} = 1 if medium or large firm, 0 otherwise),

and all other variables are as defined in equation (6.1). The model is estimated twice; first by constraining the lagged debt/equity coefficients to zero, and second, removing that constraint.

6.4   EMPIRICAL RESULTS

Using the ratio of total debt to common equity (*TD/CE*), long-term debt to common equity (*LTD/CE*), and short-term debt to common equity (*STD/CE*) in 1982 as the dependent variable, the cross-section regression is estimated for 315 firms. Simple statistics for all the model variables are presented in Table 6.3. As shown in Table 6.4 (column 1), using total debt to common equity (*TD/CE*) as the dependent variable, the emergence of a negative and statistically significant coefficient for R/S suggests that asset specificity is inversely related to debt. This is consistent with the findings of Bradley, Jarrell and Kim (1984) and Balakrishnan and Fox (1993). The negative and statistically significant coefficient of *OPM* suggests that high levels of internal cash flow are associated with lower levels of debt. This is consistent with the findings of Titman and Wessels (1988). The negative coefficient on innovation suggests that even after controlling for internal cash flow, innovative firms use less and

Table 6.3 Descriptive characteristics of the regression sample

Variable	Mean	Std. dev.	Minimum	Maximum
*Innov./*Ln (total Assets) (82)	0.452	0.798	0.000	6.747
STD/CE (82) (%)	12.783	26.493	0.000	244.538
LTD/CE (82) (%)	46.374	56.141	0.000	361.630
TD/CE (82) (%)	59.157	70.372	0.330	492.904
STD/CE (77) (%)	13.178	30.846	0.000	320.813
LTD/CE (77) (%)	53.902	93.775	0.000	1111.320
TD/CE (77) (%)	67.080	113.910	0.000	1264.020
R/S (82) (%)	2.942	2.818	0.000	16.641
Operating Profit Margin (82) (%)	11.089	8.567	-40.260	54.530
Ln (Total Assets) (82)	6.334	1.581	2.794	11.040

Table 6.4 Regression results (OLS) for short-term, long-term and total debt to common equity equations for all firms in 1982 (t-statistics in parentheses)

Variable	(1) TD/CE	(2) TD/CE	(3) LTD/CE	(4) LTD/CE	(5) STD/CE	(6) STD/CE
Intercept	95.824	48.008	65.342	33.476	30.481	17.005
	(5.871)	(3.604)	(5.071)	(3.090)	(4.663)	(2.828)
INNOV/A	-1.944	-1.197	-3.505	-2.799	1.561	1.571
	(-0.411)	(-0.321)	(-0.939)	(-0.917)	(0.825)	(0.931)
R/S	-6.701*	-3.927*	-5.135*	-2.868*	-1.574*	-1.186*
	(-4.899)	(-3.578)	(-4.751)	(-3.181)	(-2.87)	(-2.419)
OPM	-1.872*	-1.869*	-1.356*	-1.433*	-0.515*	-0.439*
	(-3.872)	(-4.909)	(-3.554)	(-4.597)	(-2.664)	(-2.554)
Assets	0.954	2.805	2.143	2.897*	-1.189	-0.207
	(0.386)	(1.437)	(1.099)	(1.816)	(-1.202)	(-0.233)
STD/CE t-5						0.391*
						(9.036)
LTD/CE t-5				0.407*		
				(12.479)		
TD/CE t-5		0.424*				
		(13.816)				
Adj. R-squared	0.045	0.2417	0.113	0.408	0.118	0.4526
F-statistic	4.719	21.084	11.048	44.281	11.568	53.808
Sample size	315	315	315	315	315	315

Note: Statistically significant at the 95 percent level of confidence, two-tail test.

not more debt, relying on a discretionary governance structure as suggested by Williamson (1988). However, the results are not statistically significant. The positive coefficient on assets suggests that larger firms are more diversified that smaller ones.

When lagged D/CE is included in column (2), neither the sign nor significance of any of the other coefficients changes. The coefficient of the lagged debt term is positive and statistically significant, implying that current capital structure is closely related to its prior characteristics. This supports the hypothesis that capital structure is stable over time, as advanced by Fischer et.al. (1989). These results are robust for different specifications of the dependent variable in columns (3)–(6). The negative and statistically significant coefficient for R/S in columns (5) and (6) suggests that short-term debt may be a more important strategy variable than long-term debt, since it can be increased and/or decreased more easily to 'hit a target', for firms that are actively managing their capital structure.

Table 6.5 shows separate regression estimates for large and small firms.[9] R/S and OPM apparently have similar effects on small- and large-firm capital structure. The negative and significant coefficient for R&D is consistent with the hypothesis that R&D is a risky growth option. All of the arguments regarding the difficulty of using external finance, especially debt, for R&D should apply most strongly to small firms. Such firms have access to a narrower range of capital market instruments, and are less likely to be able to trade off externally financed physical investment and R&D at the margin. Although operating cash flow is negatively associated with both large- and small-firm capital structure, the coefficient for large firms is not statistically significant. The positive and statistically significant coefficient for OPM in column (1) for small firms is consistent with other findings that small firms rely more on retained earnings than large firms to finance investment.

In column (2) the coefficient for large-firm innovation is negative and statistically significant. Firms that tend to invest heavily in firm-specific assets and firm-specific know-how will find it more difficult to fund such investments with debt. The results are consistent with a discretionary governance structure (Williamson 1988). However, the positive and statistically significant coefficient for innovation suggests that small firms use more, not less, long-term debt to finance innovation. These results suggest that small innovative firms must use higher levels of debt and a more simple governance structure to finance investment. Governance patterns for small firms may differ from large firms because they tend to be more closely held, subject to greater proprietary control and different monitoring costs. However, this should indicate a lower cost of equity, resulting in the use of less debt.[10]

Columns (3)–(4) in Table 6.5 report analogous results for short-term debt.

Table 6.5 Regression results for debt to common equity for large and small firms in 1982 (t-statistics in parentheses)

Variable	(1) LTD/CE OLS SF	(2) LTD/CE OLS LF	(3) STD/CE OLS SF	(4) STD/CE OLS LF	(5) LTD/CE SUR SF	(6) LTD/CE SUR LF
Intercept	104.01	-3.718	81.945	18.391	82.623	6.717
	(2.431)	(-0.173)	(4.116)	(1.571)	(1.861)	(0.267)
INNOV/A	32.389*	-8.461*	14.636*	-1.818	35.931*	-10.377*
	(3.111)	(-2.168)	(3.021)	(-0.858)	(3.253)	(-1.911)
R/S	-5.819*	-5.892*	-2.285*	-0.801	-5.502*	-3.048*
	(-3.647)	(-4.087)	(-3.075)	(-1.023)	(-2.866)	(-2.014)
OPM	-3.771*	-0.511	-0.784*	-0.594*	-3.962*	-1.803*
	(-4.842)	(-1.155)	(-2.166)	(-2.469)	(-4.572)	(-3.555)
Assets	-2.109	10.481*	-12.222*	0.602	1.793	9.120*
	(-0.227)	(3.582)	(-2.814)	(0.378)	(0.185)	(2.543)
Sys. weighted R-squared	–	–	–	–	0.357	0.357
Adj. R-squared	0.242	0.146	0.201	0.028	–	–
F-statistic	8.596	10.353	6.954	2.603	–	–
Sample size	95	219	95	219	89	89

Note: * Statistically significant at the 95 percent level of confidence, two-tail test.

111

For both large and small firms higher levels of cash flow are associated with less short-term debt. For small firms the positive and statistically significant coefficient of innovation suggests that even after holding the level of R/S constant, innovative activity results in higher levels of short-term debt. The statistically insignificant coefficient of both innovation and R/S in column (4) suggests that for large firms, *the short-term capital structure choice is independent of long-term investment decisions.*

This somewhat surprising finding suggests that, ceteris paribus, small firms use more debt than large firms to finance innovation, but not R&D. For small firms this result holds for both short-term debt, as well as long-term debt. This result is robust for different specifications of the model. These results would simply not go away. Therefore, we cannot reject the hypothesis that innovation will have a disparate effect on small- and large-firm capital structure. Brouwer and Kleinknecht (forthcoming) found that R&D expenditures account for only about a third of total investment for an innovation. One possible explanation is that small firms may face binding liquidity constraints and must rely on both short- and long-term debt as permanent capital, that is, short-term debt is used for more than smoothing transitory shortages of internal cash flow in small firms. The amount that must be invested in new equipment and plant to produce a new product, or embody a new process, generally exceeds the R&D costs many fold. This finding is consistent with the conclusion of Evans and Jovanovic (1989), Fazzari, Hubbard and Petersen (1986), Hao and Jaffe (1993), and Holtz-Eaklin, Joulfaian and Rosen (1994) that small firms face binding liquidity constraints.[11]

The results in columns (5) and (6) using the SUR model are similar to the OLS results. All of the coefficients have the hypothesized sign and are statistically significant. While not reported here, these results are robust for different sample size and specification of the model, with the exception of lagged debt. Table 6.6 shows regression results for large and small firms with lagged debt to common equity. All the variables have the expected sign and are statistically significant. The positive and statistically significant coefficient of lagged debt suggests that the capital structure choice of large and small firms is a long-run decision.

6.5 CONCLUSION

This chapter uses a new measure of specificity to examine the effect of uniqueness on capital structure choice in the context of corporate governance and firm size. The results suggest that innovation is an important determinant of capital structure choice, and that the exact relationship may depend on firm size. For small firms, innovation coincides with greater

Table 6.6   *Regression results for debt to common equity for large and small firms in 1982 corrected for heteroskedasticity (t-statistics in parentheses)*

Variable	(1) LTD/CE OLS SF	(2) STD/CE OLS SF	(3) LTD/CE OLS LF	(4) STD/CE OLS LF
Intercept	77.902	50.246	–7.442	17.677
	(1.827)	(1.831)	(–0.405)	(1.147)
INNOV/A	18.856*	11.764*	–4.388*	–0.772
	(2.262)	(3.197)	(–2.248)	(–0.842)
R/S	–4.207*	–1.646*	–3.287*	–0.588
	(–3.464)	(–3.148)	(–3.787)	(–1.226)
OPM	–3.353*	–0.568*	–0.685	–0.586*
	(–4.073)	(–2.285)	(–1.860)	(–1.960)
Assets	–1.359	–7.510*	7.280*	–0.558
	(–0.161)	(–4.425)	(2.889)	(–0.034)
LTD/CE t-5	0.293*	–	0.411*	–
	(4.787)		(6.859)	
STD/CE t-5		0.335*		0.424*
	–	(3.559)	–	(9.449)
Adj. R-squared	0.33	0.46	0.48	0.16
F-statistic	10.54	17.25	42.90	9.48
Sample size	95	95	219	219

Note: * Statistically significant at the 95 percent level of confidence, two-tail test.

levels of debt financing, while for large firms asset specificity is associated with a more flexible governance structure.

There are at least three conclusions to be drawn from these results. First, the results for small firms may be spurious. Second, governance patterns for small firms may be different from large firms. Structural differences in governance costs may explain the lack of fit of the TCE model to all firms. Third, small innovative firms may face binding liquidity constraints, relying more on debt (both short and long term) as permanent capital, instead of equity. Liquidity constraints would suggest that capital markets may not be perfect as assumed in much of the literature. While these findings are not without ambiguity they do suggest that future research should examine the *impact* of leverage on the survival of small firms.

NOTES

1. For a review of the literature see Harris and Raviv (1991).
2. Balakrishnan and Fox (1993) find that advertising to sales ratio is positively related to capital structure. This result implies that firms that spend more on reputational assets such as brand names can leverage more. These goods may be bought and sold without many transaction costs.
3. A firm's relative innovative advantage is likely to be roughly proportional to the number of suitably qualified people exposed to the knowledge base from which innovative ideas might derive. The key feature of a particular environment constitutes what Winter (1984) terms a 'technological regime'. For a test of the Winter hypothesis see Acs and Audretsch (1988).
4. The *Business Week* data include the company-financed R&D expenditures of 735 companies. Although the *Business Week* sample excludes the smallest enterprises, firms which can be considered as relatively small are included in the data. One hundred and thirty firms have fewer than 500 employees, which is the standard used by the US Small Business Administration to distinguish small from large firms. The mean asset size of the whole sample in 1977 was $1 164 million with the largest being $38 453 million and the smallest $9 527 million. Slightly more than one-quarter of the sample is composed of firms with less than $100 million sales.
5. Short-term debt does not include non-debt current liabilities, and is defined as that which matures in one year or less. Long-term debt includes capitalized leases, and is defined as that which matures in more than one year.
6. This would retard technological change because technological progress itself depends on the creation of firm-specific assets as new products or new production processes. Porter (1992: 66) has recently suggested that, 'many American companies invest too little, particularly in those intangible assets and capabilities required for competitiveness' – R&D, employee training and skills development, information systems, organizational development, and supplier relations.
7. The marginal cost of debt includes two components: the cost of the debt instrument itself and the change in the cost of equity capital that results from the higher debt ratio. Although the cost of debt must be lower than the cost of equity (on average) at all times, when one considers the cost of debt at the margin, including the implicit increase in the cost of equity, it is possible for the two to be equal, as assumed in this example.
8. The large and medium groups were combined into one group because the small firm roughly corresponds to the US Small Business Administration's definition of what a small firm is. A small firm is defined as a firm with less than 500 employees.
9. In order to estimate a SUR model a balanced data set is required. Since the small-firm category used in this study is half the size of the large-firm category, a special selection process was designed to match pairs from each sub-sample to run the SUR regressions. First, the large-firm sample was ranked by size, and every other firm was selected. This preserves the distribution within the sub-sample. Each of the large firms was then matched to a firm in the small-firm sample. First, the sub-sample was matched by firm size and second by innovation rate. The same process was then repeated with the large firms omitted from the first sub-sample. The sample size varied from run to run depending on how it was sorted. The SUR results were virtually identical for all of the different sorts.
10. Indeed, we know that small biotechnology companies in the R&D phase have very low debt levels and are equity financed, as suggested by the theory. Biotechnology companies in the innovation phase also have low levels of debt. However, they have been the recipients of billions of dollars of venture capital investment!
11. Hao and Jaffe (1993) find that financial conditions, whether measured as cash flow, the stock of liquid assets or the ratio of liquid assets to current liabilities, do affect the R&D spending of small firms. For large firms there is no evidence of such an effect.

7. Employment growth in metropolitan areas

7.1 INTRODUCTION

Shift-share analysis has become a very popular tool for analyzing regional employment change. While earlier papers have focused on one version of the shift-share technique, this chapter looks at shift-share analysis from both absolute and relative perspectives. The purpose of this chapter is to utilize the traditional approach to shift-share analysis to analyse high-technology employment change in 37 metropolitan areas. A new variable, labor force, is introduced to permit inter-metropolitan comparison by converting absolute numbers into relative numbers. High technology in metropolitan areas has received little attention in shift-share analysis and little has been done in analyzing high technology at the industry level.

This chapter has two objectives: (1) to utilize the traditional shift-share technique in both absolute and relative terms and illustrate why both are necessary, and (2) to give the first account of the recent trend of high-technology employment in US metropolitan areas. In Section 7.2 we introduce the data, followed by a description of technique in Section 7.3. Section 7.4 provides a regional analysis and Section 7.5 provides an industry by industry analysis of high technology employment. We find that shift-share analysis is a useful tool to study employment shifts in metropolitan areas. Most of the gains and losses in an MSA can be explained by the region's competitiveness component.

7.2 DATA

The Bureau of Labor Statistics (BLS) supplied employment, or ES-202 series data, for the years 1988 and 1991. Employment data are reported to the BLS by State Employment Security Agencies (SESAs) and cover 98 percent of civilian employees. While an initial year prior to 1988 may be desirable in terms of increasing the length of the period of analysis, we chose 1988 to avoid complications caused by the reclassification of SIC codes in 1987. Labor force data are also supplied by the BLS and reflect data gathered as part of the Local Area Unemployment Statistics (LAUS) program.

Thirty-two three-digit SIC industries were chosen and grouped in six high-technology industries as identified by Acs (1996). These industries are: biotechnology and biomedical, defense and aerospace, information technology, energy and chemicals, high-technology machinery and instruments, and high-technology research (Appendix E).

A sample of 37 metropolitan statistical areas (MSAs) was selected using the criteria of high-technology development, venture capital, innovation and university R&D. For instance, urban centers like San Jose, Boston and San Francisco have large venture-capital communities while New York, Baltimore and Los Angeles have a high concentration of university research. Finally, the MSAs were grouped into three main categories depending on the size of the average labor force between 1988 and 1991. The first category, small-sized MSAs (SSM), has 11 MSAs with an average labor force of less than 0.6 million. The second category, medium-sized MSAs (MSM), has 13 MSAs with an average labor force between 0.6 million and 1.2 million. The last category, large-sized MSAs (LSM), has 13 MSAs with an average labor force greater than 1.2 million. The 37 MSAs represent 52.9 percent of US high-technology employment. On an industry basis, the sample ranges from 30.51 percent for energy and chemicals to 77.63 percent for information technology and services.

Table 7.1 ranks clusters by high-technology importance and growth. Between 1988 and 1991, 17 of the MSAs in the sample have more than 1 percent of the US high-technology employment. Los Angeles leads the sample with 6.17 percent of US high-technology employment. The cities with the highest employment growth rates are Austin (36.8), Charlotte (21.85), San Francisco (21.6) and Raleigh/Durham (17.8).

7.3   SHIFT-SHARE TECHNIQUE

Ever since Creamer (1943) set the tone of shift-share analysis and Perloff et al. (1960) revived it by using it in regional economic analysis, the model has been a subject of controversies. The debate has centered around the model's effectiveness as a predictive and analytical tool. Praskevopoulos (1971), Ashby (1964), James and Hughes (1973), Andrikopoulos et al. (1990), Ireland and Moomaw (1981) – just to name a few – have written in support of the model, while Houston (1967) and Brown (1969) have questioned the validity of the model. By the same token, Kalbacher (1979), Klaasen and Paelinck (1972) and McDonough and Sihag (1991) have proposed different versions of shift share either by including multiple bases or by including relative weights for variables used in computations.

In this study a traditional shift-share analysis is used to describe employment

Table 7.1 US high-technology employment*

Metropolitan area	High-tech employment in 1988	Rank	High-tech employment in 1991	Rank	Percentage of US high tech (1991)	Rank	Employment growth rate (1988–1991) (%)	Rank
Austin	33 696	(28)	46 118	(23)	0.76	(23)	36.86	(1)
Charlotte	1 263	(37)	1 539	(37)	0.03	(37)	21.85	(2)
San Francisco	36 288	(26)	44 127	(25)	0.73	(25)	21.60	(3)
Raleigh	46 228	(22)	54 472	(20)	0.90	(20)	17.83	(4)
Houston	124 939	(9)	145 289	(9)	2.39	(9)	16.29	(5)
Seattle	135 751	(8)	157 607	(6)	2.60	(6)	16.10	(6)
Miami	18 664	(36)	21 427	(32)	0.35	(32)	14.80	(7)
Portland	38 002	(25)	41 887	(26)	0.69	(26)	10.22	(8)
Atlanta	60 346	(18)	65 617	(16)	1.08	(16)	8.73	(9)
Salt Lake City	32 052	(30)	34 711	(28)	0.57	(28)	8.30	(10)
Washington	141 291	(7)	150 045	(7)	2.47	(7)	6.20	(11)
San Diego	96 909	(12)	100 232	(12)	1.65	(12)	3.43	(12)
Richmond	18 866	(35)	19 399	(33)	0.32	(33)	2.83	(13)
Indianapolis	50 024	(21)	50 795	(22)	0.84	(22)	1.54	(14)
Cincinnati	52 883	(20)	53 303	(21)	0.88	(21)	0;79	(15)
Denver	56 585	(19)	56 955	(18)	0.94	(18)	0.65	(16)
Cleveland	60 958	(17)	61 173	(17)	1.01	(17)	0.35	(17)
Dallas	150 134	(6)	149 249	(8)	2.46	(8)	-0.59	(18)
Phoenix	83 273	(15)	82 176	(14)	1.35	(14)	-1.32	(19)
Columbus	34 403	(27)	33 544	(29)	0.55	(29)	-2.50	(20)

Table 7.1 continued

Metropolitan area	High-tech employment in 1988	Rank	High-tech employment in 1991	Rank	Percentage of US high tech (1991)	Rank	Employment growth rate (1988–1991) (%)	Rank
Philadelphia	167 770	(5)	162 587	(5)	2.68	(5)	-3.09	(21)
Pittsburg	45 687	(23)	44 206	(24)	0.73	(24)	-3.24	(22)
Chicago	204 009	(4)	192 830	(4)	3.18	(4)	-5.48	(23)
San Jose	255 600	(3)	239 256	(2)	3.94	(2)	-6.39	(24)
Minneapolis	121 955	(10)	113 378	(10)	1.87	(10)	-7.03	(25)
Louisville	28 914	(31)	26 781	(31)	0.44	(31)	-7.38	(26)
Nashville	19 854	(33)	18 385	(34)	0.30	(34)	-7.40	(27)
St Louis	95 555	(13)	88 201	(13)	1.45	(13)	-7.70	(28)
Kansas City	38 136	(24)	35 161	(27)	0.58	(27)	-7.80	(29)
Rochester	86 703	(14)	79 277	(15)	1.31	(15)	-8.56	(30)
Baltimore	61 732	(16)	55 378	(19)	0.91	(19)	-10.29	(31)
Orlando	33 565	(29)	29 793	(30)	0.49	(30)	-11.24	(32)
New York	115 904	(11)	102 801	(11)	1.69	(11)	-11.31	(33)
Boston	268 574	(2)	234 134	(3)	3.86	(3)	-12.82	(34)
Providence	19 080	(34)	16 597	(36)	0.27	(36)	-13.01	(35)
Los Angeles	436 065	(1)	374 781	(1)	6.17	(1)	-14.05	(36)
Tucson	20 975	(32)	16 999	(35)	0.28	(35)	-18.96	(37)
Total	3 292 633		3 200 210		52.70		-2.81	

Note: *Ranked by growth rate.

Source: US Bureau of Labor Statistics, ES-202 data, special run.

growth in each of the 37 metropolitan statistical areas under study by taking into account employment in all MSAs combined. The change in high-technology employment in industry i in MSA j can be broken up into three components: (1) the national growth component, (2) the industry mix component and (3) the competitive or regional share component.

We define the national growth component as the high-technology employment change of metropolitan area j and industry i assuming i is growing at the national growth rate. The growth rate of all metropolitan areas combined will be used for national growth. We also define the actual growth as the difference between high-technology employment in 1988 and 1991 for industry i and MSA j. The net relative growth is equal to the difference between the national growth and the actual growth. The sum of net relative growth for all the six industries makes up the total net relative growth of a metropolitan area. Net relative growth is calculated as follows:

$$NRG_j = \sum (r_{ij} - s)HTEMP_{ij}$$
$$\text{for } i = 1,\ldots,6 \quad j = 1,\ldots,37$$

(7.1)

where NRG_j is the net relative growth of high-technology employment for the metropolitan statistical area $(MSA)_j$ between 1988 and 1991, $HTEMP_{ij}$ is 1988 employment for high technology industry i and metropolitan area $(MSA)\,j$, r_{ij} is the employment growth rate for high-technology industry i and MSA j between 1988 and 1991, and s is the employment growth rate for all high-technology industries and all MSAs between 1988 and 1991.

To control for the size of a metropolitan area, we introduce a new variable, labor force, to carry out a common size analysis. As the economic interest is the creation of jobs, it is crucial to compare jobs created or lost to the number of people who are able and willing to work (labor force). We define the controlled net relative growth as the net relative growth per 1 000 persons in the labor force. Since the span of our study is 1988 and 1991, labor force refers to the average of the two years' labor force. Thus, equation (7.1) is modified as follows,

$$CNRG_j \frac{\sum (r_{ij} - s)HTEMP_{ij}}{LF_j}$$

(7.2)

$$\text{for } i = 1,\ldots 6 \quad j = 1,\ldots 37$$

where $CNRG_j$ is the controlled net relative growth of high-technology employment for the metropolitan statistical area (MSA) j between 1988 and 1991, and LF_j is the average labor force for MSA j between 1988 and 1991.

The net relative growth is a measure of the shift of high technology jobs in and out of the economic activity of the metropolitan area. The net relative growth, which can be negative or positive, is determined by two factors: (1) industry mix and (2) the regional share or competitive component. The industry mix is itself influenced by growth in a given industry. The employment growth in a metropolitan area is affected positively or negatively by the performance of each individual industry that makes up its economy. These industries may have a higher or a lower growth rate than the national average. The following equation is used to calculate the industry mix:

$$IM_j = \sum (s_i - s) HTEMP_{ij}$$
$$\text{for } i = 1, \ldots, 6 \quad j = 1, \ldots, 37 \tag{7.3}$$

where s_i is the employment growth rate for industry i for all MSAs, and IM_j is the industry mix of high-technology employment for MSA j.

The controlled industry mix is calculated by dividing the competitive component by the average labor force between 1988 and 1991. Thus, equation (7.3) becomes

$$CIM_j \frac{\sum (s_i - s) HTEMP_{ij}}{LF_j} \tag{7.4}$$
$$\text{for } i = 1, \ldots 6 \quad j = 1, \ldots 37$$

where CIM_j is the controlled industry mix of high-technology employment for MSA j.

The other component of net relative growth is the competitive component. The competitive component measures the part of a metropolitan area's growth that is due to its competitiveness. For instance, two metropolitan areas may have the same industry structure and the same industry mix, but may have different growth because one is more competitive than the other. Given the net relative growth and the industry mix, the competitive component is computed by subtracting equation (7.3) from equation (7.1). Therefore, the competitive component equation is:

$$CC_j = \sum (r_{ij} - s) HTEMP_{ij}$$
$$\text{for } i = 1, \ldots, 6 \quad j = 1, \ldots, 37 \tag{7.5}$$

where CC_j is the competitive component of the net relative growth for MSA j.

The controlled competitive component is calculated by dividing the competitive component by the average labor force between 1988 and 1991. Thus, equation (7.5) becomes

$$CCC_j \frac{\sum (r_{ij} - s_i) HTEMP_{ij}}{LF_j} \qquad (7.6)$$

$$\text{for } i = 1, \ldots 6 \quad j = 1, \ldots 37$$

where CCC_j is the controlled competitive component of the net relative growth for MSA j.

The controlled components of shift share are introduced to supplement the traditional shift share. They are introduced to capture the performance of all MSAs and remove any bias that may be due to the size of the metropolitan area.

The shift-share technique answers three questions: (1) how is a metropolitan area doing compared to the national average? (2) what is the impact of industry mix on the metropolitan economy? and (3) how competitive is the metropolitan area? However, shift share does not explain why the metropolitan area is growing. For a discussion of this, see Acs, FitzRoy and Smith (1999).

The analysis below is different from previous shift-share analyses in that it views the growth of high technology in both absolute and relative terms. Relative values should be understood as the values of controlled components of shift share. In other words, relative values are absolute values per 1 000 persons in the civilian labor force.

7.4   REGIONAL ANALYSIS

Table 7.2 presents a summary of our results. The net relative growth indicates the number of jobs that should have moved in or out of the economy. The industry mix indicates how a region performed because of its industry mix, while the competitive component captures the number of jobs gained or lost not because of the industry mix, but because the region is competitive. For the whole sample, 16 of the 37 MSAs had a negative industry mix; that is, they lost jobs because of the portfolio of their high-tech industries. Seventeen regions lost high-tech employment because of a lack of regional competitiveness.

Between 1988 and 1991 Los Angeles lost 49 385 jobs. Los Angeles lost 7 378 jobs partly because 48.4 percent of its high-tech jobs are concentrated in the defense and aerospace industry, an industry in decline. However, the competitive components show that Los Angeles lost 42 000 jobs because of the poor competitiveness of the city. Seattle gained 25 560 jobs in the same period. It lost 4 203 jobs because it had an unfavorable mix of industries; however, it gained 29 762 jobs because of its overall competitiveness. Figure

Table 7.2 Shift-share analysis

Metropolitan area	Industry mix				Competitive component				Net relative growth			
	Absolute	Rank	Relative	Rank	Absolute	Rank	Relative	Rank	Absolute	Rank	Relative	Rank
Atlanta	(105)	(23)	-0.07	(22)	7 023	(7)	4.72	(10)	6 918	(7)	4.69	(11)
Austin	642	(10)	1.46	(4)	12 272	(3)	27.96	(1)	12 914	(3)	30.02	(1)
Baltimore	(129)	(24)	-0.11	(23)	(4 541)	(31)	-3.80	(30)	(4 670)	(29)	-3.97	(30)
Boston	156	(20)	0.10	(21)	(27 268)	(36)	-17.58	(37)	(27 112)	(36)	-17.38	(37)
Charlotte	539	(12)	0.85	(6)	3 474	(10)	5.47	(9)	4 013	(10)	6.40	(8)
Chicago	1 367	(5)	0.42	(14)	(6 979)	(33)	-2.17	(25)	(5 612)	(33)	-1.76	(25)
Cincinnati	(453)	(29)	-0.59	(28)	2 316	(14)	2.99	(12)	1 863	(17)	2.45	(14)
Cleveland	(633)	(31)	-0.67	(29)	2 511	(13)	2.67	(15)	1 878	(16)	2.01	(17)
Columbus	172	(18)	0.24	(19)	(92)	(21)	-0.13	(21)	80	(20)	0.11	(20)
Dallas	955	(8)	0.66	(11)	2 256	(15)	1.57	(16)	3 212	(13)	2.23	(15)
Denver	724	(9)	0.82	(9)	1 190	(18)	1.34	(18)	1 914	(15)	2.17	(16)
Houston	3 056	(2)	1.80	(2)	20 703	(2)	12.20	(4)	23 759	(2)	14.51	(4)
Indianapolis	168	(19)	0.25	(18)	1 968	(16)	2.91	(13)	2 136	(14)	3.18	(13)
Kansas City	465	(13)	0.54	(13)	(2 399)	(27)	-2.80	(26)	(1 934)	(25)	-2.28	(26)
Los Angeles	(7 378)	(37)	-1.70	(34)	(42 008)	(37)	-9.69	(34)	(49 385)	(37)	-11.86	(36)
Louisville	(952)	(34)	-1.87	(35)	318	(19)	0.62	(19)	(634)	(23)	-1.25	(23)
Miami	606	(11)	0.64	(12)	2 667	(12)	2.81	(14)	3 272	(12)	3.50	(12)
Minneapolis	146	(21)	0.10	(20)	(5 395)	(32)	-3.85	(32)	(5 249)	(31)	-3.79	(29)

Nashville	(288)	(27)	-0.54	(26)	(639)	(23)	-1.20	(24)	(927)	(24)	-1.73	(24)
New York	2 717	(3)	0.83	(8)	(12 657)	(35)	-3.87	(32)	(9 940)	(35)	-3.08	(27)
Orlando	(667)	(32)	-1.09	(33)	(2 189)	(26)	-3.58	(29)	(2 856)	(27)	-4.90	(31)
Philadelphia	2 026	(4)	0.84	(7)	(2 631)	(28)	-1.08	(23)	(605)	(22)	-0.25	(22)
Phoenix	(258)	(26)	-0.25	(25)	1 433	(17)	1.37	(17)	1 175	(18)	1.14	(18)
Pittsburg	339	(16)	0.34	(16)	(573)	(22)	-0.58	(22)	(234)	(21)	-0.24	(21)
Portland	(365)	(28)	-0.54	(27)	5 287	(9)	7.84	(6)	4 922	(9)	7.58	(6)
Providence	(63)	(22)	-0.18	(24)	(1 900)	(25)	-5.56	(33)	(1 962)	(26)	-5.71	(32)
Raleigh	1 097	(6)	2.65	(1)	8 060	(5)	19.47	(3)	9 157	(5)	22.93	(3)
Richmond	356	(15)	0.77	(10)	83	(20)	0.18	(20)	439	(19)	0.98	(19)
Rochester	(3 747)	(35)	-7.38	(37)	(1 762)	(24)	-3.47	(28)	(5 510)	(32)	-10.96	(34)
Saint Louis	(827)	(33)	-0.77	(31)	(3 919)	(30)	-3.08	(27)	(4 747)	(30)	-3.76	(28)
Salt Lake City	338	(17)	0.27	(17)	3 196	(11)	6.29	(7)	3 534	(11)	7.11	(7)
San Diego	(453)	(30)	-0.89	(32)	6 421	(8)	5.58	(8)	5 967	(8)	5.30	(10)
San Francisco	1 017	(7)	0.88	(5)	7 813	(6)	8.85	(5)	8 829	(6)	10.08	(5)
San Jose	359	(14)	0.41	(15)	9 729	(34)	-11.77	(36)	(9 370)	(34)	-11.17	(35)
Seattle	(4 203)	(36)	-5.08	(36)	29 763	(1)	27.74	(2)	25 560	(1)	24.74	(2)
Tucson	(235)	(25)	-0.75	(30)	(3 169)	(29)	-10.13	(35)	(3 404)	(28)	-10.85	(33)
Washington	3 514	(1)	1.59	(3)	9 096	(4)	4.12	(11)	12 609	(4)	5.77	(9)
Large-sized MSAs	5 626		0.23		(61 779)		-2.54		(56 153)		-2.31	
Medium-sized MSAs	(2 449)		-0.20		36 780		3.00		34 331		2.80	
Small-sized MSAs	(3 177)		-0.41		24 999		3.76		21 822		3.34	

Note: Relative numbers refer to the number of employees per 1 000 persons in civilian labor force.

123

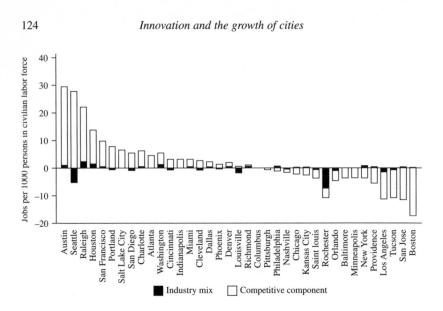

Figure 7.1   High-technology employment growth in US metropolitan areas:
a shift-share analysis

7.1 ranks the metropolitan areas by competitiveness. It is clear that most of the gains and losses come from a negative competitiveness.

7.5   SECTORIAL ANALYSIS

Since industry mix refers to a portfolio of industries and is therefore applicable to total high-technology industries, it should be understood as industry performance whenever the term is used for a particular industry. For example, job growth due to industry mix for the biotechnology and biomedical industry should be understood as job growth due to the performance of that industry in the nation. However, when this term is used for an MSA's total high-technology industry, it refers to job growth due to the kind of mix (portfolio) making up a metropolitan area's high technology industry. An industry-by-industry analysis has proved necessary in this chapter since each metropolitan area has its own strengths and weaknesses for each of the six industry groups. Those strengths and weaknesses may or may not appear in the aggregate results shown earlier. Tables 7.3 to 7.5 provide data on the six industry groups for 37 metropolitan areas.

The biotechnology and biomedical industry grew by 7.64 percent between 1988 and 1991. This high growth is reflected in the industry mix which is positive for all MSAs under study. The findings reveal that this particular industry

Table 7.3   Shift-share analysis: net relative growth

Metropolitan area	Biotechnology & biomedical		Defence & aerospace		Energy & chemicals		Information technology & services		Machinery & instruments		High-tech research	
	Absolute	Relative	Absolute	Relative	Absolute	Relative	Absolute	Relative	Absolute	Relative	Absolute	Relative
Atlanta	2 130	1.45	(2 860)	−1.94	34	0.02	5 116	3.47	1 373	0.93	1 125	0.76
Austin	820	1.91	NA	NA	NA	NA	10 025	23.30	939	2.18	1 131	2.63
Baltimore	982	0.83	(3 745)	−3.18	26	0.02	(1 500)	−1.27	(667)	−0.57	235	0.20
Boston	25	0.02	(3 511)	−2.25	(326)	−0.21	(15 122)	−9.69	(7 933)	−5.09	(245)	−0.16
Charlotte	310	0.50	(115)	−0.18	848	1.35	2 163	3.45	638	1.02	170	0.27
Chicago	(801)	−0.25	2 990	0.94	2 151	0.67	2 522	0.79	(6 899)	−2.16	(5 576)	−1.75
Cincinnati	194	0.26	524	0.69	733	0.96	1 289	1.69	(341)	−0.45	(536)	−0.70
Cleveland	23	0.02	(305)	−0.33	805	0.86	1 262	1.35	(184)	−0.20	277	0.30
Columbus	155	0.22	(202)	−0.28	144	0.20	2 176	3.06	(1 218)	−1.71	(976)	−1.37
Dallas	792	0.55	(1 904)	−1.32	195	0.13	3 486	2.42	(154)	−0.11	796	0.55
Denver	144	0.16	(1 350)	−1.53	132	0.15	2 420	2.75	(115)	−0.13	684	0.78
Houston	213	0.13	1 446	0.88	6 627	4.05	8 384	5.12	5 973	3.65	1 117	0.68
Indianapolis	2 611	3.89	(299)	−0.45	73	0.11	(711)	−1.06	(243)	−0.36	705	1.05
Kansas City	(237)	−0.28	5 675	6.68	(46)	−0.05	(7 081)	−8.33	(726)	−0.85	480	0.56
Los Angeles	(2 083)	−0.50	(32 177)	−7.73	(52)	−0.01	(6 639)	−1.59	(8 385)	−2.01	(50)	−0.01
Louisville	173	0.34	NA	NA	NA	NA	1 124	2.22	(1 879)	−3.71	(52)	−0.10
Miami	995	1.06	(85)	−0.09	(98)	−0.11	1 625	1.74	576	0.62	259	0.28
Minneapolis	2 876	2.08	(1 366)	−0.99	274	0.20	(6 851)	−4.94	11	0.01	(193)	−0.14
Nashville	(22)	−0.04	(510)	−0.95	115	0.22	127	0.24	(772)	−1.44	133	0.25
New York	573	0.18	(367)	−0.11	(994)	−0.31	(6 841)	−2.12	(4 191)	−1.30	1 880	0.58

Table 7.3 *continued*

Metropolitan area	Biotechnology & biomedical		Defence & aerospace		Energy & chemicals		Information technology & services		Machinery & instruments		High-tech research	
	Absolute	Relative	Absolute	Relative	Absolute	Relative	Absolute	Relative	Absolute	Relative	Absolute	Relative
Orlando	(91)	-0.16	(4 630)	-7.95	(52)	-0.09	2 125	3.65	(5)	-0.01	(203)	-0.35
Philadelphia	3 355	1.39	(687)	-0.28	2 339	0.97	(4 384)	-1.81	(2 437)	-1.01	1 210	0.50
Phoenix	(990)	-0.96	2 028	1.97	229	0.22	(1 610)	-1.56	1 165	1.13	354	0.34
Pittsburg	284	0.29	(153)	-0.16	(903)	-0.94	1 197	1.24	(1 476)	-1.53	818	0.85
Portland	526	0.81	225	0.35	164	0.25	5 471	8.43	(1 622)	-2.50	159	0.24
Providence	(6)	-0.02	(10)	-0.03	(461)	-1.34	651	1.89	(2 139)	-6.23	3	0.01
Raleigh	1 178	2.95	NA	NA	NA	NA	5 575	13.96	860	2.15	1 544	3.87
Richmond	(433)	-0.97	NA	NA	NA	NA	(180)	-0.40	899	2.02	153	0.34
Rochester	584	1.16	NA	NA	NA	NA	1 213	2.41	(6 930)	-13.78	(377)	-0.75
Saint Louis	(12)	-0.01	(6 416)	-5.08	1 691	1.34	(469)	-0.37	(218)	-0.17	678	0.54
Salt Lake City	1 629	3.28	666	1.34	(112)	-0.23	203	0.41	58	0.12	1 089	2.19
San Diego	2 871	2.55	(446)	-0.40	(124)	-0.11	(378)	-0.34	2 319	2.06	1 726	1.53
San Francisco	201	0.23	(348)	-0.40	325	0.37	6 937	7.92	645	0.74	1 069	1.22
San Jose	1 612	1.92	(4 551)	-5.43	571	0.68	543	0.65	(6 609)	-7.88	(935)	-1.11
Seattle	1 189	1.15	18 916	18.31	177	0.17	4 329	4.19	(283)	-0.27	1 232	1.19
Tucson	26	0.08	(1 258)	-4.01	32	0.10	(2 034)	-6.48	(490)	-1.56	320	1.02
Washington	190	0.09	1 994	0.91	(335)	-0.15	6 498	2.97	497	0.23	3 766	1.72

Note: Relative numbers refer to the number of employees per 1 000 persons in civilian labor force.

Table 7.4 Shift-share analysis: industry mix

Metropolitan area	Biotechnology & biomedical		Defence & aerospace		Energy & chemicals		Information technology & services		Machinery & instruments		High-tech research	
	Absolute	Relative	Absolute	Relative	Absolute	Relative	Absolute	Relative	Absolute	Relative	Absolute	Relative
Atlanta	274	0.18	(740)	-0.50	206	0.14	507	0.34	(497)	-0.33	145	0.10
Austin	245	0.56	NA	NA	NA	NA	421	0.96	(249)	-0.57	224	0.51
Baltimore	236	0.20	(964)	-0.81	240	0.20	322	0.27	(449)	-0.38	486	0.41
Boston	1 712	1.10	(1 988)	-1.28	311	0.20	2 418	1.56	(3 367)	-2.17	1 071	0.69
Charlotte	131	0.21	(12)	-0.02	500	0.79	227	0.36	(334)	-0.53	26	0.04
Chicago	1 162	0.36	(72)	-0.02	861	0.27	1 587	0.49	(3 773)	-1.17	1 603	0.50
Cincinnati	453	0.59	(884)	-1.14	352	0.46	145	0.19	(713)	-0.92	194	0.25
Cleveland	229	0.24	(372)	-0.40	743	0.79	196	0.21	(1 552)	-1.65	124	0.13
Columbus	172	0.24	(77)	-0.11	203	0.28	205	0.28	(647)	-0.89	316	0.43
Dallas	393	0.27	(1 318)	-0.91	981	0.68	1 542	1.07	(841)	-0.58	198	0.14
Denver	450	0.51	(694)	-0.78	776	0.87	280	0.32	(268)	-0.30	179	0.20
Houston	135	0.08	(42)	-0.02	3 808	2.24	397	0.23	(1 582)	-0.93	340	0.20
Indianapolis	1 146	1.69	(636)	-0.94	64	0.09	186	0.27	(727)	-1.07	135	0.20
Kansas City	547	0.64	(144)	-0.17	136	0.16	322	0.38	(505)	-0.59	109	0.13
Los Angeles	2 025	0.47	(10 021)	-2.31	1 256	0.29	1 684	0.39	(3 670)	-0.85	1 349	0.31
Louisville	45	0.09	NA	NA	NA	NA	66	0.13	(1 116)	-2.19	53	0.10
Miami	722	0.76	(103)	-0.11	43	0.05	89	0.09	(191)	-0.20	46	0.05
Minneapolis	1 264	0.90	(686)	-0.49	139	0.10	1 080	0.77	(1 903)	-1.36	251	0.18
Nashville	99	0.18	(153)	-0.29	98	0.18	118	0.22	(464)	-0.87	14	0.03
New York	1 824	0.56	(220)	-0.07	374	0.11	897	0.27	(1 175)	-0.36	1 017	0.31

Table 7.4 continued

Metropolitan area	Biotechnology & biomedical		Defence & aerospace		Energy & chemicals		Information technology & services		Machinery & instruments		High-tech research	
	Absolute	Relative	Absolute	Relative	Absolute	Relative	Absolute	Relative	Absolute	Relative	Absolute	Relative
Orlando	87	0.14	(677)	-1.11	13	0.02	208	0.34	(353)	-0.58	55	0.09
Philadelphia	2 390	0.99	(892)	-0.37	1 249	0.51	1 081	0.45	(2 267)	-0.93	465	0.19
Phoenix	217	0.21	(1 174)	-1.13	34	0.03	874	0.84	(346)	-0.33	137	0.13
Pittsburg	299	0.30	(12)	-0.01	417	0.42	225	0.23	(975)	-0.99	384	0.39
Portland	208	0.31	(107)	-0.16	36	0.05	311	0.46	(921)	-1.37	107	0.16
Providence	194	0.57	(5)	-0.01	117	0.34	120	0.35	(516)	-1.51	27	0.08
Raleigh	600	1.45	NA	NA	NA	NA	521	1.26	(335)	-0.81	312	0.75
Richmond	274	0.60	NA	NA	NA	NA	100	0.22	(62)	-0.13	43	0.09
Rochester	570	1.12	NA	NA	NA	NA	163	0.32	(4 567)	-8.99	86	0.17
Saint Louis	811	0.76	(2 140)	-1.99	696	0.65	269	0.25	(646)	-0.60	183	0.17
Salt Lake City	386	0.30	(325)	-0.26	110	0.09	276	0.22	(186)	-0.15	77	0.06
San Diego	642	1.26	(1 424)	-2.80	70	0.14	585	1.15	(943)	-1.86	617	1.21
San Francisco	402	0.35	(92)	-0.08	173	0.15	318	0.28	(165)	-0.14	380	0.33
San Jose	1 071	1.23	(1 687)	-1.93	45	0.05	2 792	3.20	(2 691)	-3.08	829	0.95
Seattle	385	0.47	(4 655)	-5.63	25	0.03	297	0.36	(530)	-0.64	274	0.33
Tucson	58	0.19	(356)	-1.14	4	0.01	165	0.53	(165)	-0.53	59	0.19
Washington	127	0.06	(163)	-0.07	103	0.05	1 664	0.75	(272)	-0.12	2 054	0.93

Note: Relative numbers refer to the number of employees per 1 000 persons in civilian labor force.

Table 7.5 Shift-share analysis: competitive component

Metropolitan area	Biotechnology & biomedical		Defence & aerospace		Energy & chemicals		Information technology & services		Machinery & instruments		High-tech research	
	Absolute	Relative	Absolute	Relative	Absolute	Relative	Absolute	Relative	Absolute	Relative	Absolute	Relative
Atlanta	1 856	1.25	(2 119)	-1.42	(172)	-0.12	4 609	3.09	1 870	1.26	980	0.66
Austin	574	1.31	NA	NA	NA	NA	9 603	21.88	1 187	2.70	907	2.07
Baltimore	746	0.62	(2 781)	-2.33	(214)	-0.18	(1 821)	-1.52	(218)	-0.18	(252)	-0.21
Boston	(1 687)	-1.09	(1 523)	-0.98	(636)	-0.41	(17 540)	-11.31	(4 566)	-2.94	(1 316)	-0.85
Charlotte	180	0.28	(103)	-0.16	348	0.55	1 935	3.04	972	1.53	143	0.23
Chicago	(1 963)	-0.61	3 062	0.95	1 290	0.40	936	0.29	(3 126)	-0.97	(7 179)	-2.23
Cincinnati	(259)	-0.33	1 408	1.82	381	0.49	1 144	1.48	372	0.48	(730)	-0.94
Cleveland	(205)	-0.22	67	0.07	62	0.07	1 066	1.13	1 369	1.46	153	0.16
Columbus	(16)	-0.22	(125)	-0.17	(59)	-0.08	1 971	2.71	(571)	-0.78	(1 292)	-1.78
Dallas	399	0.28	(586)	-0.41	(786)	-0.55	1 944	1.35	687	0.48	598	0.41
Denver	(307)	-0.35	(657)	-0.74	(643)	-0.73	2 140	2.41	153	0.17	504	0.57
Houston	78	0.05	1 488	0.88	2 819	1.66	7 987	4.71	7 555	4.45	777	0.46
Indianapolis	1 464	2.16	337	0.50	9	0.01	(897)	-1.32	483	0.71	570	0.84
Kansas City	(784)	-0.92	5 819	6.80	(182)	-0.21	(7 402)	-8.65	(221)	-0.26	371	0.43
Los Angeles	(4 108)	-0.95	(22 155)	-5.11	(1 308)	-0.30	(8 323)	-1.92	(4 715)	-1.09	(1 399)	-0.32
Louisville	128	0.25	NA	NA	NA	NA	1 058	2.07	(763)	-1.50	(105)	-0.21
Miami	273	0.29	18	0.02	(141)	-0.15	1 536	1.62	767	0.81	213	0.22
Minneapolis	1 612	1.15	(680)	-0.48	135	0.10	(7 931)	-5.65	1 914	1.36	(444)	-0.32
Nashville	(121)	-0.23	(357)	-0.67	17	0.03	9	0.02	(308)	-0.58	120	0.22
New York	(1 251)	-0.38	(147)	-0.05	(1 368)	-0.42	(7 738)	-2.37	(3 016)	-0.92	862	0.26

Table 7.5 continued

Metropolitan area	Biotechnology & biomedical		Defence & aerospace		Energy & chemicals		Information technology & services		Machinery & instruments		High-tech research	
	Absolute	Relative	Absolute	Relative	Absolute	Relative	Absolute	Relative	Absolute	Relative	Absolute	Relative
Orlando	(178)	-0.29	(3 953)	-6.46	(66)	-0.11	1 917	3.13	348	0.57	(258)	-0.42
Philadelphia	965	0.40	205	0.08	1 090	0.45	(5 465)	-2.25	(170)	-0.07	745	0.31
Phoenix	(1 207)	-1.16	3 202	3.07	195	0.19	(2 484)	-2.38	1 511	1.45	216	0.21
Pittsburg	(15)	-0.02	(141)	-0.14	(1 320)	-1.34	971	0.99	(501)	-0.51	433	0.44
Portland	318	0.47	331	0.49	128	0.19	5 160	7.66	(702)	-1.04	52	0.08
Providence	(200)	-0.58	(5)	-0.01	(578)	-1.69	530	1.55	(1 623)	-4.75	(24)	-0.07
Raleigh	578	1.40	NA	NA	NA	NA	5 054	12.20	1 196	2.89	1 233	2.98
Richmond	(707)	-1.54	NA	NA	NA	NA	(280)	-0.61	960	2.09	109	0.24
Rochester	14	0.03	NA	NA	NA	NA	1 050	2.07	(2 363)	-4.65	(463)	-0.91
Saint Louis	(824)	-0.65	(4 276)	-3.36	995	0.78	(738)	-0.58	429	0.34	495	0.39
Salt Lake City	1 242	2.45	991	1.95	(221)	-0.44	(73)	-0.14	244	0.48	1 013	1.99
San Diego	2 229	1.94	978	0.85	(194)	-0.17	(963)	-0.84	3 262	2.83	1 108	0.96
San Francisco	(201)	-0.23	(257)	-0.29	152	0.17	6 619	7.58	810	0.93	689	0.79
San Jose	541	0.65	(2 864)	-3.46	526	0.64	(2 249)	-2.72	(3 918)	-4.74	(1 764)	-2.13
Seattle	804	0.75	23 571	21.97	152	0.14	4 031	3.76	247	0.23	958	0.89
Tucson	(32)	-0.10	(903)	-2.89	28	0.09	(2 199)	-7.03	(325)	-1.04	262	0.84
Washington	62	0.03	2 157	0.98	(438)	-0.20	4 834	2.19	769	0.35	1 712	0.78

Note: Relative numbers refer to the number of employees per 1 000 persons in civilian labor force.

130

experienced sustained growth during the period under study. However, the competitive component which captures the growth due to the competitiveness of the MSA rather than the industry tells a different story. Five large MSAs, Los Angeles, Chicago, Boston, New York and Phoenix, lost more than 1 200 jobs each due to competition; while San Diego, Atlanta, Minneapolis and Indianapolis gained more than 1 400 jobs each.

As argued earlier, although it is important to know the gains and losses in absolute terms, the employment growth in small and medium metropolitan areas is neglected if no analysis is conducted in relative terms. Metropolitan areas like Salt Lake City and Indianapolis gained more than two jobs per 1 000 persons in the labor force due to competition. This is by far the greatest gain if the size of labor force is considered. Fortunately for this industry, only three metropolitan areas – Richmond, Phoenix and Boston – lost more than one job per 1 000 persons in the labor force. Overall, Salt Lake City, Indianapolis and Raleigh/Durham dominated the growth of the biotechnology and biomedical industries. Raleigh/Durham's strengths are conspicuous in industry mix.

The defense and aerospace industry experienced a large decline (–7.29 percent) during the period under study. The decline in this particular industry affected Los Angeles and Seattle more than any other metropolitan areas. The two lost more than 14 500 jobs due to the industry mix. However, in terms of competitiveness, Seattle gained 23 571 jobs while Los Angeles lost 22 155. For that reason, the trend in the defense and aerospace industry affected Seattle less than any other metropolitan area. Other MSAs with a high competitive advantage include Kansas City, Chicago, Phoenix, Washington, Houston and Cincinnati. On the opposite side, Saint Louis, Orlando, San Jose, Baltimore and Atlanta lost a considerable number of jobs due to corn petition.

Relatively speaking, Seattle gained approximately 20 jobs per 1 000 persons in the labor force because of its competitiveness, although five jobs were lost because of a weak industry performance. Overall, Los Angeles and Orlando each lost eight jobs per 1 000 persons in the labor force. It is worth mentioning that in absolute terms, Tucson lost 1 258 jobs, a number that is reasonable since it lost fewer jobs than 12 other MSAs. However, because of the small size of the metropolitan area, Tucson is ranked fifth in terms of jobs lost per 1 000 persons in the labor force (four jobs).

The energy and chemicals industry experienced a positive growth (2.69 percent) between 1988 and 1991. Houston, which had 8.5 percent of the US energy and chemicals industry, experienced the highest growth due to industry mix with 3 808 jobs gained. Los Angeles and Philadelphia have also benefited from the strengths of the energy and chemicals industry by gaining more than 1 200 jobs each. Just as in other high-tech industries, Los Angeles did poorly in terms of competitive advantage. Los Angeles, along with Pittsburgh and New York, lost more than 1 000 jobs due to regional share. On the other hand, Houston, Chicago and Philadelphia each had substantial gains of more than 1 000 jobs. Controlling for the size of labor force, Houston is also the leader in the energy and chemicals industry growth, followed by Charlotte and St Louis. Providence and Pittsburgh performed worse than any other metropolitan area under study.

Information technology is an industry with a high concentration of jobs in San Jose, Boston, Washington, Chicago, Los Angeles and Dallas. These MSAs are also the greatest gainers of jobs due to the high growth in this industry during the last ten years. However, all these MSAs except Washington and Dallas experienced job losses due to competition. Austin and Houston gained more than 7 000 jobs each due to their competitiveness. Controlling for the size of labor force, Austin is by far the best performer in the information technology and services industry. Between 1988 and 1991, Austin gained 21 jobs per 1,000 persons in the labor force. Raleigh/Durham, Portland and San Francisco gained 12, eight and eight, respectively. At the same time, Boston, Kansas City and Tucson lost 11, eight and seven jobs per 1 000 persons in the labor force.

High-technology machinery is an industry heavily concentrated in Rochester, Chicago and Los Angeles. These MSAs experienced a decline due to the poor performance of this industry at the national level. There was a 9.21 percent job decline in this industry, almost 2 percent more than in the defense industry. Other losers include Boston, Philadelphia and San Jose. Houston is the greatest winner of the competition with 7 555 jobs added between 1988 and 1991. The same metropolitan area stays the most competitive in the industry if labor force is controlled. Other good performers include Raleigh/Durham, San Diego, Austin and Richmond. As a small-size MSA, Providence lost a great many jobs in this industry.

One out of ten employees in high-technology research works in the Washington metropolitan area. This MSA, along with Chicago, Los Angeles, New York and Boston has benefited from the high growth in this particular industry. However, with the exception of Washington, the other MSAs did poorly in terms of competition. Washington is by far the most competitive MSA in this industry, followed by Raleigh/Durham, San Diego and Salt Lake City. The competitiveness of Washington is not obvious when labor force is controlled. In that regard, Raleigh/Durham and Salt Lake City are growing faster than Washington. Chicago, San Jose and Columbus are losing their competitive edge.

7.6   SHIFT SHARE AND THE MSA SIZE

What is the right-size MSA for high-tech industry? It appears that it depends on the industry. As shown in Table 7.6, in biotechnology small-sized MSAs

Table 7.6 Shift-share analysis by size of metropolitan area

Industry		Competitive component			Industry mix			Net relative growth		
		Large-sized	Medium-sized	Small-sized	Large-sized	Medium-sized	Small-sized	Large-sized	Medium-sized	Small-sized
Biotechnology & biomedical	Absolute	(4 860)	1 599	3 261	12 116	5 824	4 044	7 257	7 423	7 305
	Relative	−0.20	0.13	0.61	0.50	0.47	0.76	0.30	0.60	1.37
Defence & aerospace	Absolute	(24 575)	28 236	(3 661)	(18 281)	(12 280)	(2 270)	(42 857)	15 956	(5 931)
	Relative	−1.01	2.30	−0.69	−0.75	−1.00	−0.43	−1.76	1.30	−1.12
Energy & chemical	Absolute	1 620	(1 285)	(335)	9 984	3 256	942	11 604	1 971	607
	Relative	0.07	−0.10	−0.05	0.41	0.27	0.14	0.48	0.16	0.09
Information technology & services	Absolute	(27 426)	4 559	22 867	13 125	6 650	2 884	(14 301)	11 209	25 751
	Relative	−1.13	0.37	3.45	0.54	0.54	0.44	−0.59	0.91	3.89
Machinery & instruments	Absolute	(2 370)	3 062	(693)	(19 993)	(9 976)	(9 993)	(22 363)	(6 913)	(10 686)
	Relative	−0.10	0.25	−0.10	−0.82	−0.81	−1.51	−0.92	−0.56	−1.61
High-tech research	Absolute	(4 168)	608	3 560	8 675	4 077	1 217	4 507	4 685	4 777
	Relative	−0.17	0.05	0.54	0.36	0.33	0.18	0.19	0.38	0.72
Total high tech	Absolute	(61 779)	36 780	24 999	5 626	(2 449)	(3 177)	(56 153)	34 331	21 822
	Relative	−2.54	3.00	3.76	0.23	−0.20	−0.41	−2.31	2.80	3.34

Note: Relative numbers refer to the number of employees per 1 000 persons in civilian labor force.

133

perform better than medium and large-sized ones. For example, the net relative gain in small-sized MSAs was 137 jobs per 100 000 persons in the labor force compared with 60 for medium-sized MSAs and 30 for large-sized MSAs. In defense and aerospace medium-sized MSAs perform better than small and large-sized MSAs. In high-technology research, small-sized MSAs perform better than medium and large-sized MSAs. In high-tech machinery, small-sized MSAs dominate the industry in terms of growth. In information technologies, small-sized MSAs outperform medium and large-sized MSAs. Finally, in the energy and chemicals industry, large MSAs perform better than medium-sized and small-sized MSAs.

7.7   CONCLUSION

This chapter illustrates the two perspectives of high-technology employment in 37 MSAs. Absolute values are used when one wants to pinpoint the magnitude of employment losses and gains. No matter how big a metropolitan area is, one loss of a job is always detrimental to the economy. Economists are tempted to find out why jobs are lost or gained in one region and not in another. Those losses or gains can only be measured with absolute numbers.

Large and small metropolitan areas may have different effects on job losses or gains. This chapter also calculates the magnitude of these losses or gains by taking labor force as a control variable. The results of this study also help identify the effects of high-technology trends on US metropolitan areas. It should be mentioned that the labor force variable can be replaced by any other meaningful variable depending on the analysis. The key is to carry out an analysis based on results with the same unit. This chapter identifies which metropolitan areas are weak or strong in which industries and how the industry portfolio of each MSA affects performance in its total high-technology employment. Since 1991 was a recession year, additional research should be conducted with post-recession data.

8. Employment, wages and R&D spillovers

8.1 INTRODUCTION

Localized clusters of high-technology firms, such as California's famous Silicon Valley or Boston's Route 128, are of significant interest to policy-makers and economists alike. For in addition to favorable effects on international competitiveness and their role in structural change, such clusters generate considerable regional benefits in terms of jobs, growth and economic development. Understanding the determinants of the spatial distribution of high-technology activities is therefore important for both regional and indus-trial policy.

Traditional explanations of locational choice refer to transportation costs and proximity to raw material, fuel or labor inputs as major factors in the agglomerative process. A recent body of literature in which spillovers play a major role distinguished information spillovers with respect to their origin. This literature has developed in response to research by Krugman (1991), Henderson (1988), and Glaeser et al. (1992). In the first approach externalities work within industries. Concentrated industry structures, it is argued, are advantageous due to the internationalization of spillovers. Local concentration within an industry is therefore supportive of growth (Romer 1990).

A very different position has been attributed to Jacobs (1969). Jacobs perceives information spillovers from other industries to be more important for the firm than within-industry information flows. Heterogeneity not special-ization is seen as the most important regional growth factor. Glaeser et al. analyze the six largest industries in each of 170 US cities. Their results are consistent with the presence of Jacobs-type externalities. Industries will grow sluggishly in cities with high degrees of specialization. Heterogeneity is conducive to growth in these models. The issues of specialization and hetero-geneity are also addressed by Henderson, Kuncoro and Turner (1995) and Henderson (1994). The results in these papers differ considerably from those obtained by Glaeser et al.

Another response which has received serious attention recently points to the role of geographically bounded knowledge spillovers from universities and federal laboratories in the location decision of firms. Informal evidence suggests there is a close association between high-technology clusters and major research universities in the United States (Acs 1996). Typically cited are the links between Stanford University and Silicon Valley or MIT and Route 128. Such a nexus has scarcely emerged in Europe except in the form of a few fledgling research parks such as in Cambridge, England (Lumme et al. 1993). Formal tests conducted by Jaffe (1989) provide econometric evidence for the real effects of academic research in terms of its spillover to corporate patenting activity. In addition, papers by Jaffe, Trajtenberg and Henderson (1993), Almeida and Kogut (1999) and Anselin, Varga and Acs (1997) demonstrate the significant degree of localization of these knowledge externalities with respect to patent citations and innovations. However, spillovers from university research to commercial innovation are not the only effects of relevance to theory and policy. *The ultimate economic interest lies chiefly in the product markets and jobs that are generated by R&D.* The aim of this chapter is to test for the existence of such spillovers from university R&D to local high-technology employment. This is a question of considerable policy importance (*Business Week* 1994) which has only been discussed systematically to date by Beeson and Montgomery (1993) who, in contrast to our results, find no statistically significant effect of university research and development expenditures on high-technology employment shares.

The discussion is organized into five sections. Section 8.2 outlines discursively the theoretical background. Section 8.3 provides a preliminary analysis of the data. We use unique annual data for six-high technology sectors in 36 American Standard Metropolitan Statistical Areas (SMSAs) for the period from 1988 to 1991 to investigate the relationship between university R&D expenditure and employment. Our use of MSA data should clearly subject the theoretical argument for spillovers based on spatial proximity to a more precise test. The model is specified and estimation issues are discussed in Section 8.4 and, in the Section 8.5, the econometric results are reported. A final section concludes the paper.

8.2　THEORETICAL BACKGROUND

There are two related hypotheses explaining the development of high-technology clusters in the vicinity of major university R&D activity.

8.2.1　Research Spillovers

The first explanation argues that university research is a source of significant innovation-generating knowledge which diffuses initially through personal contacts to adjacent firms, especially those based in a science park (Westhead and Storey 1995). Since both basic and applied university research may benefit private enterprise in various ways it induces firms to locate nearby. Lund (1986) in a survey of industrial R&D managers confirms the proximity of university R&D as a factor in the location decision due to the initial spillover from neighboring university research to commercial innovation. Of course, as research results are used and disseminated, the learning advantage created by close geographic proximity between local high-technology activity and the university would fade but these learning lags may be long.[1] Knowledge flows locally, therefore, through a variety of channels discussed below, more easily and efficiently than over greater distances.

There is a growing body of evidence which supports this hypothesis, especially in the United States. Spillovers from university R&D to patent activity in the same state have been identified econometrically by Jaffee (1989). Acs, Audretsch and Feldman (1992, 1994a) reinforce this result with, instead of patents, a more direct measure of economically useful knowledge production, namely the number of innovations recorded in 1982 by the US Small Business Administration from the leading technology, engineering and trade journals. Likewise, Nelson (1986), using surveys of research managers, finds university research to be a key source of innovation in some industries, especially those related to biological science where he finds some degree of corporate funding of university projects. University research spillovers may be a factor which explains how small, and often new, firms are able to generate innovations while undertaking generally negligible amounts of R&D themselves.[2] There is econometric evidence for this result based on data from both the United States (Acs et al. 1994a) and Italy (Audretsch and Vivarelli 1996).

Despite the presumed advantages of geographical proximity for receiving spillovers, the mechanisms by which knowledge is transferred are not well understood. Information flows are usually attributed to the use of faculty as technical consultants (Mansfield 1995) and postgraduate students as research assistants, the use of university library, recreation and dining facilities, informal communication between individuals at trade shows, industry conferences, seminars, talks and social activities, or joint participation in commercial ventures by university and corporate scientists through contracted research projects. The latter has grown in importance since the late 1970s as the universities established formal Offices of Technology Transfer (or Licensing) to foster interaction with industry and the commercialization of research results. This partly reflects pressure applied by US government agencies to universities, for economic growth reasons, to hasten technology transfer from their laboratories to the private sector (Parker and Zilberman 1993). Federal Acts passed in the early 1980s also promote knowledge spillovers.

The Stevenson-Wydler Technology Innovation Act of 1980, for example, encourages co-operative research and technology transfer and the 1981 Economic Recovery Tax Act gives tax discounts to firms that provide research equipment to universities. Some universities have created industry consortia to help fund research. Firms pay membership fees to join these consortia and in return benefit from access to the research output and have some voice in the research agenda. Such channels would be expected to flourish given that universities as public institutions do not face the same incentives as private corporation to keep research results secret. In both the San Francisco Bay and Boston areas, for example, the introduction and growth of the biotechnology industry is a direct result of university R&D spillovers.

Presumably, the chief benefits of geographical proximity to the spillovers' source consist in a reduction in both the transactions costs of knowledge transfer and in the costs of commercial research and product development. As a caveat, it ought to noted that we do not argue that proximity is a necessary condition for spillovers to occur, only that it offers advantages in capturing them since the marginal cost of transmitting knowledge, especially informal knowledge, rises with distance (Audretsch and Feldman 1996; Audretsch and Stephan 1996; Anselin et al. 1997).

8.2.2   The Labor Market

The second university-based explanation of clustering highlights the provision of a pool of trained and highly qualified science and engineering graduates. The high level of human capital embodied in their general and specific skills is another mechanism by which knowledge is transmitted (Beeson and Montgomery 1993). To the extent that they do not migrate, such graduates may provide a supply of labor to local firms or else a supply of entrepreneurs for new start-ups in the high-technology sector (Link and Rees 1990). Some evidence for this latter link is provided by Bania, Eberts and Fogarty (1987, 1993) who, using cross-section data, find a significant effect of university research expenditure on new firm formation. University scientists themselves, of course, may provide the entrepreneurial input, working part-time as directors of their own start-up companies, or even leaving academia to take a position in a high-technology firm, or helping to plan the scientific direction of the company. According to Audretsch and Stephan (1996), the recruitment of university-based researchers with high reputations to a firm's scientific advisory board can serve to signal the quality of the firm's research to resource and capital markets. Parker and Zilberman (1993: 97) report, for example, that MIT has incubated about 40 biotechnology firms since the late 1980s. Lumme et al. (1993) in their study of academic entrepreneurship in Cambridge (England) identified 62 high-technology companies whose business idea was based on the exploitation of knowledge developed or acquired in either a university or a research institute. However, even if university research is either negligible or irrelevant to industry, university training of new industrial scientists alone may be sufficient to generate local labor market spillovers. Nelson (1986: 187), for example, notes that industrial interest in academic departments of physics is confined mainly to their output of potential industrial scientists rather than to their research results.

A university and its associated science park may also play an important signaling role in locational choice (Shachar and Felsenstein 1992) in the sense that they signal the presence of local technological capacity. Thus firms may be attracted even if the university spillovers are not in fact that great.

8.3 PRELIMINARY DATA ANALYSIS

As is well known, no disaggregated employment data at the MSA level exists for the United States. The employment and wage data used in this chapter come from the US Department of Labor, Bureau of Labor Statistics (BLS). The data are reported to BLS by the State Employment Security Agencies (SESAs) of the 50 states as part of the Covered Employment and Wages Program (i.e. the ES-202 report). Employers in private industry provide SESAs with quarterly tax reports for an average of 90 million wage and salary workers in approximately 5.9 million reporting units. These reports covered approximately 98 percent of total wage and salary civilian employment and provide a virtual census of employees and their wages for nearly all sectors of the economy. This study utilizes specialized data runs for 36 MSAs and 32 three-digit SIC industries. There are disclosure limitations of the data. Because individual records cannot be revealed, for cities and industries where there are only a few employers the data are not available. This limits both the number of cities and the number of industries that can be studied with BLS data. We could have studied most of the 300 MSAs. However, we would *not* have been able to study specific high-technology industries because of disclosure problems. Therefore, in order to study R&D spillovers, the study is limited to cities that have a large number of high-technology industries. The advantage of this approach is that we are able to study those cities that are dominated by high-technology industries and test for spillovers.

Our data for university research expenditures follow the common approach in the literature and are compiled from the National Science Foundation Survey for Scientific and Engineering Expenditures at Universities and Colleges for the various years. The innovation variable comes from the US Small Business Administration Innovation Data Base. The data set is a compilation of innovations that were introduced to the US market in the year 1982 based on an extensive review of new product announcements in trade and technical publications. The data are disaggregated at both the industry and MSA level.

The first step[3] is to identify the high-technology sectors. We proceeded by selecting those with a relatively high ratio of R&D to industry sales. Thirty-two three-digit standard industrial classification (SIC) industries were identified in this way, and then grouped into the six sectors detailed in Appendix E: biotechnology and biomedical, information technology and services, high technology machinery and instruments, defense and aerospace, energy and chemicals, and high-technology research. This latter sector refers to development and testing services carried out by the private sector. It is necessary research for the successful commercialization of university research.

The relationship between university R&D and high-technology employment can be analysed in a preliminary fashion using scatter diagrams. Figure 8.1 plots the sum of high-technology employment for all six sectors in 1989 against university research expenditure in 1985 for all 36 SMSAs. Both variables display great variation across metropolitan areas though there is a clear positive association between them. The simple correlation coefficient is 0.60. University research expenditure and high-technology employment are both high in the major cities of Los Angeles, Boston, New York and Baltimore.

Figure 8.2 plots a scatter diagram of high-technology employment against the number of scientists and engineers per 100 workers by SMSA. The motivation is that the stock of university science graduates with good general and specific skills influences the location of a high-technology cluster.

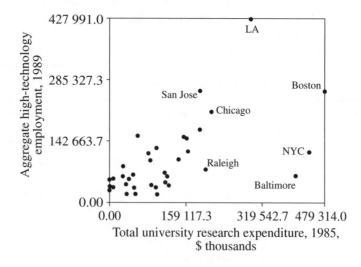

*Figure 8.1   Plot of aggregate high-technology employment, 1989 and
university research expenditure, 1985*

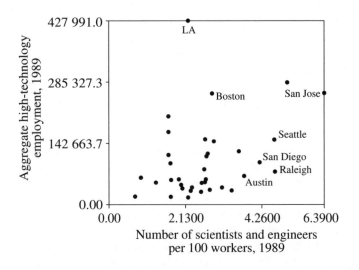

Figure 8.2   Plot of aggregate high-technology employment and the number of scientists and engineers per 100 workers, 1989

Empirically, the association with high technology employment is not that strong. The simple correlation coefficient is 0.26. The plot illustrates that Austin, San Jose, Seattle and Raleigh have a high share of engineers and scientists relative to the level of high-technology employment. In other words, the labor quality is relatively high in these SMSAs. In contrast, the large number of employees in Los Angeles appear to be concentrated in low-skilled occupations.

Our final data set only include those MSAs for which there was employment in the high-technology sector as well as university R&D and innovations. Admittedly, this excludes from consideration the joint determination of 'location' and 'magnitude' of high-technology employment and research (Henderson 1988). On the other hand, it avoids the problem of 'zeros', and is motivated by a focus on the strength of interaction between research and employment where these are present. We leave the more complex issue for further research.

8.4   EMPIRICAL SPECIFICATION

In spite of data limitations, we estimate a parsimonious structural labor market model. The main missing variable is a proxy for product demand faced by high-technology firms, such as sales, which is not available for individual MSAs.

8.4.1   The Model

Our initial specification for the employment equation is written down in natural logarithms as:

$$EMP_{MIT} = a_0 + a_1 W_{MIT} + a_2 U_{MIT} + a_3 POP_{MT} + a_4 HK_M$$
$$+ a_5 INNOV_M + aX + u_{MIT} \qquad (8.1)$$

where '*M*' indexes MSA, '*I*' indexes industry, and '*T*' indexes time: $M = 1,$ ..., 36; $I = 1, \ldots, 6$; and $T = 1988, \ldots, 1991$. EMP_{MIT} refers to high-technology employment and W_{MIT} is the corresponding annual real wage per employee, defined as nominal wages deflated by the appropriate industry producer price index. Since the panel includes only four years of annual data, cross-sectional variability dominates.[4] For this reason, attempts to estimate equations specified in terms of employment growth rates proved fruitless.

U_{MIT} refers to university R&D deflated by the gross national product price deflator. We collected data on university research and development for the years 1985 to 1991. This allows us to measure not only the flow of R&D but also to construct a stock measure UK_{MIT}. Given the time span of our data set, it seems reasonable that the use of R&D dated in 1985, $RD_{MI, T-3}$, provides an appropriate lag for the knowledge externality to be transmitted into commercial products and employment. Edwards and Gordon (1984), for example, find that innovations made in 1982 resulted from inventions made on average 4.2 years earlier. The R&D data include industry-funded university research, a component which rarely exceeds 10 percent of the total and is usually considerably less. Notice that RD_{MIT} varies by both SMSA and industry. Total university R&D spending in each city is disaggregated by broad science department and allocated to each of the six industries. This is appropriate given substantial differences in the commercial applicability of university research across academic departments. Thus employment data is disaggregated by industry sector and linked to the relevant component of university research expenditure. The assignment of research funds by academic department to industrial sector is listed in Table 8.1. This is based on the mapping of Audretsch and Feldman (1996) who in turn used the survey of industrial R&D managers conducted by Levin et al. (1987).

As a test for the local spillover hypothesis we have constructed pairs of matched cities that have high levels of R&D in close proximity to each other to test for the effect of cross-regional spillovers. This is important because R&D conducted in MSA_1 might have an impact on employment in MSA_2. In order to control for cross-border spillovers we constructed a variable OU_{MIT} that measures R&D in close proximity to our sample MSA. If the coefficient

Table 8.1   Linking university departments to industrial sectors

Industry	University departments
1. Biotechnology and biomedical	Life sciences
2. Information technology and services	Mathematical sciences
3. High-technology machinery and instruments	Environmental sciences and engineering
4. Defense and aerospace	Engineering and physical sciences
5. Energy and chemicals	Physical sciences
6. High technology research	All hard sciences

for this variable is zero then there are no cross-border spillovers, or they are different from local spillovers.[5]

POP_{MT} refers to city population and controls for local market size. Of course, the market extends beyond MSA boundaries but we do not have a more appropriate measure of demand. The number of scientists and engineers as a proportion of the labor force of each SMSA represents the potential human capital, or quality of the labor force, available for employees, HK_M. Data are only available for a single year, 1989. $INNOV_M$ is a simple count of the number of innovations by MSA in 1982, the year for which the database of commercial innovations introduced in the United States was compiled by the U.S. Small Business Administration. It attempts to control for the effect of pre-existing commercial innovation, that leads to product development and marketing with substantial time lags, on subsequent employment levels. Finally X represents a vector of industry, state and annual time dummies. These control for effects specific to each which may not have been captured by the continuous variables. Table 8.2 presents the main summary statistics by variable for the 36 MSAs in aggregate.[6]

Table 8.2   Summary statistics by variable

Variable	Maximum	Minimum	Mean	Standard deviation	Coefficient of variation
EMP_{mit}	219 500	67	15 733	25 013.8	1.59
W_{mit}	60 114	7 822	30 895	7 559	0.24
POP_{mt}	8 978 000	636 000	2 369 600	1 950 900	0.82
UD_{mit}	772 102	8	84 445	121 874	1.44
HK_m	6.39	0.76	2.72	1.14	0.42
$INNOV_m$	384	4	55.94	76.28	1.36

8.4.2   Sample Selection Bias

The disclosure limits of the BLS data outlined earlier may potentially introduce a selection bias in the results. This arises since the data are suppressed in
those MSAs where high-technology employment is low. A non-randomly
selected sample is, therefore, effectively imposed by the BLS. This bias can be
resolved econometrically by constructing a joint model which represents both
the employment equation and the selection process determining when the
dependent variable is observed. In effect we have a selection rule which states
that employment is only reported if it exceeds an unobserved disclosure
threshold, EMP^*_{MIT}. Thus the model may be described statistically as follows:

$$EMP_{MIT} = \beta' X_{MIT} + \mu_{MIT} \tag{8.2}$$

$$EMP^*_{MIT} = \gamma' Z_{MIT} + \varepsilon_{MIT} \tag{8.3}$$

$$EMP_{MIT} \text{ observed only if } EMP_{MIT} \geq EMP^*_{MIT}$$

where $(\mu_{MIT}, \varepsilon_{MIT})$ are i.i.d. drawings from a bivariate normal distribution with
zero mean, σ^2_μ variances and σ^2_ε, and covariance $\sigma_{\mu\varepsilon}$. If this covariance is non-
zero, the OLS estimates of β will be biased. X_{MIT} and Z_{MIT} are vectors of inde-
pendent variables. The dependent variable EMP^*_{MIT} is unobserved but has a
dichotomous observable realization I_{MI} which is related to EMP^*_{MIT} as
follows:

$$I_{MIT} = 1 \text{ if and only if } EMP_{MIT} \geq EMP^*_{MIT}$$

$$I_{MIT} = 0 \text{ if and only if } EMP_{MIT} < EMP^*_{MIT}$$

Equation (8.2) applies to the selected sample of 36 cities and summarizes the
specification in (8.1). Additional data were obtained on the right-hand-side
variables for a further 77 MSAs which are non-selected in the sense that no
high-technology employment data were available for these cases. The additional observations permit correction of the sample selection bias induced by
censoring of the dependent variable using the two-stage estimation procedure
proposed by Heckman (1979). In the first stage the parameters of the probability that an MSA will be in the selected sample of 36 cities are estimated
from a probit analysis of equation (8.3) using the full sample of $36 + 77 = 113$
cities. From these estimates the values of the inverse of Mills' ratio, denoted
$\hat{\lambda}_{MIT}$, are computed for each observation in the selected sample. The second
stage is to estimate the employment equation (8.2) by OLS with $\hat{\lambda}_{MIT}$ as an
additional explanatory variable. It has been shown by Heckman and others that

this correction term is a proxy variable for the probability of selection, measuring the sample selection effect arising from undisclosed observations on employment. This procedure gives consistent estimates of the parameters of equation (8.2).

Note that Z_{MIT} is a subset of X_{MIT}. Since the non-disclosure problems which apply to employment likewise afflict the wage data, the wage variable is excluded from the Z_{MIT} vector in the selection equation. The probability of high-tech employment disclosure is likely to be strongly related to city size which is proxied here by the population variable. In addition, the innovation and university R&D variables are included. Human capital was badly determined in all probit equations and so dropped from the preferred specification.

8.5   RESULTS

Three sets of results are reported. First, aggregate high-technology employment equations by MSA are estimated over a four-year time period. Corresponding to the aggregate construction of the employment variable, total university R&D expenditures are specified on the right-hand side. Second, employment and university R&D are disaggregated and matched up by industry sector in a pooled regression. Third, sectoral employment equations are estimated for each of our six industry clusters.

8.5.1   The Aggregated Unmatched Equation

Column (1) of Table 8.3 reports the aggregate OLS estimates of equation (8.1) in which the six high-technology industry clusters are pooled to form a single sector. The equation includes both state and time fixed effects to control for unmeasured state and time-specific factors. The coefficients on the fixed effects are not tabulated but their joint significance cannot be rejected by an F-test. The equation was estimated in natural logarithms over the four-year period 1988 to 1991 using 144 observations (4 years x 36 cities). The coefficients should therefore be interpreted as elasticities. Three lags are specified for the university R&D variable of which the first clearly has the strongest impact. Restricting the second and third lags to zero and re-estimating the equation gives the results reported in column (2). The coefficients have the expected signs and are statistically significant at the 5 percent level using a one-tail test. In particular the R&D elasticity of employment is 0.11 with a t-ratio of 3.51. To check for the robustness of the results, the equation was respecified by substituting the stock of research and development for the flow measure. This generated virtually identical parameter estimates. To correct for any possible simultaneity between employment and real wages, the equation

Table 8.3   Aggregate high-technology employment estimates

Dependent variable	(1) OLS EMP_{MT}	(2) OLS EMP_{MT}	(3) PROBIT I_{MT}	(4) OLS EMP_{MT}	(5) OLS EMP_{MT}
constant	13.19	13.20	−14.32	13.32	13.28
	(3.10)	(3.17)	(8.73)	(3.97)	(3.85)
W_{MT}	−0.77	−0.77		−0.68	−0.61
	(−1.84)	(−1.89)		(1.87)	(1.83)
$U_{M, T-1}$	0.12	0.11	0.56	0.04	
	(0.59)	(3.51)	(6.21)	(0.49)	
$U_{M, T-2}$	−0.02				
	(−0.08)				
$U_{M, T-3}$	0.01				
	(0.07)				
POP_{MT}	0.21	0.21	1.04	0.20	0.19
	(2.66)	(2.70)	(5.85)	(1.61)	(1.70)
HK_M	0.48	0.48		0.48	0.48
	(4.30)	(4.35)		(5.21)	(5.28)
$INNOV_M$	0.65	0.65	0.19	0.62	0.61
	(9.83)	(9.97)	(2.00)	(10.21)	(10.36)
				-0.20	-0.32
$\hat{\lambda}_{MT}$				(0.82)	(4.78)
$\bar{R}^2$	0.88	0.88		0.88	0.88
$\hat{\sigma}$	0.278	0.276		0.276	0.275
n	144	144	452	144	144

Notes: (i) Absolute *t*-statistics are in parentheses; (ii) all variables are in natural logarithms; (iii) $\bar{R}_2$ is the adjusted multiple correlation coefficient, $\hat{\sigma}$ is the estimated standard error of the regression and *n* is the number of observations; (iv) unreported dummy variables for time and state are also included in each of these regressions except the probit in column (3).

was also estimated using lagged wages. Again, however, the results were very similar and are not presented.

These simple OLS estimates provide a baseline from which to assess the impact of sample selection on the employment equation. Column (3) of Table 8.3 reports the coefficient estimates of the disclosure probability equation estimated by maximum likelihood probit on the full sample of 113 MSAs over the four-year period. The population, innovation and R&D variables are statistically significant at conventional levels, and the equation correctly predicts disclosure status in 88 percent of cases. Column (4) lists the estimated coefficients of the employment equation corrected for sample selection and again controlling for state and time fixed effects. The key difference from the results of the uncorrected equation in column (2) is the statistical insignificance of the R&D variable. Moreover, its coefficient has fallen considerably from 0.11 to 0.04 suggesting a substantial initial upward bias. Under the null hypothesis of no selection bias, the coefficient of the estimated inverse Mills' ratio, $\hat{\lambda}_{MT}$, has a t-distribution. Using a simple t-test, we cannot reject the null. However, omitting the university R&D variable from the employment equation overturns the initial statistical insignificance of the sample selection effect and increases its absolute value as reported in column (5). This outcome implies that there is a sample selection problem for these data. The absolute t-statistics in parentheses are based on White's heteroskedastic consistent estimates of the standard errors since, in the presence of selection bias, the usual OLS estimates of the standard errors of the estimates of β are also biased.

The significance of the coefficient on R&D in the probit equation demonstrates that the magnitude of total university R&D in an MSA has a strong and direct effect on the probability of employment disclosure but only affects aggregate high technology employment indirectly through the disclosure term, $\hat{\lambda}_{MIT}$. So although R&D may appear to be a statistically significant important determinant of employment when an OLS regression is fitted on the selected sample as in column (2), this is the consequence of non-random sample selection. The negative sign on the selection term, $\hat{\lambda}_{MT}$, indicates that, controlling for all observed effects, an MSA for which high-technology employment is disclosed will have lower employment than an MSA with similar characteristics for which it remains undisclosed. With respect to the remaining coefficients, a comparison of column (5) with column (2) indicates that they are overstated if sample selection is ignored.

8.5.2 The Disaggregated Matched Equation

The first column of Table 8.4 reports the least squares regression results for the disaggregated equation using 864 observations drawn from six high-technology sectors in 36 MSAs over the four-year period, 1988 to 1991. The R&D variable is constructed by matching up university R&D by department with the appropriate industry cluster. In order to test for local versus non-local spillovers we also specify a variable, denoted OU_{MIT}, representing matched university R&D from the nearest neighboring city for the same high-technology sectors.

There are three important findings in Table 8.4. First, the results suggest that no non-regional spillover from university research can be detected. The negative and statistically insignificant coefficients on the lags of OU suggest

Table 8.4   Disaggregated high-technology employment estimates

Dependent variable	(1) OLS EMP_{MIT}	(2) OLS EMP_{MIT}	(3) PROBIT I_{MIT}	(4) OLS EMP_{MIT}
constant	−20.85	−21.88	−9.64	−22.55
	(−9.84)	(−10.33)	(21.99)	(−8.26)
W_{MIT}	2.59	2.54		2.53
	(13.54)	(13.20)		(10.43)
$U_{MI, T-1}$	−0.14			
	(−1.41)			
$U_{MI, T-2}$	0.01			
	(0.06)			
$U_{MI, T-3}$	0.16	0.10	0.10	0.11
	(1.80)	(3.55)	(6.57)	(3.62)
POP_{MT}	0.36	0.37	1.08	0.44
	(3.54)	(3.67)	(17.07)	(3.68)
HK_M	0.14	0.20		0.19
	(1.00)	(1.46)		(1.55)
$INNOV_M$	0.42	0.38	0.40	0.42
	(5.27)	(4.72)	(10.94)	(4.69)
$OU_{MI, T-1}$	-0.19			
	(−1.42)			
$OU_{MI, T-2}$	0.08			
	(0.44)			
$OU_{MI, T-3}$	−0.02			
	(−0.22)			
$\hat{\lambda}_{MT}$				0.25
				(0.98)
$\bar{R}^2$	0.60	0.60		0.60
$\hat{\sigma}$	0.872	0.882		0.881
n	864	864	2712	864

Notes: (i) Absolute *t*-statistics are in parentheses; (ii) all variables are in natural logarithms; (iii) $\bar{R}^2$ is the adjusted multiple correlation coefficient, $\hat{\sigma}$ is the estimated standard error of the regression and *n* is the number of observations; (iv) dummy variables for industry, time and state are also included in each of these regressions except for the probit in column (3).

that university research conducted in other MSAs does not spill over. Experimenting with different combinations of lags did not alter the finding. This is consistent with Anselin, Varga and Acs (1997, chapter 3) who found that spillovers from university R&D were mediated within a 75-mile radius.

Second, the positive and statistically significant coefficient on $UD_{MI,T3}$ reported in columns (1) and (2) suggests that lagged university R&D is an important determinant of high-technology employment. In this richer disaggregated data set, it is the third lag of R&D rather than the first lag (preferred in the aggregate equation) which captures the dynamics of the spillover to employment. To test for selection bias, the same procedure outlined with respect to the aggregate unmatched equation was followed. The probit selection equation (column 3) estimated for 113 MSAs again performed satisfactorily: the parameter estimates were well determined and the equation correctly predicted the disclosure status of 85 percent of the observations. However, the null hypothesis of no selection bias cannot be rejected. And, unlike the aggregate equation, the coefficient on the R&D variable retains its magnitude and significance. Indeed the corrected equation in column (4) is strikingly similar to the unadjusted equation in column (2). Likewise, re-estimating this equation with a lagged real wage to correct for simultaneity or an R&D capital stock variable instead of the flow variable yields almost identical results. The equation is not sensitive to these alternative specifications. So although the magnitude of the employment elasticity is small (0.11), this is robust evidence supporting a direct spillover of university research onto high-technology employment with a three-year lag in the relationship. In unreported regressions, we found the same result when the dependent variable is specified in terms of high-technology employment shares, in striking contrast to the statistically insignificant coefficient reported by Beeson and Montgomery (1993).

Comparing the results at the aggregate and disaggregated levels, two conclusions emerge. First, disaggregating the data by industry sector appears to deal with the non-random selection problem that appeared in the aggregated data. Second, it is clear that detection of the R&D spillovers to employment requires the matching of industry clusters to relevant university department. Aggregated data are simply too coarse to provide an appropriate testbed. Indeed, in a world of full employment disclosure, finer matching of university R&D and employment at the three- or four-digit level would be expected to detect more powerful spillovers.

Finally a further result is that real wages and employment are positively related ceteris paribus. This is counter to our results in Table 8.3 and to our theoretical priors based on the perfectly competitive model. Dropping the wage variable did not markedly affect the signs and significance of the remaining regressors so this outcome does not vitiate our spillover story. Neither re-estimating with 2SLS nor as random effects models produced major differences in the results. So the results are robust with respect to estimation technique.

At first blush, this result is quite surprising. However, it is quite consistent with two important features of high-technology industries. First, output markets with continual product innovation and imperfect information are far from the traditional model of perfect competition. It follows that some proxy for product demand should be included in the employment equation but such a variable was not available. Thus we are estimating a reduced form rather than a true structural demand model. These within-industry specific skills are often required in high-technology sectors. Second, specialized skills are often required in high-technology sectors. These within-industry specific skills may not be transferable across industries, leading to a positive relationship between wages and employment. This is consistent with increasing returns. Locational advantages that attract high-technology firms may also generate shortages of skilled workers that lead to higher wages. Other wages typically follow to maintain differentials.

The positive correlation between high-technology employment and wages thus probably reflects the crucial shortages and imperfect mobility of skilled labor that has been the subject of much policy discussion and concern. Equally plausible, and without relying on market imperfections, it may simply be the demand for products produced by the most skilled and highly paid workers that has grown most rapidly.

The university-based labor market spillover story has weaker support. The proportion of engineers and scientists in a city, the human capital variable, is statistically insignificant. Our population and technical innovation variables, however, are both well determined.

8.5.3 Industry Matched Equations

We have also estimated employment functions separately for each of the six high-technology industries. Table 8.5 reports the estimates of the OLS equations corrected for sample selection bias. The uncorrected OLS and probit equations are not presented for reasons of space. Of the six equations, only the estimates for the energy and chemicals sector are generally not sensible, an outcome which holds independently of whether the sample selectivity term is included. A plausible explanation is that energy and chemicals represents a rather traditional industry dependent on both raw materials and products that are much more costly to transport than the inputs of other sectors. Access to port facilities, and other transport infrastructure, is thus likely to be much more important in the location decision, weakening considerably the role of the R&D, innovation and human capital variables.

With respect to the remaining five sectors, the R&D coefficient is positive and statistically significant in all but high-technology machinery and instruments. Sample selection bias cannot be rejected in three industry clusters, namely: defense and aerospace; information and technology services and high

Table 8.5   Industry OLS high-technology employment function estimates

	EC	DA	ITS	HTR	BB	HTM
constant	6.09	−62.01	3.79	−6.31	−5.71	−21.61
	(1.18)	(3.84)	(1.63)	(3.23)	(1.98)	(4.27)
W_{MIT}	−0.18	5.95	0.03	0.15	0.82	2.47
	(0.37)	(3.42)	(0.14)	(0.83)	(2.64)	(5.64)
HK_M	−0.50	−0.25	0.55	0.91	−0.13	−0.07
	(3.41)	(0.65)	(6.52)	(14.77)	(0.76)	(0.54)
POP_{MT}	0.72	0.18	0.24	0.84	0.30	0.43
	(2.84)	(0.45)	(4.16)	(13.57)	(2.79)	(1.85)
$INNOV_M$	−0.34	0.65	0.88	0.11	0.40	0.53
	(2.68)	(1.56)	(13.43)	(2.77)	(3.62)	(4.07)
$U_{MI, T-3}$	−0.01	0.48	0.06	0.41	0.18	0.02
	(0.09)	(2.69)	(2.50)	(11.72)	(6.03)	(0.56)
$\hat{\lambda}_{MIT}$	−1.21	1.38	0.37	0.38	0.20	0.11
	(2.70)	(1.70)	(1.71)	(2.17)	(0.65)	(0.30)
$\bar{R}^2$	0.88	0.63	0.94	0.97	0.86	0.82
$\hat{\sigma}$	0.487	1.025	0.230	0.218	0.367	0.414
n	144	144	144	144	144	144

Notes: (i) *t*-statistics are in parentheses; (ii) all variables are in natural logarithms; (iii) $\bar{R}^2$ is the adjusted multiple correlation coefficient, $\hat{\sigma}$ is the estimated standard error of the regression and n is the number of observations; (iv) unreported dummy variables for time and state are also included in each of these regressions.
Key:
EC   energy and chemicals
DA   defence and aerospace
ITS   information and technology services
HTR   high-technology research
BB   biology and biomedical
HTR   high- technology machinery and instruments

technology research. In each case, however, the effect of the sample selection is upwardly to adjust the estimated parameter on university R&D. So in these sectors, failure to correct for selectivity leads to an understatement of the R&D effect. The R&D spillovers to employment are particularly powerful in defense and aerospace and high-technology research, where the estimated coefficients exceed 0.40.

   The estimated parameters on the innovation count variable are significant and correctly signed in four of the sectors, though the coefficient on the human capital variable is only well determined in information and technology services and in high technology research. Although the results for labor quality and prior innovation are mixed in terms of both sign and statistical significance, it is the university R&D effect, our key variable of interest, which is the most consistent.

## 8.6	CONCLUSIONS

Previous empirical work on R&D spillovers has focused on their relationship with innovation and patent counts at the level of individual US states. With new data for 36 American MSAs including the main university R&D centers we have found a statistically significant and robust spillover to employment in four high-technology sectors, after controlling for state fixed effects. This confirms the popular view of high-technology clusters and provides the first quantitative evidence that academic research has a positive local high-technology employment spillover at the city level. A further result is that innovation was also strongly related to high-technology industry employment after a long time lag, again a plausible but hitherto untested proposition.

These results are clearly of relevance for regional policy. They provide support for the importance of high-technology clusters in the United States and possible lessons for Europe and Japan where such clusters are much less well developed and where there is no evidence of the localization of knowledge spillovers, at least in the semiconductor industry (Almeida and Kogut 1999). In spite of dramatic declines in the costs of information transmission, local spillovers underline the importance of personal contacts and face-to-face communication in transferring scientific progress into jobs and products. Clearly more research is required on the nature of the transmission process as well as on the skill composition of high-technology employment, and the relationship of training and skills to wages and employment in local labor markets. Another significant unexplored issue is the role of rent-sharing in an industry where human capital is particularly important. Our short panel precluded any dynamic analysis but longer time series could throw light on the determinants of high-technology employment growth that have generated the distribution and composition of existing clusters.

Naturally, university knowledge spillovers are not the only reason for high-technology clusters. Other forces for localization are quite strong. They would include the development of specialized intermediate goods industries, economies of scale and scope, and network externalities. With respect to the latter, innovations by different producers may be complementary, yielding related new products or processes when combined. On these questions too, further research is called for.

NOTES

1. Shachar and Felsenstein (1992) report evidence from studies conducted in Europe and Japan which show very few benefits arising from the close physical proximity of high-technology firms to a local university.
2. It should be noted that R&D is not a good measure of small-firm inputs into knowledge production since such inputs often arise informally without the support of an R&D laboratory.
3. See Acs (1996) for a detailed description.
4. Inclusion of a lagged dependent variable in (8.1) yielded a coefficient of almost unity and impaired the explanatory power of most other variables, suggesting a relative lack of movement in employment over time.
5. There are other logical ways to test for this, for example, weighting the values of other cities' R&D by some measure of their distance from the focal city.
6. The minimum real wage excluding the observations on Louisville in high technology research but continuing to include observations on Louisville for other sectors (DA, BB, EC, etc.) is $15 742 (the adjusted mean is $30 989, standard deviation is $7 448 and coefficient of variation is still 0.24).

9. Heterogeneity versus specialization

9.1 INTRODUCTION

What type of economic activity will promote positive externalities and, therefore, economic growth? This question is important given the debate in the literature about the nature of economic activity and how it affects economic growth. The Marshall–Arrow–Romer (MAR) externality concerns knowledge spillovers between firms in an industry. Arrow (1962) presented an early formalization; the paper by Romer (1986) is a recent and influential statement. Applied to cities by Marshall (1961 [orig. 1890]), this view says that the concentration of an industry in a city facilitates knowledge spillovers between firms and, therefore, the growth of that industry. According to this approach, externalities work within industries (Loesch 1954).

These theories of dynamic externalities are extremely appealing because they try to explain simultaneously how cities form and why they grow. MAR, in particular, predict that industries cluster geographically to absorb the knowledge spilling over between firms. In addition, they predict that regionally specialized industries grow faster because neighboring firms can learn from each other much better than geographically isolated firms.

A very different position has been attributed to Jacobs (1969). Jacobs perceives information spillovers between industry clusters to be more important for the firm than within-industry information flows. Heterogeneity, not specialization, is seen as the most important regional growth factor, so Jacobs' theory predicts that industries located in areas that are highly industrially diversified should grow faster.[1] Glaeser et al. (1992) analyze the six largest industries in each of 170 US cities. Their results are consistent with the presence of Jacobs-type externalities. Industries will grow sluggishly in cities with high degrees of specialization. However, as Duranton and Puga (1999) point out in their survey of this area, the results may depend on the sector concerned. Thus, Henderson (1994) finds that traditional standardized goods tend to be produced in more specialized cities, and (relative) demand for these products has declined secularly as new product demand has grown.

While Glaeser et al. (1992), Henderson, Kuncoro and Turner (1995) and Henderson (1994) have all examined the role of heterogeneity and specialization in economic growth, none of these studies has directly examined the role of university or industrial R&D, the ultimate source of new and existing knowledge for economic growth. Recently, Jaffe (1989), Jaffe, Trajtenberg and Henderson (1993) and Varga (1998) found that R&D and other knowledge spillovers not only generate externalities, but that such knowledge spillovers tend to be geographically bounded within the region where the new economic knowledge was created. Anselin, Varga and Acs (1997 and 2000a) confirmed the positive relationship between university research and innovative activity, and provided the first direct measure on the extent of knowledge spillovers that extended over a range of 50 miles from the innovating Metropolitan Statistical Area (MSA). However, these studies have only examined the effect of knowledge spillovers on patent and/or innovation counts but not on employment. The ultimate economic interest lies chiefly in the product markets and jobs that are generated by R&D.

In the last chapter we examined the spillover effects of university R&D on high-technology employment at the metropolitan level. While our data was for a much shorter time period than Glaeser et al. (1992) and we only looked at high-tech employment, by using BLS data instead of County Business Patterns data, we did not have to estimate missing values. Moreover, we had data at the three-digit level, instead of the two-digit level, permitting a more disaggregated analysis. We found that after controlling for wages, prior innovations, state fixed effects and sample selectivity bias, university R&D spillovers have a significant effect on high-technology employment within narrow industry bounds in MSAs.

In other words, university R&D spillovers appear to operate locally within a narrow set of industries from university research through innovation to high-technology employment. There was no strong evidence of university R&D spillovers across industries or MSAs. The transmission of university knowledge spillovers across industries appears to be unimportant. It is certainly plausible that the usefulness of university research to the firm is greatest if it is in the same three- or four-digit SIC classification. Differing technologies and professional specializations also suggest that university research is likely to be less valuable to the firm if it is carried out in different two-digit SIC codes. Thus, we found no support for Jacobs-type externalities for university R&D spillovers across industry clusters.

The purpose of this chapter is to extend this research to industrial R&D. We test the MAR hypothesis that industrial R&D does not 'spill over' across regional industry clusters. This is important for several reasons. First, the ratio of business R&D to total R&D is about 0.725, and even larger in selected three-digit industries. Second, industrial R&D is more applied and closer to employment and economic growth than university R&D. Third, the empirical evidence suggests that R&D spillovers operate at the industry level and proximity does matter (Jaffe 1986).

In Section 9.2 we briefly summarize the literature on the search for R&D spillovers at the industry level. In Section 9.3 we examine some of the theoretical underpinnings of the heterogeneity and specialization hypotheses. Issues concerning the measurement of high technology employment and R&D are outlined in Section 9.4. After the empirical specification and econometric issues are discussed in Sections 9.5 and 9.6, the results are presented in Section 9.7. The final section summarizes our conclusions. We find that the channels of knowledge spillover are similar for industrial R&D and university R&D. Both university and industry R&D spillovers operate within but not across narrow three-digit industry groupings, thus supporting the specialization thesis in this context. However, these essentially cross-sectional data do not permit direct conclusions about employment growth.

9.2   THE SEARCH FOR INDUSTRIAL R&D SPILLOVERS

What are R&D spillovers? There are two distinct notions. First, R&D intensive inputs are purchased from other industries at less than their full quality-adjusted price. This is a problem of measuring capital equipment, other inputs and their prices correctly and not really a case of pure knowledge spillovers. A good example of such productivity transfers would be the computer industry. It has experienced tremendous productivity growth. Different industries have benefited differentially from it depending on their rate of computer purchases. But these are not pure knowledge spillovers; instead they are just consequences of conventional measurement problems under uncertainty.

True spillovers are ideas borrowed by research teams of industry (or firm) i from the research results of industry (or firm) j. The photographic equipment industry (SIC 386) and the measuring and controlling device industry (SIC 382) may not purchase inputs from one another but may be in a sense working on similar problems and hence able to benefit considerably from each other's research.

To measure R&D spillovers directly, one has to assume either that their benefits are localized in a particular industry, or in a range of products. Or that there are ways of identifying the relevant channels of influence, so 'that one can detect the path of the spillovers in the sands of the data' (Griliches 1992: S31). Arguably the usefulness of somebody else's research to you is highest if he is in the same four-digit SIC classification as you are. It is probably still high if she is in the same three-digit industry group. While research in your two-digit industry classification is less useful, it is still more valuable to you than research outside of your two-digit industry.

If there are R&D spillovers within industries then the computed returns should be higher at the industry than the firm level. A comparison of firm-based

R&D results with those found using various industry aggregates does not, however, indicate consistently higher R&D coefficients at the aggregate level (Mairesse and Mohnen 1990). This result may be due to measurement error. These studies, for example, do not take into account explicitly the difference between private and social obsolescence rates (Griliches 1992).

Nevertheless, there are a significant number of reasonably well done studies all pointing in the same direction: R&D spillovers at the industry level are present, their magnitudes may be quite large and social rates of return remain significantly above private rates. See, for example, Jaffe (1986), Griliches and Lichtenberg (1984) and Bernstein and Nadiri (1989).

9.3 HETEROGENEITY VERSUS SPECIALIZATION

The importance of location to employment growth may seem paradoxical in a world of instant communications. However, as has been pointed out by Lucas (1988 and 1993) and Black and Henderson (1999), it is localized information and knowledge spillovers, presumably through personal face-to-face contacts, that make cities the engines of economic growth. Cities grow faster than rural areas.

Despite the general consensus that knowledge spillovers within a given location stimulate employment growth, there is little consensus as to exactly how this occurs. The MAR model formalizes the insight that the concentration of an industry in a city promotes knowledge spillovers between firms and therefore would facilitate employment growth in a city industry observation. An important assumption is that knowledge externalities with respect to firms exist, but only for firms within the same industry. Thus, the relevant unit of observation is extended from the firm to the region in the theoretical tradition of the MAR model and in subsequent empirical studies, but spillovers are limited to occur within the relevant industry. The transmission of knowledge spillovers across industries is assumed to be non-existent or at least trivial.

However, according to Jacobs (1969), the emphasis on within-industry spillovers may be misplaced. Jacobs' idea is that the crucial externality in cities is cross-fertilization of ideas across different lines of work and industries. New York grain and cotton merchants saw the need for national and international financial transactions, and so the financial services industry was born. Rosenberg (1963) discusses the spread of machine tools across industries and describes how an idea is transmitted from one industry to another. Because cities bring people together from different walks of life, they foster transmission of ideas. Lucas (1993) emphasizes metropolitan areas as the most natural context in which the compact nature of the geographic growth facilitates personal interchange, communication and knowledge spillovers both within and across industries.

Jacobs (1969) develops a theory which emphasizes that the variety of industries within a geographic region promotes knowledge externalities and ultimately employment and economic growth. A common science base facilitates the exchange of existing ideas and generation of new ones across disparate but complementary industries. Thus, in Jacobs' view, diversity rather than specialization is the operative mechanism of economic growth.

A second issue is the role of university R&D.[2] University R&D by definition exists outside the industry. However, university R&D is a source of significant innovation-generating knowledge which diffuses initially through direct personal contacts to adjacent firms. Since both basic and applied university research may benefit private enterprise in various ways, it induces firms to locate nearby (Jaffe 1989, and Anselin et al. 1997). Lund (1986) surveys industrial R&D managers and finds the proximity of university R&D to be important for the location decision due to the initial spillover from neighboring university research to commercial innovation. Of course, as research results are embodied in commercial products and disseminated, the initial learning advantage created by close geographic proximity between local high-technology industrial activity and the university would fade but may persist for significant durations. Thus knowledge, both of a formal nature and embodied in the tacit skills of mobile human capital, flows locally through a variety of channels more easily and efficiently than over greater distances.[3]

9.4   DESCRIPTION OF THE DATA

Clusters are geographic concentrations of interconnected companies and institutions in a particular field or industry. Clusters encompass an array of linked industries and other entities important to competition. They include, for example, suppliers of specialized inputs such as components, machinery and services and providers of specialized infrastructure (Porter 1990).[4] If the Marshall–Arrow–Romer (MAR) externality concerns knowledge spillovers between firms in an industry or cluster of industries, they most probably operate along these interconnections within clusters. We identified 32 three-digit standard industrial classification (SIC) industries as high-technology clusters on the basis of a relatively high ratio of R&D to industry sales (Acs 1996). These industries were grouped into the five clusters detailed in Appendix E, namely biotechnology and biomedical, information technology and services, high-technology machinery and instruments, defense and aerospace, and energy and chemicals.[5]

Employment and wage data corresponding to the five industry clusters were provided by the US Department of Labor, Bureau of Labor Statistics (BLS). These are reported to the BLS by the State Employment Security Agencies (SESAs) of the 50 states as part of the Covered Employment and Wages Program (i.e. the EC-202+ report). Employers in private industry provide SESAs with quarterly tax reports for an average of 90 million wage and salary workers in approximately 5.9 million reporting units. These reports covered approximately 98 percent of total wage and salary civilian employment and provide a virtual census of employees and their wages for nearly all sectors of the economy.

This study utilizes specialized data runs for 36 MSAs which are listed in Table 9.1 in descending order of total high- technology employment in our five clusters. There is considerable variation in employment levels both between MSAs within an industry grouping and between sectors within a given city. Unfortunately, labor market data were unavailable for additional MSAs due to disclosure limitations. In those cities and industries where there are only a few employers, the data cannot be released due to the problem of potentially revealing the details of individual records. This limits both the number of industries and the number of cities which can be studied using BLS data. Although we could study employment in most of the 300 MSAs, discloure problems prohibit access to data on specific high-technology industries. This study of R&D spillovers, therefore, is necessarily confined to those cities that have a large number of high-technology industries.

Our measure of industrial research and development (R&D) is a proxy based on data on professional employment in high-technology research laboratories in the Bowker Directories (Jacques Cattell Press 1982). While imperfect, this approach allowed us to construct a private R&D variable for all MSAs. As indicated in Anselin, Varga and Acs (1997), our proxy variables are remarkably similar to the R&D expenditures used in Jaffe (1989).

The data on university R&D are measured in expenditure rather than employment terms. Total university R&D spending in each city is disaggregated by broad science department and allocated to each of the five industries. The assignment of research funds by academic department to each industrial grouping follows that used in Acs, FitzRoy and Smith (1999) which in turn was based on the mapping of Audretsch and Feldman (1996). The data are compiled from the National Science Foundation Survey of Scientific and Engineering Expenditures at Universities and Colleges for various years. Table 9.2 reports mean industrial and university R&D across the 36 MSAs by industrial grouping. Interestingly, there is an inverse relationship between our measures of average industrial R&D and university R&D by sector. The biotechnology sector, for example, has the smallest R&D laboratories in terms of employment but the largest expenditures in terms of university R&D (departments of life sciences). This is because the more mature industries have

Table 9.1   High-technology employment by MSA and industry cluster, 1988

MSA	BB	DA	HTM	EC	ITS	TOTAL
Los Angeles	19 535	219 696	54 176	24 343	89 321	407 071
Boston	16 481	44 355	54 176	5 710	133 252	253 974
San Jose	10 301	36 315	40 134	828	147 266	234 844
Chicago	11 159	1 587	59 874	15 835	80 821	169 276
Philadelphia	22 026	19 535	36 315	22 026	59 874	159 776
Dallas	3 789	29 732	12 964	18 033	80 821	145 339
Seattle	3 714	98 715	8 184	464	15 835	126 912
Houston	1 299	925	24 343	73 130	21 162	120 859
Minneapolis	12 209	15 063	29 732	2 565	59 874	119 443
Portland	5 486	22 026	73 130	8 184	8 690	117 516
Tucson	1 224	3 568	4 188	1 900	89 321	100 201
New York City	17 676	4 817	18 215	6 905	49 020	96 633
Rochester	7 863	49 020	9 996	12 835	14 328	94 042
Phoenix	2 079	26 903	5 324	626	49 020	83 952
San Diego	6 185	29 732	14 617	1 286	29 732	81 552
Raleigh-Durham	5 767	22 026	5 166	8 184	26 903	68 046
Cleveland	2 208	8 103	24 343	13 766	10 509	58 929
Austin	2 368	22 026	3 827	8 184	22 026	58 431
Washington DC	2 643	16 155	7 631	3 789	26 903	57 121
Denver	4 359	15 214	4 146	14 328	15 063	53 110
Baltimore	2 275	21 162	6 905	4 402	17 154	51 898
Kansas City	437	22 026	17 154	8 184	3 568	51 369
Cincinnati	4 359	19 341	11 047	6 502	7 707	48 956
Atlanta	2 643	22 026	953	8 184	5 377	39 183
Pittsburgh	2 892	259	15 063	7 707	12 088	38 009
Indianapolis	5 271	3 133	7 785	2 514	17 154	35 857
Orlando	1 998	2 344	14 185	665	16 647	35 839
Nashville	837	14 764	5 431	249	11 047	32 328
Salt Lake City	3 714	7 115	2 864	2 018	14 764	30 475
San Francisco	3 866	1 998	2 540	3 197	16 983	28 584
Charlotte	1 261	262	5 166	9 228	12 209	28 126
Columbus	1 652	1 685	9 996	3 751	10 938	28 022
St Louis	561	7 785	2 540	66	8 866	19 818
Miami	953	3 361	7 186	1 808	6 310	19 618
Providence	1 863	111	7 942	2 143	6 438	18 497
Louisville	6 974	2 253	2 951	796	4 769	17 743

Key:
BB   Biotechnology and biomedical
DA   Defense and aerospace
HTM   High-technology machinery and instruments
EC   Energy and chemicals
ITS   Information technology and services

Table 9.2   Mean industrial and university R&D by cluster

Industrial cluster	Industrial R&D (laboratory employment in 1985)	University R&D (annual expenditure 1988 to 1991 in $ m.)
Biotechnology and biomedical	644.6	112.8
Defense and aerospace	962.4	47.9
High-technology machinery and instruments	1 071.4	36.9
Energy and chemicals	1 258.4	22.6
Information technology and services	1 909.9	7.9

higher industrial R&D and the newer clusters, such as biotechnology and biomedical that are rather young, have larger university expenditures.

9.5   THE EMPIRICAL MODEL

Since the data do not permit us to estimate a well-specified labor demand equation, the employment equation is written down as a simple log linear reduced form in equation (9.1):

$$EMP_{MIT} = \alpha_0 + \alpha_1 W_{MIT} + \alpha_2 R_{MI} + \alpha_3 RSPILL_{MI} + \alpha_4 U_{MI,\, T-3}$$
$$+ \alpha_5 USPILL_{MI,\, T-3} + \alpha_6 INNOV_M$$
$$+ \alpha_7 POP_{MT} + \alpha V + u_{MIT} \tag{9.1}$$

where $M = 1 \ldots 36$ indexes the MSA, $I = 1 \ldots 5$ indexes industry grouping, and $T = 1988 \ldots 1991$ indexes time, and all variables are in natural logarithms. EMP_{MIT} refers to high-technology employment, W_{MIT} is the corresponding annual real wage per employee, defined as nominal wages deflated by the appropriate producer price index. Note that the panel is very short, including only four years of annual data, which compares unfavourably with, say, Glaeser et al. (1992), who use observations drawn from 1956 and 1987 to estimate employment growth equations. Since cross-section variability dominates in our data set, attempts to estimate equations specified in terms of employment growth rates, rather than in levels, proved fruitless.

$U_{MI,\, T-3}$ refers to university R&D deflated by the gross national product price deflator. Given the time span of the data set, it seems reasonable that the use of R&D with a three-year lag provides an appropriate delay for the university research knowledge externality to be transmitted into commercial products and employment. Edwards and Gordon (1984), for example, find that innovations made in 1982 resulted from inventions made on average just over four years previously.

To test directly for spillovers to employment in each sector from university R&D expenditure outside of that matched to each industrial grouping, the variable $USPILL_{MI, T-3}$ was constructed. It is the sum of all hard science university R&D spending by MSA less the expenditure which corresponds to each industry.

R_{MI} is the industrial R&D proxy measured using employment in R&D laboratories. Data were collected by sector and city for a single year, namely 1985. The variable $RSPILL_{MI}$ captures any spillover from industrial R&D which is not specific to each industry grouping. It is constructed using the same method as that described for the university spillover variable.

$INNOV_M$ is a count of the number of product innovations by MSA in 1982, the year for which the database of US commercial innovations was compiled by the Small Business Administration. The count is based on an extensive review of new product announcements in trade and technical publications. The data are disaggregated by MSA but not by industry, so cross-industry spillover effects from the innovation count cannot be directly tested here.[6] In this model, the variable attempts to control for the effect of pre-existing commercial innovation, that ultimately leads to product development and marketing with substantial time lags, on subsequent employment levels.

POP_{MT} refers to MSA population and controls for local market size. Although the market may well extend beyond MSA boundaries, we do not have a more appropriate measure of demand. Finally V represents a vector of industry, state and annual time dummies. These control for fixed effects which may not have been captured by the continuous variables.

9.6   SAMPLE SELECTION BIAS

The disclosure limits of the BLS data described previously may introduce a selection bias in the results. This arises since the data are suppressed in those MSAs where high-technology employment is low. A non-randomly selected sample is, therefore, effectively imposed by the BLS. This bias can be resolved econometrically by constructing a joint model which represents both the employment equation and the selection process determining when the dependent variable is observed, as in Chapter 8.[7]

Table 9.3 provides basic summary statistics for all the variables in the model, disaggregated by disclosure status, and presented in their raw

Table 9.3   Summary statistics by variable

Variable	36 MSAs Mean	36 MSAs Coefficient of variation	77 MSAs Mean	77 MSAs Coefficient of variation
EMP_{MIT}	17 308	1.55		
W_{MIT}	31 723	0.24		
POP_{MT}	2 370 200	0.82	647 000	0.96
$INNOV_M$	56	1.36	7	1.53
R_{MI}	1 169	1.79	187	2.93
$RSPILL_{MI}$	4 678	1.51	761	2.08
$U_{MI, T-3}$	46	1.44	10	2.13
$USPILL_{MI, T-3}$	149	0.91	33	1.53

Note: (a) For ease of reading the table, the means are rounded to the nearest integer value; (b) the university R&D variables are measured in $ millions.

(unlogged) form.[8] The 77 MSAs for which high-technology employment is not disclosed are clearly much smaller, with substantially fewer innovations and considerably lower R&D than those 36 MSAs for which employment and wage data are available.

9.7   RESULTS

The first column of Table 9.4 reports the ordinary least squares regression results using 720 observations drawn from five high-technology clusters in 36 MSAs over the four-year period, 1988 to 1991. The absolute *t*-statistics in parentheses are based on White's heteroskedastic consistent estimates of the standard errors. The equation includes both state, time and industry fixed effects to control for unmeasured factors. The coefficients on the fixed effects are not tabulated but their joint significance cannot be rejected by an *F*-test. Since the equation is estimated in natural logarithms the coefficients should therefore be interpreted as elasticities.

These simple OLS estimates provide a baseline from which to assess the impact of sample selection on the employment equation. Column (2) of Table 9.4 reports the coefficient estimates of the disclosure probability equation estimated by maximum likelihood probit on the full sample of 113 MSAs over the four-year period. The probit equation performs satisfactorily. All of the variables with the partial exception of industrial R&D, R_{MI}, are statistically significant at conventional levels, and the equation correctly predicts disclosure

Table 9.4   High-technology employment estimates

Dependent variable	(1) OLS EMP_{MIT}	(2) PROBIT I_{MIT}	(3) OLS EMP_{MIT}	(4) OLS EMP_{MIT}
	−22.69	−10.56	−22.03	−21.70
	(6.8)	(19.5)	(6.2)	(5.3)
W_{MIT}	2.61		2.61	
	(8.8)		(8.8)	
$W_{MI, T-1}$				2.60
				(7.6)
POP_{MT}	0.26	1.08	0.22	0.20
	(2.4)	(15.2)	(1.7)	(1.3)
$INNOV_M$	0.29	0.38	0.26	0.27
	(2.8)	(8.2)	(2.0)	(1.9)
R_{MI}	0.12	0.03	0.12	0.11
	(4.1)	(1.4)	(4.2)	(3.6)
$RSPILL_{MI}$	0.02	−0.07	0.03	0.04
	(0.5)	(3.1)	(0.7)	(0.7)
$U_{MI, T-3}$	0.09	0.08	0.09	0.07
	(3.5)	(3.5)	(3.0)	(2.3)
$USPILL_{MI, T-3}$	0.06	0.15	0.05	0.06
	(1.5)	(5.1)	(1.0)	(1.1)
$\hat{\lambda}_{MIT}$			−0.19	−0.23
			(0.6)	(0.6)
$\bar{R}_2$	0.59	0.57	0.59	0.59
$\hat{\sigma}$	0.899		0.900	0.903
n	720	2260	720	540

Notes: (a) Absolute *t*-statistics based on White's heteroskedastic consistent standard errors are in parentheses; (b) all variables are in natural logarithms; (c) $\bar{R}_2$ is the adjusted multiple correlation coefficient, $\hat{\sigma}$ is the estimated standard error of the regression, and n is the number of observations; (d) unreported dummy variables for industry, time and state are also included in each of these regressions except for the probit in column (2).

status in 84 percent of cases. Curiously, the signs on the two inter-industry spillover variables are opposite. Larger values for R&D spillovers assigned to a given MSA and industry (university) are likely to be associated with a smaller (greater) probability of employment disclosure, all else equal. Note, however, that the magnitudes of the R&D coefficients are comparatively small. It is mainly MSA size, in terms of population, and to a smaller degree, the number of innovations, that most powerfully determine disclosure probability.

Column (3) lists the estimated coefficients of the employment equation corrected for sample selection. Under the null hypothesis of no selection bias, the coefficient of the estimated inverse Mills' ratio, $\hat{\lambda}_{MIT}$, has a t-distribution. Using a t-test, we cannot reject the null at conventional levels of statistical significance. This outcome implies that there is no sample selection problem for these data. Hence including a term to capture sample selection makes very little difference with respect to the remaining coefficients, as a comparison of the corrected equation in column (3) with the unadjusted equation in column (1) indicates.

There are several important findings in column (3). First, the major result is that the estimates suggest, if anything, a rejection of the heterogeneity hypothesis. Although the coefficient on the university R&D spillovers in other clusters, $USPILL_{MI, T-3}$, is slightly larger than that for the corresponding industrial R&D spillover, $RSPILL_{MI}$, both are statistically insignificant at conventional levels.

Second, industrial and university R&D are positive and statistically significant determinants of high-technology employment. The employment elasticities are similar in magnitude, 0.12 and 0.09 respectively, though they are not strictly comparable given the different bases of measurement.

Third, and perhaps surprisingly, real wages and employment are positively related ceteris paribus. To correct for any possible simultaneity between employment and real wages, the equation was also estimated using lagged wages. The results are reported in column (4) and are very similar to those in columns (1) and (3). Neither unreported re-estimates with 2SLS or random effects models produced any difference in this result which thus appears to be robust to estimation technique.

Without a measure of output we cannot estimate a production function or a structural model of labor demand. Our reduced form relationship between wages and high technology employment suggests that we may have captured the dynamics of labor supply in the face of mobility costs and specific skills. Faster growing local industries may need higher wages to recruit scarce skills from further afield to compensate for relocation and transport costs. There is an analogy with the well-known firm size–wage correlation, and of course higher employment is likely to imply larger firms on average.[9]

9.8 CONCLUSIONS

We have established a striking correlation between local R&D and subsequent high-technology employment in the same MSA and three-digit industry cluster. There is apparently no spillover relationship from R&D in the other industry groups. This result may seem surprising in the light of much recent research which seems rather to support the Jacobs' (1969) view of the benefits of diversity. Of course, our essentially cross-sectional data cannot directly address the key issues of growth performance, which require longer panels. And we have only focused on a narrow subset of industries, albeit important ones in the context of knowledge spillovers. Also, our industry groupings offer no evidence on spillovers within groups, between the industries we have aggregated and listed in Appendix E.

From a microeconomic perspective, our evidence for the benefits of specialization, following MAR, does appear plausible in our context and raises several challenges for future research. These include extensions to other industries and longer panels which allow for further direct testing of spillovers from R&D to growth and productivity in other industries.

NOTES

1. This chapter does not address the issue posed by these studies and also Porter (1990) and Schumpeter (1942) on the role of competition and monopoly in promoting innovation and growth.
2. This is discussed in more detail in Acs, FitzRoy and Smith (1999).
3. Note that we do not present here any tests for geographical spillovers, such as those conducted by Anselin, Varga and Acs (2000a). Research and development occurring in a given MSA may well have cross-regional employment impacts but consideration of the distinction between local and non-local spillovers is outside the scope of this chapter.
4. A rich literature has recently developed on industry clusters. See for example, Porter (1998); Braunerhjelm and Carlsson (1999); Acs (1996) and Storper (1995). For a review of the literature see Muizer and Hospers (1998).
5. In our previous paper (Acs, FitzRoy and Smith 1999) which did not consider industrial R&D, we were able to include the effect of university R&D on employment for the high-technology research sector.
6. For a discussion of their limitations see Edwards and Gordon (1984), Feldman and Audretsch (1999) and Varga (1998).
7. See Maddala (1983).
8. A human capital, labour supply variable for MSAs that was used with mixed results in our previous work was insignificant and hence omitted here.
9. Higher wages and employment may be a legacy of faster growth in previous years not included in our short panel.

10. Regional innovation systems

10.1 INTRODUCTION

In the introductory chapter of Nelson's *National Innovation Systems*, a central hypothesis is formulated about 'a new spirit of what might be called "tech-nonationalism" . . . combining a strong belief that the technological capabilities of a nation's firms are a key source of their competitive prowess, with a belief that these capabilities are in a sense national, and can be built by national action' (Nelson 1993: 3). While Richard Nelson and Nathan Rosenberg are careful to explain that one of the central concerns of their 15-country study is to establish 'whether, and if so in what ways, the concept of a "national" system made any sense today', they also add that *de facto* 'national governments act as if it did' (Nelson 1993: 5). The purpose of this chapter is to raise some questions about this hypothesis and to provide a framework to study 'local' systems of innovation as an alternative hypothesis.

In Section 10.2, we deal with the process of *globalization* of economic activities and of its impact on the national production and governance systems. This forces one to confront both what John Naisbitt has called the 'global para-dox' and what we have called elsewhere the 'dispersive revolution' (Naisbitt 1994; de la Mothe and Paquet 1994a). In Section 10.3, we review quickly the main features of *network dynamics* and the way it is stalled by the phenome-non of *centralized mindset*: a strong attachment to a tendency to bet on central-ized means of problem-solving that almost inevitably lead to compulsive centralization and misguided approaches. In Section 10.4, we provide some *evidence* in support of our local systems of innovation hypothesis. Section 10.5 outlines systems of innovation and the Section 10.6 presents the elements of the system. Section 10.7 summarizes the argument.

10.2 THE PARADOXICAL CONSEQUENCES OF GLOBALIZATION

Real-life economies are 'instituted processes', that is, sets of rules and conventions that vest the wealth-creation process with relative unity and stability by harmonizing the geo-technical constraints that are imposed by the environment with the values and plans found in decision-makers (Polanyi 1968). Modern economies have evolved substantially over the last century. The wealth-creation process of the late nineteenth century was mainly instituted as a 'social armistice' between fairly rigid constraints imposed by technology, geography and natural resources endowments, on the one hand, and the less than perfectly co-ordinated plans of private and public decision-makers, on the other hand. As both constraints and preferences evolved, national economies came to be instituted differently. They evolved often quite differently because of the degrees of freedom afforded them by the extent to which they were protected from the rest of the world by relatively high transportation costs, transaction costs and tariff walls.

In the recent past, the wealth-creation process has changed dramatically. It has become increasingly dematerialized as its mainsprings ceased to be natural resources and material production and became knowledge and information activities. Transportation costs, transaction costs and tariff walls tumbled. And, as a result of important information economies and of growing organizational flexibility, transitional firms have become capable of organizing production globally and thus escape to a great extent the constraints nation-states might wish to impose on them. Therefore, economic activity has become less constrained by geography and, in many instances, has become truly deterritorialized.

There is little question that economic activity of all types is moving in the direction of globalization. At the start of the twenty-first century, a worldwide system of production and distribution is evolving, in much the same way as national markets evolved from local and regional networks during the nineteenth century (Chandler 1990). In nearly every economically active country of the world, the importance of international trade and foreign direct investment (FDI) has risen significantly over the last decade.[1] The growth of FDI has been particularly dramatic, increasing more rapidly than either world production or world trade. As a result, both inbound and outbound FDI stocks have increased relative to total investment and gross domestic product in nearly every country (Dunning 1995). Cross-border intra-firm activities are now the norm rather than the exception.

Globalization refers to the web of linkages and interconnections between states, societies and organizations that make up the present world economic system. Globalization creates new structures and new relationships, with the result that business decisions and actions in one part of the world have significant consequences in other places. The growth of global markets stimulates competition and forces governments to adopt market-oriented policies, both domestically and internationally. Modern technologies have greatly reduced the cost of information and the capabilities to participate in the global economy (Dunning 1993). Countries must join the club. Policies that aim to exclude global participation via trade and investment barriers can be easily circumvented, and they keep no hostages but deprive the countries concerned of global prosperity.

The pressures of global competition force producers continually to innovate, and to upgrade the quality of existing products. Yet, at the same time, many firms can no longer acquire or afford all the knowledge and human resources that they need. Increasingly, they form interdependent and flexible relationships with other firms – including suppliers and competing firms – to fully capitalize on their core competencies (Gomes-Casseres 1996). Interdependence calls for a capacity on the part of firms, individuals and governments to interact with speed, flexibility and creativity in response to the actions of other agents (de la Mothe and Paquet 1996).

Globalization cannot be characterized as a simple process of trade liberalization. To be sure, there has been much liberalization, but firms and nations which have become more exposed internationally have also become increasingly dependent on intangibles like know-how, synergies and untraded interdependencies. This new techno-economic world has required important changes in the managerial, strategic and political rules of the game.

First, 'firms', 'governments' and 'third-sector organizations' have become rather fuzzy concepts. It is often no longer possible to distinguish the inside and the outside in the complex web of networks and alliances they are enmeshed in. Second, the knowledge/information fabric of the new economy has led to the development of a large number of non-market institutions as information and knowledge proved to be poorly handled by the market. Finally, the traditional and narrow economic notion of competition has been replaced by the broader and more sophisticated notion of competitiveness as a benchmark for assessing the process of wealth-creation and as a guide in designing the requisite web of explicit and organic co-operative links between all stakeholders (Paquet 1990).

As a result, private and public organizations have become more footloose and as such they have become more compatible with a variety of locations, technologies and organizational structures (de la Mothe and Paquet 1994b). They have also been potentially affected to a much greater extent by the synergies, interdependencies, socio-cultural bonds or trust relationships that are capable of producing comparative advantages. Indeed, the central challenge of the new economy has been to find ways to create an environment in which knowledge workers do as much learning as possible from their experience, but also from each other, from partners, clients, suppliers and so on. This entails that, for learning to occur, there must be *conversations* between and among partners. But since working conversations that create new knowledge can only emerge where there is trust and proximity, these have proved to be essential inputs (Webber 1993).

Two very significant transformations in our modern political economies in the last decades have been ascribable to a large extent to the challenges posed by the new socio-economy: a balkanization of existing national economies *and* a concurrent massive devolution in the governance system of both private and public organizations.

10.2.1 Balkanization of National Economies

There are many reasons for balkanization to proceed as globalization sets in. First, global competitiveness has led advanced industrial nations to specialize in the export of products in which they have 'technological' or 'absolute' advantages, and since those export-oriented absolute-advantage industries tend to be found in sub-national regions, this has led to the emergence of a mosaic of sub-national geographical agglomerations and regional 'worlds of production' characterized by *product-based technological learning systems* resting, in important ways, on conventions rooted in the cultures of local economic actors (Storper 1992, 1993).

Second, the pressures of globalization have put so much strain on the nation-state that sub-national regions and communities have felt strongly a need for roots and anchors in local/regional bonds of ethnicity, language and culture. This *tribalism* (to use Naisbitt's term) has been reinforced by the fact that it often proved to be the source of a robust entrepreneurial culture and therefore of competitive advantage in the new context (Stoffaes 1987).

Third, the dysfunctionality of the nation-state has triggered the emergence of a genuine shared community of economic interests at the regional level, and the dynamics of collective action has led to the *rise of the region-state*, when sub-national governments or loose alliances among local authorities have become active as partners of foreign investors and providers of the requisite infrastructure to leverage regional policies capable of making the region an active participant in the global economy (Ohmae 1993; *The Economist* 1994).

Fourth, as the region-state emerged, it has been in a position to provide support for the sub-national development blocs through the nurturing of complementarities, interdependencies and externalities via infrastructure, networking of economic and business competence, and so on and to dynamize the transformation process at the meso-economic level (Dahmen 1988; de la Mothe and Paquet 1994c). This has in turn reinforced the separate internal dynamics and the resilience of the sub-national systems.

10.2.2 Devolution of the Governance System

Global competitiveness has also triggered a massive devolution in the governance systems of both public and private organizations. The reasons for this are:

first, the search for speed of adjustment, variety, flexibility and innovation gener-ated by global competitiveness has forced corporations to adapt ever faster and this has led them to 'deconstruct' themselves into networks of quasi-autonomous units capable of taking action as they see fit in the face of local circumstances. Managers ceased to be 'drivers of people' and became 'drivers of learning' (Wriston 1992). This required a shift from hierarchical structures of governance to networking structures that were conducive to innovative conversations.

Second, the same process has been witnessed in the governance of public organizations where the need to do more with less and the growing pressure for more sub-national states to co-operate actively with private organizations to ensure success on the global scene has led governments into massive priva-tization or the devolution of power to lower-order public authorities (Rivlin 1992; Osborne and Gaebler 1992; Paquet 1994).

Third, this has led to general praise for the flexibility and genuine souplesse of the federal system as a system of governance for both private and public organizations, and to the general celebration of bottom-up management (O'Toole and Bennis 1992; Handy 1992, 1994).

Fourth, in transforming the governance of economic, social and political organizations, the growing search for flexibility has not stopped at decentral-ization and privatization strategies. There has been a growing pressure to dissolve permanent organizations so as to allow a maximum open use of all the possibilities of networking. This has led to the proposal that virtual enter-prises and governments might provide the ultimate flexibility (Davidow and Malone 1992; de la Mothe and Paquet 1994a). This form of dissolution of governance systems has not only proved to be dynamically efficient but has also led to a reinforcement of community bonds as private and public organi-zations ceased to be the main source of identification.

10.3 NETWORK DYNAMICS AND CENTRALIZED MINDSET

Sub-national areas have proved to be better loci for 'conversations' likely to foster fast learning. Indeed, it is argued by the defenders of the notion of local systems of innovation that such sub-national areas are a more supportive underground for the development of multi-stakeholder networks and new forms of co-operation and relational exchange. But this has not deterred those who have a strong taste for national across-the-board interventions. The techno-nationalists emphasize the importance of the national network of insti-tutions, acting as a system and providing the foundations and the underpin-nings of the innovation system. This leads them to bet on policies designed to act on the national institutions to stimulate innovations.

The opposition between local and national systems of innovation is rooted in the contrast between two dynamics: the bottom-up dynamics of networks and the top-down dynamics built on the centralized mindset.

10.3.1 Bottom-up network dynamics

The paradoxical consequences of globalization have been not only to generate balkanization but also to create the need for new forms of organization. Hierarchies have limited learning abilities and markets have limited capacities to process information effectively. Networks and alliances are ways to counter these failures, ways to combine the benefit of being large and small at the same time.

The network is not, as is usually assumed, a mixed form of organization existing halfway on a continuum ranging from market to hierarchy. Rather, it is a generic name for a third type of arrangement built on very different integrating mechanisms: networks are consensus/inducement-oriented organizations and institutions. This suggests that instead of the market-hierarchy dichotomy, one should bet on a partition of institutions and organizations according to three principles of integration: (a) those associated with threat/coercion, (b) those associated with exchange and (c) those associated with consensus and inducement-oriented systems. This more useful way of classifying institutions has been used by Karl Polanyi (1968 [orig. 1957]); François Perroux (1960); Kenneth Boulding (1970) and more recently by Shumpei Kumon (1992).

Networks have two sets of characteristics: those derived from their dominant logic (consensus and inducement-oriented systems) and those derived from the dominant intelligence that emerges from their structure. The consensus dominant logic does not abolish power but it means that power is distributed. A central and critical feature of networks is the emphasis on *voluntary* adherence to norms. While this voluntary adherence does not necessarily appear to generate constraints *per se* on the size of the organization, it is not always easy for a set of shared values to spread over massive disjointed transitional communities: free-riding, high transaction costs, problems of accountability, and so on impose extra work. So the benefits in terms of leanness, agility and flexibility are such that many important multinationals have chosen *not* to manage their affairs as a global production engine, but as a multitude of smaller quasi-independent units co-ordinated by a loose federal structure, because of the organizational diseconomies of scale in building a clan-type organization (O'Toole and Bennis 1992; Handy 1992).

As for the structural characteristics of the network, these complement nicely the dominant logic for networked intelligence, as embodied for instance in a company or an organization. The network will have the following traits:

it will be distributed, decentralized, collaborative and adaptive (Kelly 1994: 189). This network structure based on reciprocity and trust is a self-reinforcing mechanism for it breeds trust and reciprocity, thereby increasing the social capital and generating increasing returns. In that sense, reciprocity that is based on voluntary adherence generates lower costs of co-operation and therefore stimulates more networking as social capital accumulates with trust. The experiences in Emilia-Romagna described by Putnam (1993), its echo effect in Denmark or parallel developments in the Silicon Valley described by Saxenian (1994) are all pointing in the same direction. The site of a dense concentration of overlapping networks of solidarity generates wealth-creation on a surprising scale.

Some have argued that new technologies might well generate 'cyberhoods' that would be as potent as neighborhoods and that maybe the 'local' setting for such networks of solidarity or for a cultural milieu likely to generate much innovation could become truly deterritorialized and completely 'virtual'. But even network enthusiasts are not quite ready to consider the 'virtual community' as anything more than a poor simulacrum of the real community and consequently see it as being unlikely to generate the requisite degree of passion and commitment that is needed to fuel social capital accumulation on the appropriate scale (Rheingold 1993).

The growth of network markets in a number of sectors where mass customizations are important has generated a new form of externalities that has yielded important increasing returns, some snowballing effects and some possibilities of lock-in. This is the logic of network economies. But the network externalities and spillovers are not spreading in a frictionless world. Networking casts much more of a local shadow than is usually presumed: 'space becomes ever more variegated, heterogeneous and finely textured in part because the processes of spatial reorganization ... have the power to exploit relatively minute spatial differences to good effect (Harvey 1988). Consequently, a network does not extend boundlessly but tends instead to crystallize around a unifying purpose, mobilizing independent members through voluntary links, around multiple leaders in integrated levels of overlapping and superimposed webs of solidarity. This underscores the enormous importance of 'regional business cultures' and explains the relative importance of the small- and medium-sized enterprise networks in generating new ideas (Lipnack and Stamps 1994).

Not only are networks generating social capital and wealth, they have also been closely associated with a greater degree of progressivity of the economy, that is, with a higher degree of innovativeness and of capacity to transform because networks cross boundaries. Indeed, boundary-crossing networks are likely to ignite much innovativeness because they provide an opportunity for reframing and recasting perspectives and for questioning the assumptions that have been in good currency. One might suggest a parallel between boundary-crossing and migration into another world in which one's home experience serves as a useful contrast to the new realities. Much of the buoyant immigrant entrepreneurship is rooted in this dual capacity to see things differently and to network within and across boundaries. In the face of placeless power in a global economy, seemingly powerless places with their own communication code on a historically specific territory are fruitful terrains for local collaborative networks.

10.3.2   Top-down centralized mindset

In the face of strong *presumptions* regarding the existence of *regional innovation systems*, it is surprising to find that so little has been done to escape the mindset of 'national systems of innovation'. The reason for this bias is, however, not very difficult to understand. Since the cost of thinking is not zero, humans adopt paradigms and mindsets to routinize their thinking. Technonationalism's appeal is of this sort.

Mitchel Resnick has analysed the *travers* that explains that, in an era of decentralization in every domain, centralized thinking is remaining prevalent in our theories of knowledge, in our ways of analyzing problems, and in our search for policy responses. 'Politicians, managers and scientists are working with blinders on, focusing on centralised solutions even when decentralised approaches might be more appropriate, robust, or reliable' (Resnick 1994: 36). As Resnick explained, 'the centralised mindset is not just a misconception of the scientifically naive', one may find ample evidence that in science, in governance, there is a strong resistance to the idea of complexity being formed from a decentralized process. The resistance to evolutionary theory is of that ilk. It is more reassuring to presume that every pattern must have a single cause, and therefore an ultimate controlling factor.

This explains the opposition to a bottom-up explanation when this alternative cosmology has been suggested – (Science Council of Canada 1984, 1990) even when documentary evidence had been mounted to show that such an approach was not only promising but *de facto* building on already impressive accomplishments in a number of metropolitan areas (Davis 1991). More than a decade after the suggestion by the Science Council that metropolitan technology councils might be the appropriate lever to energize local systems of innovation, the idea is still in limbo. The centralized 'national system of innovations' continues to dominate the policy scene, and the view of a fragmented and localized *set of systems of innovation* that could only be nurtured from the periphery is still not in good currency (Paquet 1992; de la Mothe and Paquet 1994d; Paquet and Roy 1995).

10.4   CORROBORATIVE EVIDENCE: SOME COMPARATIVE VIGNETTES

We draw from three sets of corroborative evidence. First, recent exploratory work on network economies have underlined the importance of local spillovers or externalities, but the extent to which these spillover effects are indeed localized has not been sufficiently emphasized. Second, a whole body of observations and descriptive/ethnographical and empirical studies using alternative databases on innovative activities would appear to provide collateral evidence. Finally, the existing literature of the historical and case-study variety shows that indeed innovation systems have blossomed locally.

10.4.1   Network Economies

A first element of support has emerged in a somewhat oblique way from some recent work on network economies. The economic literature on networks has generated a rekindling of interest in the role of externalities in supply after decades of neglect. At the core of this renewal is the explosion of the new information and communication technologies. These technologies are at the core of a wave of innovations generated and diffused over the last decades and underpin the new centrality of increasing returns and economies of scale. It is to the increased centrality of communication networks that one may ascribe the new emphasis on the basic characteristics of information: interdependence, inappropriability and externality (Antonelli 1992: 6).

The analysis of telecommunication networks has served as a *révélateur*. They represent a sector with a particularly high degree of heterogeneity of components, of technical interrelatedness, of complexity of technological change, and they are exemplars of a sector with much irreversibility in investment, important scale economies and increasing returns and a broad array of externalities. Indeed, in the 'paradigmatic network industry the market demand schedule slopes *upwards* (due to demand externalities) and the market supply schedule slopes *downwards* (due to indivisibilities and supply externalities)' (David 1992: 104; Acs, FitzRoy and Smith 1999). But the most crucial aspect of this literature is the component suggesting that 'these features apply not only to the increasing number of sectors affected by the spreading of information and communication technologies, but more generally to all the processes of growth and change' (Antonelli 1992: 15).

If such is the case, some interesting results are emerging in six major areas (Antonelli 1992):

- the rate of introduction of innovations by a firm would appear to be more and more influenced by its capacity to co-operate with other firms;

- the success of a new technology depends on adoption externalities;
- network externalities are determinant in the selection of a technology;
- key sectors are the providers of externalities through an array of untraded interdependencies and linkages;
- proximity is a strong necessary condition to take advantage of externalities generated by others;
- network firms are the result of attempts by firms to internalize externalities.

A critical examination of this new world reveals that three factors will be central to the new dynamics:

1. networks represent an intermediate solution between the dynamic efficiency of markets and the static efficiency of hierarchical integrated organizations;
2. selective co-operation is the new pivotal tool for economic agents to internalize externalities;
3. any change is likely to have a strong *local character* (Piore 1992: 443; Antonelli 1992: 23).

These factors may vary from sector to sector but are at the source of the various clusterings that lead to social learning and to the dynamic reinforcement of the cluster (Porter 1990).

10.4.2 Empirical evidence

The chapters in this volume provide extensive evidence of the important innovative activity of small firms and throw some light on the important sectoral/locational/organizational factors that explain the different dynamics of innovative activity of large and small firms in different types of industries and locations. These studies have suggested that small firms are the recipients of important spillovers from knowledge generated in larger centers in firms and universities. These external effects differ from industry to industry but depend much on organizational and locational factors. These studies have provided important new evidence to help us understand the texture of local systems of innovation and the potential levers that might be used to design a new generation of public policies based on this new learning.

One of the important results generated by these chapters is the detailed documentation that R&D spillovers which are one of the sources of externalities are greatly facilitated by the 'geographical coincidence' of the different partners (universities, research labs, firms) within the state. Not only does innovative activity increase as a result of high private corporate expenditures on R&D, but it increases also as a result of research undertaken by universities within the area.

While it is difficult to generalize because of the fact that the patterns of innovative activity vary greatly from industry to industry and because of the fact that local embedding is often intermingled with global networks, it is clear from the literature that the local milieu can be regarded very often as the collective entrepreneur and innovator rather than the firm. Obviously the capacity for collective entrepreneurship depends a lot on socio-cultural factors resulting from the history of the region as Putnam has shown in the case of Italy. But much can be gained from the creation of a robust and decentralized system of institutional support to ensure that technical and commercial knowledge is diffused fast and as widely as possible, thereby catalysing the process of social learning (Best 1990; Todtling 1994; Cooke and Morgan 1994; Audretsch, 1995).

There has been a little more systematic work on the landscape of innovative activity in the United States using both traditional R&D expenditures and direct measures of innovative activity like the number of innovations commercially introduced derived from a score of technology, engineering and trade journals listing innovations and new products. This has shown that innovative activity is not evenly spread over the territory. Both R&D expenditures by industry and universities are clustered and they have important spatial spillovers that territorialize innovative activity. While small firms or large firms may dominate the scene, the clustering effect is quite clear in the data presented in Chapter 2 (Table 2.6).

This sort of clustering activity is even more evident at the county level. Chapter 1 (Table 1.1) shows the number of innovations for the 26 most innovative counties in the United States. One can see clearly that most of the innovations are clustered in a few counties. For instance, five counties in California accounted for 80 percent of the innovations in the state.

None of this is a robust proof that local systems of innovation exist or that public policy should be mainly directed to the local level. We only suggest that there are undeniably important spatial spillovers and that, in an oblique way, the available data on state and county innovative activity would appear to corroborate the local systems of innovation hypothesis.

10.4.3 Case Studies

The dossier of case studies tending to show some evidence that local systems of innovation exist and have a dynamic of their own is very extensive. It ranges from commemorative and boosterism writings, to carefully documented cases in monographs and books, to anecdotal evidence quoted on the occasion of a paper covering a broader territory, to tentative syntheses on the basis of all of the above. While it is difficult to derive precise general propositions from this variegated material, it provides a very rich file documenting the ways in which local systems of innovation have emerged and evolved.

There is no unanimity in this dossier. One finds strident critics and vehement apologists of local systems of innovation. But the vast majority of the case work is strongly in support of the existence and importance of local systems of innovation, and very much can be learned from these documents about the types of policies that have had determining impacts on the success of these ventures. They all document the importance *of proximity and the centrality of community, linguistic and related dimensions as the fabric of the socio-cultural underground on which sub-national systems of innovation are built.* From these case studies, one may derive a few elements of learning:

1. a common thread is the way in which relationships develop between private concerns and both the community and the public actors, and the way in which 'enabling agencies' foster collaboration; whether these agencies have materialized in formal mechanisms of governance like metropolitan technology councils or have simply crystallized in the form of an ethos, the instruments of collective co-ordination based on appeals to solidaristic local values, vision and culture are of central import (Hollingsworth 1993);

2. another common thread is the importance of leadership; leadership is 'what enables the complex inter-institutional and inter-sectoral partnerships to develop and become operational' and it would appear that the ability of communities to shape their future depends much more on social than on technological processes (Davis 1991: 12);

3. a third common thread is the great fragility of many local systems of innovations because of the fact that they are 'weakly institutionalized'; this is the sort of weakness that suggests the way in which the senior governments might be of most help in getting the local communities to help themselves, that is, in providing the enabling support to get the communities to invent new instruments and design new policy approaches. But there is also evidence of very robust local systems of innovations (Cooke and Morgan 1994; Saxenian 1994).

10.5   SYSTEMS OF INNOVATION

Systems of innovation are a new approach to the study of innovations in the economy that has emerged during the last decade. The systems approach is certainly not a formal theory. It does not provide convincing propositions as regards established and stable relations between variables. The most it does in this direction is to provide a basis for the formulation of conjectures that various factors are important for technological innovation.

The systems approach – like many other institutionally oriented approaches – is a conceptual framework that many scholars and policy-makers consider useful for the analysis of innovation (Edquist 1997). Although the systems of innovation approach is not considered a formal and established theory, its development has been influenced by different theories of innovation such as interactive learning theories (Arrow 1962) and evolutionary theories (Nelson and Winter 1982).

Much work has been done in the tradition of neo-Schumpeterian evolutionary economics to advance our understanding of the microfoundations of innovation. Perhaps the touchstone volume of this tradition is Nelson and Winter's *An Evolutionary Theory of Economic Change* (1982). In recent years, efforts have been made to percolate general theoretical and empirical observations from this literature up into a conceptual framework capable of guiding policy and loosely organized around the idea of a 'national system'.

Despite their different interpretations of innovation, all versions of the systems of innovation approach place innovation at the very center of focus. Technological innovation is a matter of producing new knowledge or combining existing knowledge in new ways, and of transforming this into economically significant products and processes. Many different kinds of actors and agents in the system of innovation are involved in these processes. Such activities involve learning by doing, increasing the efficiency of production operations, learning by using, increasing the efficiency of the use of complex systems, and learning by interacting, involving users and producers in interaction resulting in product innovations (Lundvall 1992: 9).

In the systems approach, innovation is viewed as a ubiquitous phenomenon. In all parts of the economy, and at all times, we expect to find ongoing processes of learning, searching and exploring, which results in new products, new techniques, new forms of organization and new markets. The first step in recognizing innovation as a ubiquitous phenomenon is to focus upon its gradual and cumulative aspects. Such a perspective gives rise to simple hypotheses about the dependence of future innovation on the past. In this context, an innovation may be regarded as a new use of pre-existing possibilities and components. Almost all innovations reflect existing knowledge combined in new ways.

The systems of innovation approaches can be characterized as holistic in the sense that they have the ambition to encompass a wide array of the determinants of innovation that are important. The systems approach allows for the inclusion not only of economic factors influencing innovation but also of institutional, organizational, social and political factors. In this sense, it is an interdisciplinary approach. Elements of the systems approach, such as firms, behave differently concerning innovation in different contexts. In order to understand such phenomena it is important to have a structural concept. The systems of innovation approach can fruitfully serve as such, because it can be considered to have a structural and actor-orientated approach.

The institutional set-up is the second important dimension of the systems of innovation approach. One of the most striking characteristics the systems of innovation approaches have in common is their emphasis on the role of institutions. Institutions are of crucial importance for innovation processes. However, what is meant by institutions varies from author to author. The concept of institutions can be quite heterogeneous and very complex. It includes normative structures, regimes, as well as organizations of various kinds. For others, it includes firms and industrial research laboratories involved in innovation. It can also include supporting institutions that include research universities, government laboratories, as well as technology policies.

The systems of innovation of various countries can be quite different. In addition, the organizations and institutions constituting elements of the systems of innovation may be different in various countries, regions or sectors. In the systems of innovation approaches the differences between the various systems are stressed and focused upon rather than abstracted from. This makes it not only natural but vital to compare various systems. Without comparisons between existing systems it is impossible to argue that one national system is specialized in one way or the other. We cannot define an optimal system of innovation because evolutionary learning processes are important in such systems and they are thus subject to continuous change. The system never reaches equilibrium.

In the real world, the state and the public sector are rooted in national states, and national borders define their geographical sphere of influence. The focus upon national systems reflects the fact that national economies differ regarding the structure of the production system and regarding the general institutional set-up. Specifically, we assume that basic differences in historical experience, language and culture will be reflected in national idiosyncrasies in the internal organization of firms, inter-firm relationships, the role of the public sector, the institutional set-up of the financial sector, and R&D organizations.

The concept of a national system of innovation was proposed virtually simultaneously by Lundvall (1988), Freeman (1988) and Nelson (1988), and examined in two volumes by Lundvall (1992) and Nelson (1993). These two approaches were different. Lundvall was influenced by theories of interactive learning and Nelson approached innovation systems from an evolutionary perspective. One of the central concerns the Nelson's 15-country study was to establish, 'Whether, and if so in what ways, the concept of a national system made any sense today'.

For Nelson there were two issues. First, unless one draws the analysis of innovation very narrowly, it is inevitable that analysis of innovation in a country gets drawn into discussions of labor markets, financial systems, monetary policy and trade policy. Second, the national level may be at the same time too broad since policies that support industry *j* might not support industry *k* and in some industries a number of the institutions may act internationally making the concept of national systems too narrow.

The concept of a national innovation system may be problematic. Lundvall recognizes that both globalization and regionalization weaken the nation-state. However, Lundvall (1992) suggested that we focus on the national level precisely because of the weakened position of the nation-state. We are therefore left with the question, 'What is the proper unit of analysis for innovation systems?' In other words, at what level should innovation systems be defined: nation, industrial sector, technology, a region or globally?

Of course, this depends in part on the size of the nation-state. For small states, the system might very well be larger than the nation. For large countries the nation-state might be too large. Nevertheless, there are many reasons for balkanization to proceed as globalization sets in. For example, the dysfunctionality of the nation-state has triggered the emergence of a genuinely shared community of economic interests at the regional level (Acs, de la Mothe and Paquet 1996).

Krugman (1995) has suggested that as economies become less constrained by national frontiers (as globalization spreads), they become more geographically specialized. Important elements of the process of innovation tend to become regional rather than national. The trends are more important in the science-based and high-technology industries. Some of the largest corporations are weakening their ties to their home country and are spreading their innovation activities to source different regional systems of innovation. Regional networks of firms are creating new forms of learning and production. These changes are important and challenge the traditional role of national systems of innovation. According to Porter (1998: 77), 'Paradoxically, the enduring competitive advantages in a global economy lie increasingly in local things – knowledge, relationships, and motivation that distant rivals cannot match'.

10.6 THE ELEMENTS OF THE SYSTEM

In this section we sketch out the institutional infrastructure that supports systems of innovation (Acs 2000). In the previous sections we sketched out three elements of the contemporary political economy that support regional innovation. They are inter-firm relations, the knowledge infrastructure and the public sector. In addition to the three above we also focus on four others: internal firm organization, the financial sector, physical and communication infrastructure, and firm strategy, structure and rivalry. Table 10.1 outlines the elements of national and regional systems of innovation.

In order to gain some insight into why some regions have a competitive advantage over others, at least in some industries, it is insightful to look at the dynamics of the types of innovation: process and product. Since the technology and market knowledge that underpins innovation is often tacit, learning by doing, interacting with customers and related industries is important. In the early stage of an innovation the rate of innovation is high, and product innovation is higher than process innovation. Until a dominant design emerges many ideas will be tried. In the transition stage, process innovation surpasses product innovation and there is heavy reliance on specialized equipment and less skilled labor. When the product reaches the mature stage process innovation still dominates product innovation. However, both are lower in the mature stage than in either the early stage of the product cycle or the transition stage.

In a world where product cycles are measured in decades, technologies and products become established and industries converge toward stable oligopolies. However, when product cycles are increasingly measured in months, not decades, most firms, technologies and industries will never settle down. Continuous innovation is the key and therefore it must be easy to start firms, access to knowledge must be inexpensive and entrepreneurship is crucial. According to Gary Hamel (1999: 71):

> Stewardship versus entrepreneurship: that's the fundamental distinction between the mediocre mass and the revolutionary wealth creators. Stewards polish grandma's silver – they buff up the assets and capabilities they inherited from entrepreneurs long retired or long dead. Devoid of passion and imagination, they spend their time trying to unlock wealth by hammering down costs. Outsourcing inefficient processes, buying back shares, selling off bad businesses, and spinning out good ones. But in the new economy, investors don't want stewards. They want enrepreneurial heroes – innovators who are obsessed with creating new wealth. Stewards conserve, entrepreneurs create.

The internal organization of firms must become like Silicon Valley: organic, innovative and non-hierarchical. To capture the Valley's entrepreneurial spirit, companies need to move from resource allocation to resource attraction. In the mass production economy resource allocation was carried out by organization. In the new economy of organization it needs to be market driven.

This brings us to the financial sector. In the mass production economy, there were formal financial institutions, the capital markets that allocated funds from the economy to the firm. However, most funds were internal and were allocated by managers. In the knowledge economy, venture capital plays a critical role in technological innovation and economic development. Venture

Table 10.1 *Systems of innovation*

Elements of the system	National systems of innovation Mass production economy Process innovation	Regional systems of innovation Knowledge economy Product innovation
Inter-firm relationships	• Market • Authoritarian relationships • Emphasis on competition • Arm's length supplier relationships	• Network economics • Clusters • Supplier chains as source of innovation • Co-operation and trust
The knowledge infrastructure	• Formal R&D laboratories • Focus on process R&D • Federal R&D laboratories • Focus on defence	• University research • Focus new product R&D • External sources of knowledge • Local R&D spillovers
Community and the public sector	• Emphasis on federal level • Paternalistic relationship • Regulation	• Emphasis on regional level • Public private partnerships • Community, co-operation and trust
Internal organization of the firm	• Mechanistic and authoritarian • Separation of innovation and production • Multi-divisional firm • Hierarchical	• Organic organization • Continuous innovation • Matrix organizations
Institutions of the financial sector	• Formal savings and investment • Formal financial sector	• Venture capital • Informal financial sector
Physical and communication infrastructure	• National orientation • Physical infrastructure	• Global orientation • Electronic data exchange
Firm strategy, structure and rivalry	• Difficult to start new firms • No access to new knowledge • Little or no entrepreneurship	• Easy to start new firms • Inexpensive access to knowledge • Entrepreneurship is crucial

183

capitalists invest in new, unproven enterprises, exchange their investment capital for an equity ownership stake in the companies they finance. The past ten years have witnessed an explosion in the number of venture capital investments. The total venture capital pool increased by over 800 percent between 1980 and 1995, from $4.5 billion to $37 billion, with most of the increase occurring between 1980 and 1987, when the venture capital pool surged from $4.5 billion to $29 billion. Then again in 1999–2000 the venture capital industry exploded investing $46 billion in 1999 and close to $60 billion in 2000 according to the National Venture Capital Association (NVCA). This represents a total pool of venture capital of over $150 billion. The informal venture capital, while more difficult to measure, is estimated to be between $60 and $100 billion (Acs and Prowse 2001).

A presumption, put forward very cautiously and tentatively by a few scholars a few years ago, suggested that the most effective way to analyse the innovation system and to intervene strategically in it is to tackle the problem at the 'national' level. Yet, much recent work has raised serious questions about this hypothesis. Too many forces at work in the world economy would appear to suggest that, as globalization proceeds, national disintegration occurs, and sub-national components gain more importance. Consequently, focusing on sub-national units of analysis would, in all likelihood, provide better insights into the workings of the 'real worlds of production' and better levers for policy interventions on the innovation front.

One might have expected that observers, researchers and policy-makers would have been led to focus more of their work and analyses on local innovation systems. However, this would be discounting unduly the power of the centralized mindset at work in so many sectors of politics, management and science. This mindset has maintained the dominion of the centralized machine-model of the socio-economy in place and has kept the decentralized garden-model at bay. The result is a rather misguided pursuit of 'national systems' where there are only 'regional/sectoral' systems.

The costs of such 'national' strategies are likely to be very high if, as we surmise, what is called for is a bottom-up policy. Consequently, it may not be unimportant to call for a return to the cautious and tentative language used by Richard Nelson and to the realization that the hypothesis of 'national systems of innovation' has not been validated yet.

10.7   ENTREPRENEURSHIP AND GLOBALIZATION

The widespread fear vis-à-vis the Soviet Union pervasive throughout the West at the end of the 1950s and early 1960s was not just that the Soviets might bury the West because they were the first into space with the launching of the

Sputnik, but that the superior organization of industry facilitated by centralized planning was generating greater rates of growth in the Soviet Union. After all, the nations of Eastern Europe, and the Soviet Union in particular, had a 'luxury' inherent in their systems of centralized planning – a concentration of economic assets on a scale beyond anything imaginable in the West, where the commitment to democracy seemingly imposed a concomitant commitment to economic decentralization.

10.7.1 The Old Economy

Although there may have been considerable debate about what to do about the perceived Soviet threat some three decades ago, there was little doubt at that time that firm size mattered. And even more striking, when one reviews the literature of the day, there seemed to be near unanimity about the way in which industrial organization mattered. It is no doubt an irony of history that a remarkably similar version of the giantism embedded in Soviet doctrine, fueled by the writings of Marx and ultimately implemented by the iron fist of Stalin, was also prevalent throughout the West. This was the era of mass production when economies of scale seemed to be the decisive factor in dictating efficiency. This was the world so colorfully described by John Kenneth Galbraith (1956) in his theory of countervailing power, in which the power of big business was held in check by big labor and by big government. This was the era of the man in the gray flannel suit and the organization man,[2] when virtually every major social and economic institution acted to reinforce the stability and predictability needed for mass production (Piore and Sabel 1984; and Chandler 1977).

It became the task of a generation of scholars spanning a broad spectrum of academic fields and disciplines to sort out the issues involving this perceived trade-off between economic efficiency on the one hand and political and economic decentralization on the other. Scholars responded by producing a massive literature focusing on essentially three issues: (1) What are the gains to size and large-scale production? (2) What are the economic welfare implications of having an oligopolistic market structure, i.e. is economic performance promoted or reduced in an industry with just a handful of large-scale firms? and (3) Given the overwhelming evidence that large-scale production resulting in economic concentration is associated with increased efficiency, what are the public policy implications?

Not only was the large corporation thought to have superior productive efficiency, but it was also believed to be the engine of technological change and innovative activity. Schumpeter wrote in 1942 (p. 106), 'What we have got to accept is that the large-scale enterprise has come to be the most powerful engine of progress'.

A fundamental characteristic of this literature was not only that it was obsessed with the oligopoly question but that it was essentially static in nature. There was considerable concern about what to do about the existing firms and industrial structure, but little attention was paid to where they came from and where they were going. Oliver Williamson's classic 1968 article 'Economies as an Antitrust Defense: The Welfare Tradeoffs', became something of a final statement demonstrating what appeared to be an inevitable trade-off between the gains in productive efficiency that could be obtained through increased concentration and gains in terms of competition, and implicitly democracy, that could be achieved through decentralizing policies. But it did not seem possible to have both, certainly not in Williamson's completely static model.

The fundamental issue confronting western societies at that time was how to live with this apparent trade-off between concentration and efficiency on the one hand, and decentralization and democracy on the other. The public policy question of the day was, *How can society reap the benefits of the large corporation in an oligopolistic setting while avoiding or at least minimizing the costs imposed by a concentration of economic power?* The policy response was to constrain the freedom of firms to contract. Such policy restraints typically took the form of public ownership, regulation and competition policy or antitrust. At the time, considerable attention was devoted to what seemed like glaring differences in policy approaches to this apparent trade-off by different countries. France and Sweden resorted to government ownership of private business. Other countries, such as the Netherlands and Germany, tended to emphasize regulation. Still other countries, such as the Untied States, had a greater emphasis on antitrust. In fact, most countries relied upon elements of all three policy instruments. While the particular instrument may have varied across countries, they were, in fact, manifestations of a singular policy approach – how to restrict and restrain the power of the large corporation. What may have been perceived as a disparate set of policies at the time appears in retrospect to comprise a remarkably singular policy approach – a managed economy (Audretsch and Thurik, 1999).

Thus, in the traditional, managed economies of the post-war era, small firms and entrepreneurship were viewed as a luxury, perhaps needed by the West to ensure a decentralization of decision-making, but in any case obtained only at a cost to efficiency.

10.7.2　The New Economy

When the Berlin Wall fell in 1989 many people expected even greater levels of economic well-being resulting from the dramatic reduction of the economic burden in the West that had been imposed by four decades of Cold War. Thus, the substantial unemployment and general economic stagnation during the subsequent eight years has come as a shock. Unemployment and stagnant growth are the twin economic problems confronting Europe and much of the OECD. The traditional comparative advantage in mature, technologically moderate industries such as metalworking, machine tools and automobile production had provided an engine for growth, high employment and economic stability throughout Western Europe for most of the post-war economic period. This traditional comparative advantage has been lost in the high-cost countries of Europe and North America in the last decade for two reasons. The first has to do with globalization, or the advent of competition from not just the emerging economies in Southeast Asia but also from the transforming economies of Central and Eastern Europe. The second factor has been the computer and telecommunications revolution. The new communications technologies have triggered a virtual spatial revolution in terms of the geography of production

Globalization has triggered a virtual spatial revolution in terms of the geography of production. The (marginal) cost of transforming information across geographic space has been rendered to virtually nothing. Confronted with lower-cost competition in foreign locations, producers in the high-cost countries have three options apart from doing nothing and losing global market share: (1) reduce wages and other production costs sufficiently to compete with the low-cost foreign producers, (2) substitute equipment and technology for labor to increase productivity and (3) shift production out of the high-cost location and into the low-cost location.

Many of the European and American firms that have successfully restructured resorted to the last two alternatives. Substituting capital and technology for labor, along with shifting production to lower-cost locations has resulted in waves of *corporate downsizing* throughout Europe and North America (Baily et al. 1996). At the same time, it has generally preserved the viability of many of the large corporations. As record levels of both European and American stock indexes indicate, the companies have not generally suffered. For example, between 1979 and 1995 more than 43 million jobs were lost in the United States as a result of corporate downsizing. This includes 24.8 million blue-collar jobs and 18.7 million white-collar jobs. Similarly, the 500 largest US manufacturing corporations cut 4.7 million jobs between 1980 and 1993, or one-quarter of their work force. Perhaps most disconcerting, the rate of corporate downsizing has apparently increased over time in the United States, even as the unemployment rate has fallen. During most of the 1980s, about one in 25 workers lost a job. In the 1990s this has risen to one in 20 workers.

Globalization has rendered the comparative advantage in traditional moderate technology industries incompatible with high wage levels. At the same time, the emerging comparative advantage that is compatible with high wage levels is based on innovative activity. For example, employment has increased by 15 percent in Silicon Valley between 1992 and 1996, even though the mean income is 50 percent greater than in the rest of the country.

The global demand for innovative products in knowledge-based industries is high and growing rapidly; yet the number of workers who can contribute to producing and commercializing new knowledge is limited to just a few areas in the world. Economic activity based on new knowledge generates higher wages and greater employment opportunities reflecting the exploding demand for new and improved products and services. There are many indicators reflecting the shift in the comparative advantage of the high-wage countries toward an increased importance of innovative activity.

There are two fundamental characteristics of knowledge that differ from the traditional factors of production in the traditional economy. The first is that knowledge has increased the importance of geographic proximity. The second is that the greater degree of uncertainty, asymmetries and transactions cost lead to an increase in entrepreneurial activity. Systematic empirical evidence points to a marked shift across OECD countries toward a greater role played by small entrepreneurial firms (Acs and Audretsch 1993a; Loveman and Sengenberger 1991; Davis and Henrekson 1999; Henrekson and Johansson 1999).

As illustrated by the title page of *The Economist* proclaiming 'The Death of Distance'[3] the claim that geographic location is important to the process linking knowledge spillovers to innovative activity in a world of email, fax machines and cyberspace may seem surprising and even paradoxical. The resolution to the paradox posed by the localization of knowledge spillovers in an era where the telecommunications revolution has drastically reduced the cost of communication lies in a distinction between knowledge and information. *Information*, such as the price of gold on the New York Stock Exchange, or the value of the yen in London, can be easily codified and has a singular meaning and interpretation. By contrast, *knowledge* is vague, difficult to codify and often only serendipitously recognized. While the marginal cost of transmitting information across geographic space has been rendered invariant by the telecommunications revolution, the marginal cost of transmitting knowledge, and especially tacit knowledge, rises with distance. Geographic proximity matters in transmitting knowledge, because as Kenneth Arrow (1962) pointed out some four decades ago, such tacit knowledge is inherently non-rival in nature, and knowledge developed for any particular application can easily 'spill over' and have economic value in very different applications.

The empirical evidence consistently supports the notion that knowledge spills over for third-party use from university research laboratories as well as industry R&D laboratories. This empirical evidence suggests that location and proximity clearly matter in exploiting knowledge spillovers. Acs, Audretsch and Feldman (1992 and 1994), Anselin, Acs and Varga (2000a, 2000b),

Feldman and Audretsch (1999) and Audretsch and Feldman (1996) found that the propensity of innovative activity to cluster geographically tends to be greater in industries where new economic knowledge plays a more important role. This finding is supported by Audretsch and Stephan (1996) who examine the geographic relationships of scientists working with biotechnology firms. The importance of geographic proximity is clearly shaped by the role played by the scientist. The scientist is more likely to be located in the same region as the firm when the relationship involves the transfer of new economic knowledge. However, when the scientist is providing a service to the company that does not involve knowledge transfer, local proximity becomes much less important.

Globalization is shifting the comparative advantage in the OECD countries away from being based on traditional inputs of production, such as land, labor and capital, toward knowledge. As the comparative advantage has become increasingly based on new knowledge, public policy has responded in two fundamental ways. The first has been to shift the policy focus away from the traditional triad of policy instruments essentially constraining the freedom of firms to contract – regulation, competition policy or antitrust in the United States, and public ownership of business. The policy approach of constraint was sensible as long as the major issue was how to restrain large corporations in possession of considerable market power. That this policy is less relevant in a global economy is reflected by the waves of deregulation and privatization throughout the OECD. Instead, a new policy approach is emerging which focuses on enabling the creation and commercialization of knowledge. Examples of such policies include encouraging R&D, venture capital and new-firm start-ups (Armington and Acs 2002).

10.7.3 Public Policy

Probably the greatest and most salient shift in SME (small- and medium-sized enterprises) policy over the last fifteen years has been a shift from trying to preserve SMEs that are confronted with a cost disadvantage due to size-inherent scale disadvantages, toward promoting the start-up and viability of small entrepreneurial firms involved in the commercialization of knowledge, or knowledge-based SMEs.

For example, the United States Congress enacted the Small Business Innovation Research (SBIR) program in the early 1980s as a response to the loss of American competitiveness in global markets. Congress mandated each federal agency with allocating around 4 percent of its annual budget to funding innovative small firms as a mechanism for restoring American international competitiveness. The SBIR provides a mandate to the major R&D agencies in the United States to allocate a share of the research budget to innovative small firms. Last year the SBIR program amounted to around $1.2 billion. The SBIR represents about 60 percent of all public SME finance programs. Taken together, the public SME finance is about two-thirds as large as private venture capital. In 1995, the sum of equity financing provided through and guaranteed by public programs financing SMEs was $2.4 billion, which amounted to more than 60 percent of the total funding disbursed by traditional venture funds in that year. Equally as important, the emphasis on SBIR and most public funds is on early stage finance, which is generally ignored by private venture capital. Some of the most innovative American companies received early stage finance from SBIR, including Apple Computer, Chiron, Compaq and Intel (Acs 1999).

The second fundamental shift involves the locus of such enabling policies, which are increasingly at the state, regional or even local level. The downsizing of federal agencies charged with the regulation of business in many of the OECD countries has been interpreted by many scholars as the eclipse of government intervention. But to interpret deregulation, privatization and the increased irrelevance of competition policies as the end of government intervention in business ignores an important shift in the locus and target of public policy. The last decade has seen the emergence of a broad spectrum of enabling policy initiatives that fall outside of the jurisdiction of the traditional regulatory agencies. The success of a number of different high-technology clusters spanning a number of developed countries is the direct result of enabling policies, such as the provision of venture capital or research support. For example, the Advanced Research Program in Texas has provided support for basic research and the strengthening of the infrastructure of the University of Texas, which has played a central role in developing a high-technology cluster around Austin. The Thomas Edison Centers in Ohio, the Advanced Technology Centers in New Jersey, and the Centers for Advanced Technology at Case Western Reserve University, Rutgers University and the University of Rochester have supported generic, pre-competitive research. This support has generally provided diversified technology development involving a mix of activities encompassing a broad spectrum of industrial collaborators (Acs, de Groot and Nijkamp 2002).

One of the most interesting examples of entrepreneurial policy involves the establishment of five EXIST regions in Germany, where start-ups from universities and government research laboratories are encouraged (BMBF 2000). The program has the explicit goals of (1) creating an entrepreneurial culture, (2) the commercialization of scientific knowledge and (3) increasing the number of innovative start-ups and SMEs. Five regions were selected among many applicants for START funding. These are (1) the Rhein-Ruhr region (bizeps program), (2) Dresden (Dresden exists), (3) Thueringen (GET UP), (4) Karlsruhe (KEIM), and (5) Stuttgart (PUSH!).

Such enabling policies that are typically implemented at the local or regional level are part of a silent policy revolution currently under-way. The increased importance of innovative regional clusters as an engine of economic growth has led policy-makers to abandon the policy cry frequently heard two decades ago, 'Should we break up, regulate, or simply take over General Motors, IBM and US Steel' for a very different contemporary version, 'How can we grow the next Silicon Valley?'

NOTES

1. For a review of the multinational corporation in the 1980s see Kindleberger and Audretsch (1983).
2. For a description of these, see Whye (1960) and Riesman (1950).
3. 'The Death of Distance', *The Economist*, 30 September 1995.

11. Epilogue: towards a 'new model of regional economic development'?

In a recent paper Acs and Varga (2002) examined the relationship between geography, endogenous growth and innovation to probe the question, 'Why do some regions grow faster than others?' We surveyed three separate and distinct literatures that have a long and distinguished history, and all three have recently been re-examined. They are: the new economic geography (Krugman 1991), the new growth theory (Romer 1990), and the new economics of innovation (Nelson 1993). These three literatures examine the unit of analysis, how to model endogenous growth and the interactions between the actors and institutions in the innovation process. What we looked for from this new and evolving literature were insights that would help us develop a clear analytical framework which integrates economic growth, spatial interdependencies and the creation of new technology as an explicit production process to formulate production-oriented regional policies (Nijkamp and Poot 1997). Each one of the above approaches has its strengths and weaknesses that can be integrated to develop a model of technology-led regional economic development.

As emphasized in Acs and Varga (2002) a 'spatialized' theory of technology-led regional economic growth needs to reflect three fundamental issues. First, it should provide an explanation of why knowledge-related economic activities start concentrating in certain regions leaving others relatively underdeveloped, second, it needs to answer the questions of how technological advances occur and what are the key processes and institutions involved and third, it has to present an analytical framework where the role of technological change in regional economic growth is clearly explained. In order to answer these three questions we surveyed three separate and distinct literatures: the new economic geography, the new growth theory and the new economics of innovation. We suggest that each one of the above three approaches has its strengths and weaknesses that can be integrated to develop an appropriate model of technology-led regional economic development.

The *new economic geography* answers the question why economic activity concentrates in certain regions but not others, but leaves out innovation and economic growth. The contribution of Krugman's theory on economic concentration is not in its elements but in the way the system was put together. It has already been well known in economic geography and regional economics that decreasing transportation costs, economies of scale or increasing demand favor agglomeration. However, the way Krugman put these elements together in a general equilibrium model is novel. The model provides a case for the treatment of spatial issues in the way economists are accustomed to. The model provides a technique to analyze geographical concentration of economic activities as being induced by some initial combinations of basic parameters. However, the model in its current form does not seem to be suitable for modeling technology-led regional economic growth for at least two reasons. First, Krugman's definite insistence on avoiding modeling the role of technological externalities in regional economic growth prevents the model from being applicable in innovation-led regional development since spillovers in innovation networks are in the core of this type of development as exemplified in the literature of innovation systems. Second, while the model is very strong in working out the characterization of specific initial combinations of parameters favoring geographical concentration, it is weak in actually modeling the growth process.

The *new growth theory* explains the causes of economic growth, but leaves out regional considerations and ignores the key processes and institutions involved in innovation. A principal assumption in the theory of endogenous growth is that in creating new sets of technological knowledge the total stock of knowledge is freely accessible for anyone engaged in research. However, this assumption is not verified in the growing literature of geographic knowledge spillovers. New knowledge (potentially leading to either product or process innovations) is usually in such a tacit form that its accessibility is bounded by geographic proximity and/or by the nature and extent of the interactions among actors of an innovation system (see e.g. Anselin, Varga and Acs, 1997). Similar to the case of relaxing the neoclassical assumption of equal availability of technological opportunities in all countries of the world, a relaxation of the assumption that knowledge is evenly distributed across space within countries seems also to be necessary. The non-excludable part of the total stock of knowledge seems rather to be correctly classified if it is assumed to have two portions: a perfectly accessible part consisting of already established knowledge elements (obtainable via scientific publications, patent applications etc.) and a novel, tacit element, accessible by interactions among actors in the innovation system. While the first part is available without restrictions, accessibility of the second one is bounded by the nature of interactions among actors in a 'system of innovation'.

The *new economics of innovation* while explaining the institutional arrangements in the innovation process leaves out regional issues and economic growth. The systems approach is a conceptual framework that many scholars and policy-makers consider useful for the analysis of innovation.

Although the systems of innovation approach is not considered a formal and established theory, its development has been influenced by different theories of innovation such as interactive learning theories and evolutionary theories. In recent years, efforts have been made to percolate general theoretical and empirical observations from this literature up into a conceptual framework capable of guiding policy and loosely organized around the idea of a 'national system of innovation'. The concept of a 'national' innovation system may be problematic. Krugman has suggested that as economies become less constrained by national frontiers (as globalization spreads), they become more geographically specialized. Important elements of the process of innovation tend to become regional rather than national. Some of the largest corporations are weakening their ties to their home country and are spreading their innovation activities to source different regional systems of innovation. Regional networks of firms are creating new forms of learning and production. These changes are important and challenge the traditional role of 'national systems of innovation'.

Perhaps the most important missing element in the institutional arrangements is the role of entrepreneurship in the innovation process (Acs 2000). None of these literatures answers the question, '*How is the stock of knowledge (A) in society discovered and exploited?*' Entrepreneurial discovery and the competitive market process approach, which has emerged in modern Austrian economics during the past quarter of a century, was developed out of elements derived from Mises and from Hayek. From Mises, the modern Austrians learned to see the market as an entrepreneurially driven process. From Hayek they learned to appreciate the role of knowledge and its enhancement through market interaction for the equilibrative process.

We suggest that a specific combination of the Krugmanian theory of initial conditions for spatial concentration of economic activities with the Romerian theory of endogenous economic growth complemented with a systematic representation of interactions among the actors of Nelson's innovation system could be a way of developing an appropriate model of technology-led regional economic development. It is not the purpose of the current chapter to present an explicit solution for this problem. However, a brief outline of a possible synthesis may be provided here. The central element of the model could be the 'regional knowledge production equation' distilled from the predominantly empirical literature of innovation networks as presented in the literature of the new economics of innovation. This equation would facilitate the presence of knowledge in the Krugmanian economic geography model. Here the analytical technique for deriving initial conditions of spatial concentration could be adapted to come up with the preconditions for the emergence of knowledge-induced agglomerations. Together with other parameters of the model, threshold values of knowledge may be calculated following the technique developed by Krugman. Finally, to actually model the equilibrium path of regional economic growth induced by the threshold values of knowledge and other regional parameters, the combined framework of the new economic geography and the new economics of innovation could be complemented with the Romerian analytics of economic growth.

Appendix A: The innovation database

The original innovation database consists of 8 074 innovations introduced into the United States in 1982. Of these innovations, 4 476 were identified as occurring in manufacturing industries. These data are classified according to four-digit SIC industry, the firm, and the location of the innovation.

A private firm, The Futures Group, constructed the database and performed quality-control analyses for the U.S. Small Business Administration by examining over 100 technology, engineering, and trade journals, covering each manufacturing industry. From the sections in each trade journal listing innovations and new products, a database consisting of the innovations by four-digit SIC industry was formed. The entire list of trade journals used to compile these data is available from the authors. The Small Business Administration defines an innovation as 'a process that begins with an invention, proceeds with the development of the invention, and results in introduction of a new product, process or service to the marketplace' (Edwards and Gordon 1984: 1).

Because the innovations recorded in 1982 were the result of inventions made, on average, 4.3 years earlier, in some sense the innovation database represents the inventions made around 1978 that were subsequently introduced to the market in 1982. The data were also checked for duplication. In fact, 8 800 innovations were actually recorded, but it was subsequently found that 726 of them appeared either in separate issues of the same journal or else in different journals. Thus, double-counting was avoided.

The innovation data were classified according to the industry of origin based on the SIC code of the innovating enterprise. The Futures Group assigned the innovation to an industry based on the information given in the trade journal. When no such information was given and the relevant industry could not be determined from other sources, no industry was assigned to the innovation. The data were then classified into innovations by large firms, defined as firms with at least 500 employees, and innovations by small firms, defined as firms with fewer than 500 employees. For example, an innovation made by a subsidiary of a diversified firm would be classified by industry according to the SIC industry of the innovating subsidiary (establishment) and not by the SIC industry of the parent firm (enterprise). However, the innovation would be classified by size according to the size of the entire firm and not just by the size of the subsidiary. Because 67 innovations could not be classified according to firm size, the number of total innovations does not always equal the sum of large- and small-firm innovations.

There are several other qualifications that should be made concerning the innovation data. The trade journals report relatively few process, service and management innovations and tend to capture mainly product innovations. The most likely effect of this bias is to underestimate the number of innovations emanating from large firms, since larger enterprises tend to produce more process innovations than do their smaller counterparts. However, because it was found that the largefirm innovations are more likely to be reported in trade journals than are small-firm innovations, the biases are perhaps at least somewhat offsetting.

One potential concern might be that the significance and 'quality' of the innovations vary considerably between large and small firms. Based on 4 938 of the innovations, each innovation was classified by Edwards and Gordon (1984) according to one of the following levels of significance: (1) the innovation established an entirely new category of product, (2) the innovation is the first of its type on the market in a product category already in existence, (3) the innovation represents a significant improvement in existing technology and (4) the innovation is a modest improvement designed to update an existing product.

The distribution of innovative significance according to firm size is shown in Table A.1. While none of the innovations in the sample was in the highest level of significance, 80 were in the second level, 576 in the third level and 4 282 were classified in the fourth level. Within each level of significance, the

Table A.1   Distribution of large- and small-firm innovations according to significance levels (percentages in parentheses)

Innovation significance	Description	Number of innovations			
		Large firms		Small firms	
1	Establishes entirely new category	0	(0.00)	0	(0.00)
2	First of its type on the market in existing categories	50	(1.76)	30	(1.43)
3	A significant improvement in existing technology	360	(12.70)	216	(10.27)
4	Modest improvement designed to update existing products	2 424	(85.53)	1 858	(88.31)
Total		2 834	(99.99)	2 104	(100.00)

distribution between large- and small-firm innovations proved to be remarkably constant. In both the second and third significance categories, the large firms accounted for 62.5 percent of the innovations and the small firms for the remaining 37.5 percent. In the fourth significance category, the large firms accounted for a slightly smaller share of the innovations, 56.6 percent, while the small firms contributed the remaining 43.4 percent. A chi-square test for the hypothesis that there is no difference in the frequency of innovation with respect to innovation significance and firm size cannot be rejected at the 99 percent level of confidence. Thus, based on the classification of the significance level of innovations, there does not appear to be a great difference in the 'quality' and significance of the innovations between large and small firms.

To provide a test for any biases that might arise in the assignment of the innovation significance classification, The Futures Group undertook telephone interviews based on a subset of 600 innovating companies that were randomly selected. Of these selected companies, 529 were reached and 375 telephone interviews were actually carried out. Of those selected companies not participating in the telephone interview, the most frequent reason for not participating was the inability of The Futures Group to contact the innovating firm or targeted person responsible for the innovation. The respondents of the interviews tended to rate their innovation as being more important than the rating assigned by The Futures Group. For example, while The Futures Group did not assign any innovations to the most significant category, 25 of the interviewed firms considered their innovation to be worthy of the highest significance rating. Confronted with this disparity in ratings, Edwards and Gordon (1984: 66) conclude,

> The liberalism on the part of the respondents, especially in the assignation of 1's, may be attributed to product loyalty on the part of some respondents and, perhaps, unfamiliarity with other products on the market on the part of some of the non-technical respondents. Alternately, The Futures Group may really have underrated the innovations.

The telephone interviews also enabled the length of time between the invention and innovation to be determined, so that it could be tested whether this time interval varies systematically with firm size. Not only was the mean number of years to innovation 4.3 for both large and small firms, but a chi-square test leads to the conclusion that the time interval between invention and innovation is independent of firm size (Edwards and Gordon 1984).

Table A.2 lists the total number of innovations in those industries that had the greatest number of innovations in 1982, along with the corresponding number of large- and small-firm innovations. In some industries, the large firms exhibit considerably more innovative activity than do their smaller counterparts, while in other industries the small firms are apparently more innovative.

Table A.2   Number of innovations for large and small firms in the most innovative industries, 1982

Industry	Total innovations	Large-firm innovations	Small-firm innovations
Electronic computing equipment	395	158	227
Process control instruments	165	68	93
Radio and TV communication equipment	157	83	72
Pharmaceutical preparations	133	120	13
Electronic components	128	54	73
Engineering and scientific instruments	126	43	83
Semiconductors	122	91	29
Plastics products	107	22	82
Photographic equipment	88	79	9
Office machinery	77	67	10
Instruments to measure electricity	77	28	47
Surgical appliances and supplies	67	54	13
Surgical and medical instruments	66	30	36
Special industry machinery	64	43	21
Industrial controls	61	15	46
Toilet preparations	59	41	18
Valves and pipe fittings	54	20	33
Electric housewares and fans	53	47	6
Measuring and controlling devices	52	3	45
Food products machinery	50	37	12
Motors and generators	49	39	10
Plastic materials and resins	45	30	15
Industrial inorganic chemicals	40	32	8
Radio and TV receiving sets	40	35	4
Hand and edge tools	39	27	11
Fabricated platework	38	29	9
Fabricated structure metal	35	12	17
Pumps and pumping equipment	34	18	16
Optical instruments and lenses	34	12	21
Polishes and sanitation goods	33	13	19
Industrial trucks and tractors	33	13	20
Medicinals and botanicals	32	27	5
Aircraft	32	31	1
Environmental controls	32	22	10

*Table A.3   Innovation, R&D lab employment and university research
expenditures for US SMSAs*

SMSA	Text	Innovation	R&D employment	University research ($ thousands)
7400	San Jose SMSA	374	9 727	127 897
1123	Boston NECMA	282	22 391	325 474
5600	New York NY–NJ SMSA	222	11 136	285 776
1600	Chicago	164	15 416	145 814
4480	Los Angeles–Long Beach SMSA	161	20 226	199 028
5640	Essex County	143	26 780	17 500
6160	Philadelphia PA–NJ SMSA	139	16 967	134 499
5380	Nassau–Suffolk SMSA	120	2 534	31 881
360	Anaheim–Santa Ana–Garden Grove SMSA	108	2 904	31 037
5120	Minneapolis–St. Paul	80	7 181	103 235
1920	Dallas–Fort Worth	77	1 900	46 974
7360	San Francisco–Oakland SMSA	75	7 856	154 824
1163	Bridgeport NECMA	67	3 221	14
7320	San Diego SMSA	59	4 823	79 857
1680	Cleveland SMSA	54	5 195	42 792
2160	Detroit SMSA	51	11 599	21 511
6280	Pittsburgh	39	4 357	68 160
5080	Milwaukee SMSA	34	2 130	18 832
7600	Seattle–Everett SMSA	34	798	85 514
6840	Rochester SMSA	32	4 554	60 999
5460	New Brunswick–Perth Amboy–Sayreville SMSA	30	2 338	20 408
8480	Trenton SMSA	29	2 836	24 680
6200	Phoenix SMSA	29	3 809	8 037
3360	Houston SMSA	29	2 545	120 942
3283	Hartford NECMA	27	2 087	52 297
2080	Denver–Boulder	26	3 386	65 379
520	Atlanta	26	661	71 321
6040	Paterson–Clifton–Passaic SMSA	25	3 098	226
1280	Buffalo SMSA	24	4 404	25 591

The innovation database also exists at the state, SMSA and county level.
Table A.3 lists the number of innovations, R&D lab employment and university research expenditures by SMSA. San Jose had the most innovations with
374, followed by Boston and New York City. However, San Jose did not have
the most R&D employees or the largest university R&D budget. The complete
list of SMSAs with innovations is in Appendix B.

The innovation database also exists at the firm level. These data were first
introduced in Acs and Audretsch (1991). The firm-level database was

constructed along the lines of a study by Soete (1979), using the R&D and firm-size measures from the *Business Week* sample of over 700 corporations for which R&D expenditures play an important role. An important feature of this sample is that it includes more than 95 percent of the total company R&D expenditures undertaken in the United States. Table A.4 compares the frequency of innovation for the 30 most innovative firms to firm size, measured by sales (in millions of dollars), company expenditures on R&D (in

Table A.4   Most innovative firms, sales and R&D expenditure

Firm	Number of innovations	Sales ($ millions)	R&D expenditure ($ millions)	R&D/ sales (%)
Hewlett-Packard	55	981.0	89.6	9.1
Minnesota Mining & Mfg	40	3 127.0	143.4	4.6
General Electric	36	13 399.0	357.1	2.7
General Signal	29	548.0	21.2	3.9
National Semiconductor	27	235.0	20.7	8.8
Xerox	25	4 054.0	198.6	4.9
Texas Instruments	24	1 368.0	51.0	4.7
Pitney Bowes	22	461.0	10.5	2.3
RCA	21	4 790.0	113.6	2.4
IBM	21	14 437.0	946.0	6.6
Digital Equipment	21	534.0	48.5	9.1
Gould	20	773.0	23.1	3.0
Motorola	19	1 312.0	98.5	7.5
Wheelabrator Frye	18	332.0	2.0	0.6
United Technologies	18	3 878.0	323.7	8.3
Hoover	18	594.0	4.3	0.7
Honeywell	18	2 760.0	164.2	5.9
Rockwell International	17	4 943.0	31.0	0.6
Johnson & Johnson	17	2 225.0	97.9	4.4
Eastman Kodak	17	4 959.0	312.9	6.3
Data General	17	108.0	11.6	10.8
Exxon	16	44 865.0	187.0	0.4
Du Pont	16	7 222.0	335.7	4.6
Stanley Works	15	464.0	3.5	0.7
Sperry Rand	15	3 041.0	163.5	5.4
Pennwalt	15	714.0	15.7	2.2
North American Philips	14	1 410.0	22.5	1.6
Harris	14	479.0	21.1	4.4
General Motors	14	35 725.0	1 113.9	3.1
Becton, Dickinson	14	456.0	17.8	3.9

millions of dollars) and the R&D/sales ratio. Three important observations can be made from this table. First, the distribution of' frequency of innovation is apparently skewed, with a few firms making numerous innovations, and most firms contributing just several innovations. In fact, of the 732 firms included in our sample, 306 contributed at least one innovation, while the remaining 426 did not produce a single innovation. Second, there is a concentration of the most innovative firms in several sectors of manufacturing – electrical equipment and electronics, instruments, computers and office equipment, and non-electrical machinery. Finally, there is obviously no precise correspondence between R&D expenditures and innovative activity, or between the firm R&D/sales ratio and the frequency of innovation. Nor is there a clear tendency for the number of innovations to increase along with firm size.

Although the *Business Week* sample excludes the smallest enterprises, firms which can be considered to be relatively small are included in the data. A number of firms have fewer than 500 employees, which is the standard used by the US Small Business Administration to distinguish small from large firms. More than one-quarter of the sample is composed of firms with less than $100 million of sales. Thus, an advantage of using the *Business Week* sample over, say, the Fortune 500, is that we are able to include a much greater spectrum of firm sizes.

There is, however, an inherent bias that may affect the results when these *Business Week* R&D data are used. In compiling the survey, a materiality criterion is imposed, such that companies only need to report if their R&D is 'material', which means greater than 1 percent of sales. This results in only high R&D/sales companies reporting, which may tend to be larger firms. The effect of this censoring would then be to exclude low R&D performers among small firms from the sample, while including the high R&D performers, resulting in a twisting of the fitted regression line to the right and a tendency to indicate increasing returns where none exist. However, to the extent that this censoring is consistent across all firm sizes and R&D levels, the results will not be biased.

Appendix B: Innovations, R&D lab employment and university research by state

State	Innovations	R&D	University research
Alabama	4	1 868	45 293
Arizona	38	4 086	62 206
Arkansas	4	187	12 303
California	851	48 552	658 487
Colorado	40	4 244	87 230
Connecticut	117	8 799	136 435
Delaware	11	6 173	6 962
Florida	49	2 298	105 177
Georgia	29	1 585	102 981
Illinois	185	20 574	207 669
Indiana	38	6 970	92 986
Iowa	13	1 939	77 435
Kansas	11	2 029	21 849
Kentucky	8	571	21 224
Louisiana	4	701	48 509
Maine	3	430	5 527
Maryland	26	5 244	131 229
Massachusetts	316	24 753	364 871
Michigan	84	21 816	149 432
Minnesota	82	7 478	103 549
Mississippi	4	142	18 220
Missouri	23	4 863	100 942
Nebraska	4	275	21 893
Nevada	1	103	3 966
New Hampshire	28	624	19 368
New Jersey	352	42 907	67 887
New Mexico	3	339	57 745
New York	347	27 709	585 312
North Carolina	23	5037	111 994

State	Innovations	R&D	University research
Ohio	139	18 886	161 911
Oklahoma	14	2 630	39 175
Oregon	29	310	44 788
Pennsylvania	197	22 702	267 614
Rhode Island	22	1 083	22 035
South Carolina	11	1 131	27 019
Tennessee	16	1 397	55 692
Texas	136	9 896	296 114
Utah	13	1 926	62 249
Vermont	3	67	14 166
Virginia	27	8 023	72 208
Washington	41	1 385	95 530
West Virginia	2	1 471	13 589
Wisconsin	69	4 504	127 440

Sources: Compiled from US SBA Innovations Data Base; compiled from R.R. Bowker Company Directories; compiled from NSF Survey of Scientific and Engineering Expenditures at Universities and Colleges.

Appendix C: Innovations, R&D lab employment and university research by MSA

MSA	Innovations	R&D	University research
Akron	7	2 989	4 504
Albany–Schenectady–Troy	1	2 475	33 600
Albuquerque	2	273	26 064
Allentown–Bethlehem–Easton, PA–NJ	7	946	9 455
Anaheim–Santa Ana–Garden Grove	108	2 904	31 037
Ann Arbor	7	1 428	84 876
Atlanta	26	661	71 321
Austin	12	1 003	45 079
Baltimore	12	2 499	88 697
Bellingham	1	78	255
Benton Harbor	1	388	19
Binghamton, NY–PA	2	152	2 988
Birmingham	1	646	35 162
Bloomington–Normal	2	16	356
Boston	282	22 391	325 474
Bridgeport	67	3 221	14
Bryan–College Station	2	37	40 178
Buffalo	24	4 404	25 591
Burlington	3	41	13 952
Charlotte–Gastonia	6	191	627
Chicago	164	15 416	145 814
Cincinnati Ohio, KY–IN	13	1 247	26 709
Cleveland	54	5 195	42 792
Colorado Springs	6	726	52
Columbia	1	135	23 448
Columbus	20	2 733	52 252
Dallas–Fort Worth	77	1 900	46 974
Davenport–Rock Island–Moline, IA–IL	5	4 535	3

MSA	Innovations	R&D	University research
Dayton	11	2 538	22 608
Daytona Beach	1	97	31
Denver–Boulder	26	3 386	65 379
Detroit	51	11 599	21 511
El Paso	7	1 160	834
Fort Collins	6	83	21 717
Fort Lauderdale–Hollywood	9	285	99
Fresno	1	48	276
Gainesville	1	158	45 324
Galveston, TX	2	99	11 882
Grand Rapids	4	359	21
Greensboro–Winston–Salem–High Point	5	1 010	9 159
Greenville–Spartanburg	10	506	9 085
Hamilton–Middletown	4	39	709
Hartford	27	2 087	52 297
Houston	29	2 545	120 942
Huntsville	3	847	1 843
Janesville–Beloit	2	207	49
Jersey City	11	709	4 352
Johnson City–Kingsport–Bristol, TN–VA	2	737	736
Kalamazoo–Portage	5	950	146
Kansas City	12	1 325	956
Knoxville	1	356	32 526
Lafayette–West Lafayette	1	121	45 048
Lancaster	4	671	69
Lansing–East	4	140	35 951
Lincoln	2	127	13 236
Lorain–Elyria	2	204	75
Los Angeles–Long Beach	161	20 226	199 028
Louisville	7	414	4992
Madison	4	741	107 915
Melbourne–Titusville–Cocoa	11	81	779
Memphis, TN–AK–MS	3	122	799
Miami	4	177	32 677
Milwaukee	34	2 130	18 832
Minneapolis–St Paul	80	7 181	103 235
Nashville–Davidson	5	113	20 604
Nassau–Suffolk	120	2 534	31 881

MSA	Innovations	R&D	University research
New Bedford	6	95	569
New Brunswick–Perth Amboy–Sayreville	30	2 338	20 408
New Haven–West Haven	19	1 708	83 974
New London–Norwich	1	1 659	156
New Orleans	1	320	14 394
New York, NY–NJ	222	11 136	285 776
Essex County	143	26 780	17 500
Newburgh–Middletown	3	324	206
Newport News–Hampton	2	310	1 676
Norfolk–Virginia Beach–Portsmouth	1	136	2 819
Northeast	2	25	70
Oklahoma City	1	204	19 703
Orlando	5	514	4 704
Paterson–Clifton–Passaic	25	3 098	226
Peoria	1	27	146
Philadelphia, PA–NJ	139	16 967	134 499
Phoenix	29	3 809	8 037
Pittsburgh	39	4 357	68 160
Pittsfield	2	14	354
Portland	1	286	463
Portland, OR–WA	22	285	20 750
Portsmouth–Dover–Rochester	5	166	5 468
Providence–Warwick–Pawtucket	15	480	22 036
Provo–Orem	3	281	3 419
Raleigh–Durham	8	2 317	10 1136
Reading	1	423	123
Reno	1	26	3 226
Riverside–San Bernardino–Ontario	13	193	9 494
Rochester	32	4 554	60 999
Sacramento	7	311	32 634
St Louis	13	3 312	69 825
Salem	1	44	20
Salt Lake City	10	1 585	40 785
San Antonio	3	1 674	19 539
San Diego	59	4 823	79 857
San Francisco–Oakland	75	7 856	154 824
San Jose	374	9 727	127 897
Santa Barbara–Santa Maria–Lompoc	9	1 945	10 269

Innovation and the growth of cities

MSA	Innovations	R&D	University research
Santa Cruz	2	30	7 168
Seattle–Everett	34	798	85 514
South Bend	5	166	11 192
Spokane	3	11	230
Springfield	3	131	19
Springfield–Chicopee–Holyoke	3	449	29 455
Stockton	2	10	648
Syracuse	9	1 020	31 844
Tacoma	2	269	76
Tampa–St. Petersburg	12	668	4 790
Toledo, OH–MI	6	1 129	6 705
Trenton	29	2 836	24 680
Tucson	9	209	53 599
Tulsa	12	89	1 317
Waco	3	37	363
Washington DC	21	8 274	38 311
Waterloo–Cedar Falls	1	14	5
Wichita	5	1 490	909
Wilmington, DE–NJ–MD	11	6 706	6 962
Worcester	17	861	4 628
Youngstown–Warren	1	167	75

Sources: Compiled from US SBA Innovations Data Base; compiled from R.R. Bowker Company Directories; compiled from NSF Survey of Scientific and Engineering Expenditures at Universities and Colleges.

Appendix D: Innovation, private R&D lab employment and university research by MSA and industry sector

MSA	INN28	INN35	INN36	INN38	RD28	RD35	RD36	RD38	URD28	URD35	URD36	URD38
Akron	2	4		1	1 001	1 507	1 500	1 500	1 824	2 355	937	3 584
Albany–Schenectady–Troy		1			1 288	1 158	557	41	18 242	14 460	6181	28 226
Albuquerque			1		40	113	141		15 865	9 964	2 294	25 380
Allentown–Bethlehem–Easton	2	3		2	930	730	678		2 953	5 926	1 164	6 237
Anaheim–Santa Ana–Garden	2	48	24	31	1 688	863	729	86	22 917	8 061	6 457	29 037
Ann Arbor	1	2	2	2	825	516	105	300	62 110	20 856	11 618	79 533
Asheville					10							
Atlanta	2	9	6	9	339	181	125	21	26 688	41 457	27 318	59 344
Austin	1	4	4	3	876	757	176	149	17 225	25 604	22 496	35 458
Baltimore	1	7	1	3	1 317	615	332	723	82 816	5 406	3 665	85 040
Bay City												
Bellingham												
Benton Harbor		1		1	27	49	51	39	91	164	0	241
Binghamton NY–Pa		1	1		279				16	3	3	16
Birmingham		1			107		45		2 471	326	517	2 030
Bloomington–Normal		1		1	643				35 019	50	93	35 042
Boise City			1	1	15		1		351	2	5	201
Boston	19	88	60	114	6 414	6 907	5 497	7 860	183 096	127 736	88 683	284 713
Bridgeport	6	31	15	12	2 243	745	770	223	1	13	13	14
Bryan–College Station		2			17	20			15 328	22 521	3 849	31 021
Buffalo	3	8	3	10	2 218	584	40	962	22 008	3 248	2 551	22 256
Burlington		3					25	16	13 422	463	462	13 308
Canton	1	3			510	737	188	106				
Cedar Rapids		1		2	840	155	160	5				
Champaign–Urbana–Rantoul		1		1					18 703	34 881	18 935	46 273
Charleston				1			6	8				
Charlotte–Gastonia		4	1	1	122	55	14	25	135	446	123	526
Chicago	17	70	25	50	11 971	4 559	4 654	1 655	118 050	25 607	20 312	131 808
Cincinnati Ohio–Ky–Ind.	1	8	2	2	794	192	405	6	24 977	1 305	1 093	24 607

MSA	INN28	INN35	INN36	INN38	RD28	RD35	RD36	RD38	URD28	URD35	URD36	URD38
Cleveland	4	20	14	15	3 726	1 493	1 475	359	30 182	12 467	3 753	39 378
Colorado Springs		4	1	1	46	511	187		36	11	5	20
Columbia		1			62	11	62		19 655	3 546	686	22 790
Columbus	6	2	3	10	1 058	1 405	684	470	34 465	16 575	7 280	47 629
Cumberland Md.–W. Va.		2			217							
Dallas–Fort	4	42	24	5	589	740	257	420	41 018	5 592	5 270	44 541
Davenport–Rock Island–Moline		3		2	9	4 271	136	128	2	1	1	2
Dayton		2	2	7	933	1 269	230	89	5 671	12 883	5 901	16 933
Daytona Beach				1		97	81		0	31	31	31
Denver–Boulder		16	5	5	1 967	1 808	837	62	42 540	22 081	16 825	57 588
Detroit	1	17	4	10	4 280	2 943	2 300	730	17 714	3 713	1 642	17 955
Dubuque		1							5	1	1	6
El Paso			3	4	4		1 156	16	620	214	168	697
Elkhart			1				71					
Erie	1	2	1	2	209	89	170					
Evansville Ind.–Ky		1	1		170		144	343				
Flint			1		52		52					
Florence		1				1 028						
Fort Collins		1	2	4	83	1	181		15 640	5 733	3 583	18 894
Fort Lauderdale–Hollywood		5	3	1	100	1		3	90	9	9	99
Fort Myers–Cape Coral		2	2	1			4					
Fort Smith Ark.–Okla.						12	44					
Fresno		1			48							
Gainesville					154	4			234	42	42	201
Galveston–Texas		1		2	6		93	93	30 857	12 848	4 260	40 637
Glens Falls					153				11 882	0	0	11 882
Grand Rapids	1	3			207	12	149		14	7	2	20
Greensboro–Winston–Salem		1		4	976	34		9	9 028	129	128	9 093
Greenville–Spartanburg	1	3	2	3	466	18	10	12	3 948	4 736	1 201	7 821
Hamilton–Middletown		1	2	1	25	26			614	80	69	349
Harrisburg		1	3		75	33	85					
Hartford	3	10	4	9	519	211	1 249	113	44 948	7 012	4 306	47 316
Houston	11	2	3	13	1 865	1 182	113	31	109 045	9 351	9 835	113 496
Huntsville		2		1	14	8	411	500	278	1 565	1 148	1 729
Indianapolis	2	4	4	2	347	337	355	21				

211

MSA	INN28	INN35	INN36	INN38	RD28	RD35	RD36	RD38	URD28	URD35	URD36	URD38
Norfolk–Virginia Beach				1	60	71		5	1 207	1 531	905	2 554
Northeast		1	1		11	10			7	63	63	70
Oklahoma City			2	1	204	40	40		13 657	5 256	5 228	15 694
Orlando		3	2		64	439	396	347	423	4 194	521	4 432
Owensboro			8									
Oxnard–Simi Valley–Ventura	1	12			67	20	62					
Parkersburg–Marietta	1	1	1	1	250							
Paterson–Clifton–Passaic	6	13		5	2 953	87	92	8	213	1	13	213
Peoria			1			27			18	128	94	146
Philadelphia Pa–NJ	20	57	10	51	8 340	6 204	7 323	5 215	114 921	18 107	13 044	127 315
Phoenix		5	15	9	586	1 683	825	812	4 375	3 332	1 875	4 469
Pittsburgh	2	14	9	13	3 709	1 732	50	279	39 564	27 028	20 959	60 246
Pittsfield	1				14				167	164	187	285
Portland		10	1		257	28	6		463	0	0	64
Portland Oreg.–Wash.		3	6	6	230	6	55		18 711	2 023	1 344	19 596
Portsmouth–Dover–Rochester		3	2		12	57	45		1 528	3 885	3 106	5 139
Providence–Warwick	3	6	5	1	407	45	94		10 799	9 216	6 315	17 795
Provo–Orem		3				278	3		2 869	543	317	1 178
Racine		2		3	528	732	102	59				
Raleigh–Durham	4		4		1 947	43	301	119	85 966	13 256	9 676	92 696
Reading	1				176	24	207		3	120	120	121
Reno		1			11	4	4	8	2 682	544	147	2 748
Riverside–San Bernardino		3	3	6	67	24	7	10	7 100	1 650	2 391	8 390
Rochester		7	9	16	4 160	333	267	2 060	43 474	17 095	7 341	57 081
Rockford		6	2	1	34	36	22					
Sacramento		5	2		193	14	33	56	29 398	3 084	1 810	30 559
Saginaw		1			45	299						
St Luis	3	6		4	2 560	336	91		61 313	7 597	6 525	67 615
Salem		1			44				0	20	20	20
Salinas–Seaside–Monterey			1	4					509	2 409	2 074	2 421
Salt Lake City		6	2	2	600	279	778	58	29 553	10 805	4 552	36 642
San Antonio		3			1 666	19			19 521	18	17	19 497
San Diego	1	16	18	20	1 085	3 303	825	289	60 590	18 534	15 698	74 753
San Francisco–Oakland	1	41	19	14	4 152	1 335	2 362	391	123 392	28 501	16 722	145 459
San Jose	3	173	151	47	2 615	3 134	5 646	200	65 686	55 560	31 134	111 400

City												
Santa Barbara–Santa Maria	1	1	3		5	584	1 197	1 330	546	3 868	5 620	4 885	7 249
Santa Cruz		2	2					30	16	2 723	4 236	4 445	6 331
Santa Rosa		4			67	2	72						
Sarasota		2					20						
Seattle–Everett		15	13	4	357	201	426	287	73 050	10 254	8 589	80 057	
Sheboygan			1	1	4	81							
Shreveport			1		84	124			6 505	4 113	1 529	5 766	
South Bend		2	1	2	163		3		226	4	4	230	
Spokane		3			9	109	2		0	18	19	18	
Springfield		3			22				18				
Springfield–Chicopee–Holyoke	1		1		426	7	12	4	21 698	7 435	6 058	23 461	
Stockton		1		1	10				645	3	3	646	
Syracuse		5	1	3	918	223	97	68	25 385	6 205	3 534	25 559	
Tacoma		2			269	35			20	56	56	69	
Tampa–St. Petersburg		3	4	4	634	7	284	27	3 738	999	628	4 256	
Toledo Ohio–Mich.		2	2	2	540	244	236	55	6 053	647	417	6 248	
Trenton	1	11	6	11	1 685	1 101	625	78	8 774	9 243	10 660	13 967	
Tucson		4	4	1	93	5	118	15	30 022	23 149	15 511	51 188	
Tulsa		4	3	5	85	4			99	1 200	271	1 200	
Utica–Rome		2		3	29	57		12					
Vineland–Millville–Bridgeton					40		6	82					
Visalia–Tulare–Porterville													
Waco	1	1		2	34	3			348	15	15	62	
Washington DC		9	6	5	1 529	2 883	2 651	622	29 386	5 124	5 444	32 511	
Waterloo–Cedar Falls		1			14				5	392	0	5	
Wichita		3	1		232	11	11	75	74		281	412	
Williamsport		1			23	5							
Wilmington Del.–NJ–Md	4	2	2		607	211	305	126	3 990	2 643	1 277	3 547	
Worcester	3	10	3		50	194	247	164	1 764	2 809	500	3 302	
York		3	3		50	415	115	18	65	0	1	18	
Youngstown–Warren		1			50	4							

213

Sources: Compiled from US SBA Innovation Data Base; compiled from R.R. Bowker Company Directories; compiled from NSF Survey of Scientific and Engineering Expenditures at Universities and Colleges.

Appendix E: Industry Groupings

Biotechnology and biomedical
  Medicinals and botanicals (283)
  Medical instruments and supplies (384)
  Ophthalmic goods (385)

Information technology and services
  Computer and office equipment (357)
  Electronic distribution equipment (361)
  Audio and video equipment (365)
  Communications equipment (366)
  Electronic components and
    accessories (367)
  Communication services (489)
  Computer and data processing services
    (737)

High-technology machinery and
  instruments
  Engines and turbines (351)
  Construction and related machinery
    (353)
  General industrial machinery (356)
  Electrical industrial apparatus (362)
  Household appliances (363)
  Electric lighting and wiring (364)
  Miscellaneous electrical equipment
    and suppliers (369)
  Measuring and controlling devices (382)
  Photographic equipment and supplies
    (386)

Defense and aerospace
  Ordnance and accessories (348)
  Aircraft and parts (372)
  Guided missiles and space (376)
  Search and navigation equipment (381)

Energy and chemicals
  Crude petroleum and natural gas (131)
  Industrial inorganic chemicals (281)
  Plastic materials and synthetics (282)
  Industrial organic chemicals (286)
  Miscellaneous chemical products
    (289)
  Petroleum refining (291)

High-technology research

  Research, development and testing
    services (873)

Source: Office of Management and Budget, Standard Industrial Classification Manual, 1987, Washington DC, 1988.

Appendix F: List of Variables

Variable	Definition
K	Knowledge measured by either patent or innovation counts.
R	Industrial R&D measured by either annual expenditures or R&D employment.
U	University Research and Development expenditures measured by the National Science Foundation.
POP	State population.
VA	Tacit knowledge as measured by the extent of industry presence in the MSA.
RANK	At the MSA level the overall academic quality of high technology departments.
EDEXP	Total educational expenditures at universities.
ENRL	A proxy for size and total employment at universities.
U50	A spatial lag for university research of 50 miles.
U75	A spatial lag for university research of 75 miles.
R50	A spatial lag for industrial research of 50 miles.
R75	A spatial lag for industrial research of 75 miles.
LQ	Location quotient for high-tech employment.
BUS	Employment in business services (SIC 73).
LARGE	Percentage of large firms (firms with more than 500 employees).
FORTUNE	Dummy variable for at least 10 Fortune 500 corporations.
NP	New product innovation rate in 1982 defined as new product innovations divided by total firm innovations.
FS	Firm size defined as firm size for firm i in industry j divided by the employment of the largest firm in industry j in 1975.
MP	Monopoly profits measured as net income in 1975 divided by total company sales in 1975.
TO	Technological opportunity measured as research and development expenditures in 1975 divided by total company sales in 1975.
INNOV/A	Total 1982 innovations divided by total assets.
R/S	Ratio of R&D expenditures divided by 1982 sales.

Variable	Definition
OPM	Operating profits margin.
ASSETS	Log of total assets.
D/CE	Total debt to common equity in 1982.
INNOV	Simple count of the number of innovations by MSA in 1982.
W	Real high-technology annual wage per employee in MSA.
EMP	High-technology employment in MSA.
HK	Science and engineering employment as a percentage of the total labor force.
OU	Matched university R&D in nearest MSA.
RSPILL	All hard sciences university R&D spending by MSA less the spending which corresponds to each industry.
USPILL	All industrial R&D measured by employment less the spending which corresponds to each industry.

References

Abernathy, W.J. and K.B. Clark (1985), 'Innovation: mapping the winds of creative destruction', *Research Policy*, 14, 3–22.

Acs, Z.J. (1984), *The Changing Structure of the U.S. Economy*, New York: Praeger Publishers.

Acs, Z.J. (1990), 'High technology networks in Maryland: a case study', *Science and Public Policy*, **17**, (5), 315–25.

Acs, Z.J. (1996), 'American high technology clusters', in J. de la Mothe and G. Paquet (eds), *Evolutionary Economics and the New International Political Economy*, London: Pinter, pp. 183–219.

Acs, Z.J. (1999), 'Small firms innovation and public policy,' *Science Policy*, **26**(4), 247–58.

Acs, Z.J. (2000) (ed), *Regional Innovation, Knowledge and Global Change*, Pinter, London.

Acs, Z.J., L. Anselin and A. Varga (2002) 'Patents and innovation counts as measures of regional production of new knowledge,' *Research Policy*.

Acs, Z.J. and D.B. Audretsch (1987), 'Innovation market structure and firm size', *Review of Economics and Statistics*, **69**, (4), 567–75.

Acs, Z.J. and D.B. Audretsch (1988), 'Innovation in large and small firms: an empirical analysis', *American Economic Review*, 78, 678–90.

Acs, Z.J. and D.B. Audretsch, (1990a), *The Economics of Small Firms: A European Challenge*, Dordrecht: Kluwer Academic Publishers.

Acs, Z.J. and D.B. Audretsch, (1990b), *Innovation and Small Firms*, Cambridge, Mass.: MIT Press.

Acs, Z.J. and D.B. Audretsch, (1991), 'R&D, firm size and innovative activity', in Z.J. Acs and D.B. Audretsch (eds), *Innovation and Technological Change: An International Comparison*, Ann Arbor: University of Michigan Press, pp. 39–59.

Acs, Z.J. and D.B. Audretsch (1993a), 'Analyzing innovation output indicator: the U. S. experience', in A. Kleinknecht and D. Bain (eds), *New Concept in Innovation Output Measurement*, London: Macmillan Press, pp. 10–41.

Acs, Z.J. and D.B. Audretsch (1993b), 'Innovation and technological change: the new learning', in G. Libecap (ed.), *Advances in the Study of Entrepreneurship*, Greenwich, Conn.: JAI Press, pp. 143–76.

Acs, Z.J. and D.B. Audretsch (1994), 'Asymmetric information, agency costs and innovative entry', working paper, Wissenschaftszentrum Berlin für Sozialforschung.

Acs, Z.J., D. B. Audretsch and M. Feldman (1992), 'Real effects of academic research: comment', *American Economic Review*, **81**, 363–7.

Acs, Z.J., D.B. Audretsch and M. Feldman (1994a), 'R&D spillovers and recipient firm size', *The Review of Economics and Statistics*, **76**, 336–40.

Acs, Z.J., D.B. Audretsch and M. Feldman (1994b), 'R&D spillovers and innovative activity', *Managerial and Decision Economics*, **15**, 131–8.

Acs, Z.J. and S. Prowse (2001), 'Angel Investors and the Angel Capital Electronic Network (ACE-Net)' in M.J. Whincop, (ed.), *Bridging the Entrepreneurial Financing Gap: Linking Government with Regulatory Policy*, Sydney: Federated Press.

Acs, Z.J., B. Carlsson and C. Karlsson (eds) (1999), *Entrepreneurship, Small and Medium-Sized Enterprises and the Macroeconomy*, Cambridge: Cambridge University Press.

Acs, Z.J., H. de Groot and P. Nijkamp (2002), *The Emergence of the Knowledge Economy: A Regional Perspective*, Berlin: Springer Verlag.

Acs, Z.J., J. de la Mothe and G. Paquet (1996), 'Local systems of innovation', in P. Howitt (ed.), *Implications of Knowledge-Based Growth for Micro-Economic Policies*, Calgary: University of Calgary Press, pp. 339–58.

Acs, Z.J., F.R. FitzRoy and I. Smith (1999), 'High technology employment, wages and university R&D spillovers: evidence from U.S. cities', *Economics of Innovation and New Technology*, **8**, 57–78.

Acs, Z.J. and S.C. Isberg (1991), 'Innovation, firm size, and corporate finance: an initial inquiry', *Economics Letters*, **35**, 323–6.

Acs, Z.J. and A. Varga (2002) 'Geography, endogenous growth and innovation', *International Regional Science Review*, **25**(1), 132–48.

Aghion, P. and P. Howitt (1998), *Endogenous Growth Theory*. Cambridge, Mass: MIT Press.

Almeida and B. Kogut, 1999, 'The Localization of Knowledge and the Mobility of Engineers', *Management Science* **45**, (7), 905–17.

Altman, E. (1984), 'A further investigation of the bankruptcy question', *Journal of Finance*, **39**, 1067–89.

Andersson, A.E., C. Anderstig and B. Harsman (1990), 'Knowledge and communications infrastructure and regional economic growth', *Regional Science and Urban Economics*, **20**, 359–76.

Andrew, C. et al. (1993), 'New local actors: high technology development and the recomposition of social action', in J. Jenson et al. (eds), *Production, Space, Identity*, Toronto: Canadian Scholars' Press, pp. 327–46.

Andrikopoulos, A., J. Brox and E. Carvalho (1990), 'Shift-share analysis and the potential for predicting regional growth patterns: some evidence for the region of Ontario', *Growth and Change*, 1, 1–10.

Anselin, L. (1988), *Spatial Econometrics, Methods and Models*, Boston: Kluwer Academic.

Anselin, L. (1990), 'Some robust approaches to testing and estimation in spatial econometrics', *Regional Science and Urban Economics*, **20**, 141–63.

Anselin, L. (1992), 'SpaceStat, a program for the analysis of spatial data', National Center for Geographic Information and Analysis, University of California, Santa Barbara, CA.

Anselin, L. (1995), 'SpaceStat version 1.80 user's guide', Regional Research Institute, West Virginia University, Morgantown, WV.

Anselin, L. and A. Bera (1997), 'Spatial Dependence in Linear Regression Models With an Introduction to Spatial Econometrics', in D. Biles and A. Ullah, (eds), *Handbook of Economic Statistics*, New York: Marcel Dekker, 237–89.

Anselin, L. and R. Florax (1995), *New Directions in Spatial Econometrics*, Berlin: Springer Verlag.

Anselin, L. and S. Hudak (1992), 'Spatial econometrics in practice: a review of software options', *Regional Science and Urban Economics*, **22**, 509–36.

Anselin, L., A. Varga and Z.J. Acs (1997), 'Local geographic spillovers between university research and high-technology innovations', *Journal of Urban Economics*, **42**, 422–48.

Anselin, L., A. Varga and Z.J. Acs (2000a), 'Geographical spillovers and university research: a spatial econometric approach', *Growth and Change*, **31**, (4), 501–15.

Anselin L., A. Varga and Z.J. Acs (2000b), 'Geographic and sectoral characteristics of academic knowledge externalities', *Papers in Regional Science*, **79**, (4), 435–43.

Antonelli, C. (ed.) (1992), *The Economics of Information Networks*, Amsterdam: North-Holland.

Armington, C. and Z.J. Acs (2002), 'The determinants of regional variation in new firm foundation', *Regional Studies*, **36**(1), 33–45.

Arrow, K. (1962), 'Economic welfare and the allocation of resources for invention', in Richard Nelson (ed.), *The Rate and Direction of Inventive Activity*, Princeton, NJ: Princeton University Press, pp. 609–26.

Arthur, W.B. (1990), 'Silicon Valley's locational clusters: when do increasing returns imply monopoly?', *Mathematical Social Sciences*, **19**, 235–51.

Ashby, L.D. (1964), 'The geographical redistribution of employment: an examination of the elements of change', *Survey of Current Business*, **44**, 13–20.

Audretsch, D.B. (1995), *Innovation and Industry Evolution*, Cambridge, Mass.: The MIT Press.

Audretsch, D.B. and M.P. Feldman (1996), 'Knowledge spillovers and the geography of innovation and production', *American Economic Review*, **86**, (3), 630–40.

Audretsch, D.B. and P.E. Stephan (1996), 'Company-scientist locational links: the case of biotechnology', *American Economic Review*, **86**, (3), 641–52.

Audretsch D.B. and R. Thurik (1999), *Innovation, Industry Evolution and Employment*, Cambridge: Cambridge University Press.

Audretsch, D.B. and M. Vivarelli (1996), 'Small firms and R&D spillovers: evidence from Italy', *Small Business Economics*, **8**, (4), 91–103.

Baily, M., E.. Bartelsman and J. Hlatiwanger, (1996), 'Downsizing and Productivity Growth: Myth or Reality?', *Small Business Economics* **8**, (4), 259–78.

Balakrishnan, S. and I. Fox (1993), 'Asset specificity, firm heterogeneity and capital structure', *Strategic Management Journal*, **14**, 3–16.

Baldwin, W.L. and J.T. Scott (1987), *Market Structure and Technological Change*, New York: Harwood Academic Press.

Bania, N., L.N. Calkins and D.R. Dalenberg (1992), 'The effects of regional science and technology policy on the geographic distribution of industrial R&D labs', *Journal of Regional Science*, **32**, 209–28.

Bania, N., R. Eberts and M. Fogarty (1987), 'The role of technical capital in regional growth', presented at the Western Economic Association Meetings, July.

Bania, N., R. Eberts and M. Fogarty (1993), 'Universities and the start-up of new companies: can we generalize from Route 128 and Silicon Valley?', *The Review of Economics and Statistics*, **75**, 761–6.

Barro, R.J. and X. Sala-I-Martin (1992), 'Convergence', *Journal of Political Economy*, **100**, (2), 223–51.

Bartel, A. and F. Lichtenberg (1987), 'The comparative advantage of educated workers in implementing new technology', *The Review of Economics and Statistics*, **69**, 1–11.

Beeson, P. and E. Montgomery (1993), 'The effects of colleges and universities on local labor markets', *Review of Economics and Statistics*, **75**, 753–61.

Bernstein, J.I. and M.I. Nadiri (1989), 'Research and development and intra-industry spillovers: an empirical application of dynamic duality', *Review of Economic Studies*, **56**, 249–69.

Best, M.H. (1990), *The New Competition: Institutions of Industrial Restructuring*, Cambridge, Mass.: Harvard University Press.

Black, D. and V. Henderson (1999), 'A theory of urban growth', *Journal of Political Economy*, **107**, (2), 252–84.

Boulding, K.E. (1970), *A Primer on Social Dynamics*, New York: Free Press.

Bowman, J. (1980), 'The importance of a market value measurement of debt in assessing leverage', *Journal of Accounting Research*, **18**, 242–54.

Braczyk, H.J., P. Cooke, M. Heidenreich (eds) (1998), 'Regional Innovation Systems', *The Role of Governances In a Globalized World*, London: UCL Press.

Bradley, M., G. Jarrell and E. Han Kim (1984), 'On the existence of an optimal capital structure: theory and evidence', *Journal of Finance*, **39**, 857–78.

Braunerhjelm, P. and B. Carlsson (1998), 'Industry clusters in Ohio and Sweden, 1975–1995', *Small Business Economics*, **1**, (4), 279-93.

Braunerhjelm, P. and B. Carlsson (1999), 'Industry Structure, Entrepreneurship and The Macroeconomy: A comparison of Ohio and Sweden, 1975–1995', in Acs, Carlsson and Karlsson, (eds), *Entrepreneurship, Small and Medium Sized Enterprises and the Macroeconomy*, Cambridge: Cambridge University Press.

Breusch T. and A. Pagan (1980), 'The LM test and its applications to model specification in econometrics', *Review of Economic Studies*, **47**, 239–54

Brock, W.A. and D.S. Evans (1989), 'Small business economics', *Small Business Economics*, **1**, 7–20.

Brouwer, E. and A. Kleinknecht (forthcoming), 'Firm size, small business presence and sales from innovative products', *Small Business Economics*.

Brown, H.J. (1969), 'Shift and share projections of regional economic growth: an empirical test', *Journal of Regional Science*, **9**, (1), 1–18.

Bureau of Labor Statistics, 'Employment and earnings', Various Issues.

Business Week (1994), 'Why Are We So Afraid of Growth?' Cover Story, May 16th 62–72.

Chandler A. (1977), *The Visible Hand*, Cambridge, MA: Harvard University Press.

Chandler A. (1990), *Scale and Scope*, Cambridge, MA: Harvard University Press.

Cockburn, I. and Z. Griliches (1988), 'Industry effects and appropriability measures in the stock market's valuation of R&D and patents', *American Economic Review* (Proceedings), **78**, 419–23.

Cohen, W.M. and S. Klepper (1991), 'Firm size versus diversity in the achievement of technological advance', in Z. Acs and D.B. Audretsch (eds), *Innovation and Technological Change: An International Comparison*, Ann Arbor: University of Michigan Press, 183–203.

Cohen, W.M. and S. Klepper (1992), 'The Tradeoff between Firm Size and Diversity in the Pursuit of Technological Progress', *Small Business Economics*, **4**, (1), March, 1–14.

Cohen, W.M., R C. Levin and D.C. Mowery (1987), 'Firm size and R & D intensity: a re-examination', *Journal of Industrial Economics*, **35**, 543–65.

Cohen, W.M. and D.A. Levinthal (1989), 'Innovation and learning', *The Economic Journal*, **99**, 569–96.

Comanor, W.S. (1967), 'Market structure, product differentiation and industrial research', *Quarterly Journal of Economics*, **81**, November, 639–57.

Connally, R.A. and M. Hirschey, 1984, 'R & D, Market Structure and Profits: A Value-Based Approach', *Review of Economics and Statistics* **66**, 682.

Cooke, P. and K. Morgan (1994), 'Growth regions under duress: renewal strategies in Baden Wurttemberg and Emilia-Romagna' in A. Amin and N. Thrift (eds), *Globalization, Institutions, and Regional Development in Europe*, Oxford: Oxford University Press, pp. 91–117.

Creamer, D. (1943), 'Shifts of manufacturing industries, industrial location and natural resources', US Government Printing Office, Washington, DC.

Cressy, R.C. (1996a), 'Are Startups Debt-Rationed?', *The Economic Journal* **106**, (438), 1253–70.

Cressy, R.C., (1996b), 'Pre-Entrepreneurial Income, Cash Flow Growth and Survival of Startup Businesses: Model and Tests on U.K. Startup Data', *Small Business Economics*, Special Issue on Financing and Firm Dynamics, edited by Gavin Reid, **8** (1), 49–58.

Dahmen, E. (1988), 'Development blocks in industrial economics', *Scandinavian Economic History Review*, **36**, 3–14.

David, P.A. (1992), 'Information network economics', in Antonelli (1992), 103–5.

David, P. and J. Rosenbloom (1990), 'Marshallian factor market externalities and the dynamics of industrial localization', *Journal of Urban Economics*, **28**, 349–70.

Davidow, W.H. and Malone, M. S. (1992), *The Virtual Corporation: Structuring and Revitalizing the Corporation for the 21st Century*, New York: Harper Collins Publishers.

Davidson, R. and J.G. MacKinnon (1993), *Estimation and Inference in Econometrics*, New York: Oxford University Press.

Davis, C.H. (1991), *Local Initiatives to Promote Technological Innovation in Canada: Eight Case Studies*, Ottawa: The Science Council of Canada.

Davis, S. J and M. Henrekson (1999), 'Explaining National Differences in the Size and Industry Distribution of Employment', *Small Business Economics* **12**(1), 59–83.

de La Mothe, J. and G. Paquet (1994a), 'The dispersive revolution', *Optimum*, **25**, (1), 42–8.

de La Mothe , J and G. Paquet (1994b), 'The technology-trade nexus: liberalization, warring blocs, or negotiated access?', *Technology in Society*, **16**, (1), 97–118.

de La Mothe, J. and G. Paquet (1994c), 'The shock of the news: a techno-economic paradigm for small economies', in M. Stevenson (ed.), *The Entry into New Economic Communities: Swedish and Canadian Perspectives on the European Economic Community and North American Free Trade Accord*, Toronto: Swedish-Canadian Academic Foundation, pp. 13–27.

de La Mothe, J. and G. Paquet (1994d), 'Circumstantial evidence: a note on science policy in Canada', *Science and Public Policy*, **21**, (4), 261–8.

de la Mothe J. and Paquet G. (eds) (1996), *Evolutionary Economics and the New International Political Economy*, London: Pinter.

de la Mothe J and Paquet G. (eds) (1998), *Local and Regional Systems of Innovation* Boston: Kluwer Academic Publishers.

de Meza, D. and D.C. Webb (1987), 'Too Much Investment: A Problem of Asymmetric Information', *Quarterly Journal of Economics* **102**, 281–92.

DeBresson, C. and F. Amesse (1992), 'Networks of innovators: a review and introduction to the issues', *Research Policy*, **20**, 363–80.

Dixit, A. and J. Stiglitz (1977), 'Monopolistic competition and optimum product diversity', *American Economic Review*, **67**, 297–308.

Dorfman, S. (1983), 'The Development of a Regional High Technology Economy', *Research Policy* **12**, 299–316.

Dosi, G. (1988), 'Sources, procedures and microeconomic effects of innovation', *Journal of Economic Literature,* **26**, 1120–71.

Dosi, G. and Nelson, R.R. (1994), 'An introduction to evoutionary theories in economics', *Journal of Evolutionary Economics*, **4**, (3), 153–72.

Dunn, T.W. (1970), 'A statistical and analytical technique of regional economic analysis', Papers and Proceedings, *Regional Science Association*, **6**, 97–112.

Dunning, J.H. (1995), 'The Role of Foreign Direct Investment in a Globalizing Economy', *Banca Nationale Del Lavoero Quarterly Review* **193**, 125–144.

Dunning, J.H. (1993), *Multinational Enterprises and the Global Economy*, New York: Addison-Wesley Publishing Company.

Duranton, G. and G. Puga (1999), 'Diversity and specialization in cities: why, where and when does it matter?' Centre for Economic Performance, Discussion Paper 433, August, London School of Economics and Political Science.

Edquist, C. (1997), *Systems of Innovation*, London: Cassell.

Edwards, K.L. and Gordon, T.J. (1984), 'Characterization of innovations introduced in the US market in 1982', Report prepared for the US Small Business Administration, The Futures Group, Washington, DC.

Evans, D.S. and B. Jovanovic (1989), 'Estimates of a model of entrepreneurial choice under liquidity constraints', *Journal of Political Economy*, **4**, 808–27.

Fazzari, S.R., G. Hubbard and B. Petersen (1986), 'Financing constraints and corporate investment', *Brookings Papers on Economic Activity*, No. 1, 19–37.

Feldman, M. (1994), *The Geography of Innovation*, Boston: Kluwer Academic Publishers.

Feldman, M.P. and D.B. Audretsch (1999), 'Innovation in cities: science-based diversity, specialization and localized competition', *European Economic Review*, **43**, 409–29.

Feldman, M. and R. Florida, (1994), 'The geographic sources of innovation:

technological infrastructure and product innovation in the United States', *Annals of the Association of American Geographers,* **84**, 210–29.

Fischer, E.O., R. Heinkel and J. Zechner (1989), 'Dynamic capital structure choice: theory and tests', *The Journal of Finance,* **44**, 19–40.

Florax, R., (1992), *The University: A Regional Booster? Economic Impacts of Academic Knowledge Infrastructure,* Aldershot, UK and Brookfield, US: Avebury.

Florax, R. and H. Folmer (1992), 'Knowledge impacts of universities on industries: an aggregate simultaneous investment model', *Journal of Regional Science,* **32**, 437–66.

Freeman, C. (1982), *The Economics of Industrial Innovation,* Cambridge, Mass.: MIT Press.

Frost, M.E. and N.A. Spence (1995), 'The rediscovery of accessibility and economic potential: the critical issue of self-potential', *Environment and Planning A,* **27**, 1833–48.

Galbraith, J.K. (1956), *American Capitalism: The Concept of Countervailing Power,* revised edition, Boston, Mass.: Houghton Mifflin.

Gibrat, R. (1931), *Les inégalités économiques,* Paris: Sirey.

Gifford, S. (1992a), 'Innovation, firm size and growth in a centralized organization', *The Rand Journal of Economics,* **23**, 284–98.

Gifford, S. (1992b), 'Allocation of entrepreneurial attention', *Journal of Economic Behavior and Organization,* **19**, 265–84.

Gifford, S. (1993), 'Heterogeneous ability, career choice and firm size', *Small Business Economics,* **5**, 249–59.

Gifford, S. (1994a), 'Limited attention and the role of venture capitalist', *Journal of Business Venturing,* **12**, (6), 459–82.

Gifford, S. (1994b), 'Limited entrepreneurial attention and the optimal completeness of contracts', Working Paper, Rutgers University.

Gifford, S. (1994c), 'Limited entrepreneurial attention and the internalization of transactions', Working Paper, Rutgers University.

Gifford, S. and C.A. Wilson (1995), 'A model of project evaluation with limited attention', *Economic Theory,* **5**, 67–78.

Glaeser, E.L., H.D. Kallal, J.A. Scheinkman and A. Shleifer, (1992), 'Growth in cities', *Journal of Political Economy,* **100**, (6), 1126–52.

Glasmeier, A. (1985), 'Innovative Manufacturing Industries: Spatial Incidence in the United States', in M. Castells, ed., *High Technology, Space and Society,* Beverly Hills: Sage.

Glasmeier, A. (1991), *The High-tech Potential: Economic Development in Rural America,* New Brunswick, NJ: Center for Urban Policy Research.

Gomes-Casseres, B. (1996), *The Alliance Revolution: The New Shape of Business Rivalry,* Cambridge, MA.: Harvard University Press.

Gomulka, S. (1990), *The Theory of Technological Change and Economic Growth*, London: Routledge.

Greene, W.H. (1993), *Econometric Analysis*, New York: Macmillan Publishing Company.

Griliches, Z. (1979), 'Issues in assessing the contribution of R&D to productivity growth', *Bell Journal of Economics*, **10**, 92–116.

Griliches, Z. (1986), 'Productivity, R&D and basic research at the firm level in the 1970's', *American Economic Review*, **76**, 141–54.

Griliches, Z. (1990), 'Patent statistics as economic indicators: a survey', *Journal of Economic Literature*, **28**, 1661–707.

Griliches, Z. (1992), 'The search for R&D spillovers', *Scandinavian Journal of Economics*, **94**, 29–47.

Griliches, Z. and Lichtenberg, F. (1984), 'Inter-industry technology flows and productivity growth: a comment', *Review of Economics and Statistics*, **66**, 324–29.

Grossman, G.E and E. Helpman (1991), *Innovation and Growth in the Global Economy*, Cambridge, Mass.: MIT Press.

Grossman, G. and E. Helpman (1994), 'Endogenous innovation in the theory of growth', *Journal of Economic Perspectives*, **8**, 23–44.

Hall, B.H. (1990), 'The impact of corporate restructuring on industrial research and development', *Brookings Papers on Economic Activity: Microeconomics*, 85–124.

Hall, B.H. (1992), 'Investment and research and development: does the source of financing matter?', Working Paper No. 92–194, Department of Economics, University of California at Berkeley.

Hall, P. and A. Markusen (1985), *Silicon Landscaped*, Boston: Allen and Unwin.

Hamel, G. (1999), 'Bringing Silicon Valley Inside', *Harvard Business Review*, September-October, 70–87.

Handy, C. (1992), 'Balancing corporate power: a new federalist paper', *Harvard Business Review*, **70**, (6), 59–72.

Handy, C.B. (1994), *The Age of Paradox*, Boston: Harvard Business School Press.

Hao, K.Y. and A.B. Jaffe (1993), 'Effects of Liquidity on Firms', *R&D Spending, Economics of Innovation and New Technology* **2**, 275–82.

Harding, C.F. (1989), 'Location choices for research labs: a case study approach', *Economic Development Quarterly*, **3**, 223–34.

Harris, M. and A. Raviv (1991), 'The theory of capital structure', *Journal of Finance*, **46**, 297–356.

Harvey, D. (1988), 'Urban places in the global village: reflections on the urban condition in late 20th century', in L. Mazza (ed.), *World Cities and the Future of the Metropolis*, Milan: Electra.

Hayek, F.A. (1945), 'The use of knowledge in society', *American Economic Review*, **35**, (40), 519–30.

Heckman, J.J. (1979), 'Sample solution bias as specification error', *Econometrica*, **47**, 153–62.

Helpman, E. (1992), 'Endogenous Macroeconomic Growth Theory', *European Economic Review* **36**, 237–67.

Henderson, J.V. (1988), *Urban Development: Theory, Fact and Illusion*, New York: Oxford.

Henderson, J.V. (1994), 'Where does an industry locate?', *Journal of Urban Economics*, **35**, 83–104.

Henderson, J.V., A. Kuncoro and M. Turner (1995), 'Industrial development in cities', *Journal of Political Economy*, **103**, (5), 1067–90.

Henrekson, M. and D. Johansson (1999), 'Institutional Effects on the Evolution of the Size Distribution of Firms', *Small Business Economics* **12**(91), 59–83.

Herzog, H.W., A.M. Schlottman and D.J. Johnson (1986), 'High-technology jobs and worker mobility', *Journal of Regional Science*, **26**, 445–59.

Himmelberg, C.P. and B.C. Petersen (1994), 'R&D and internal finance: a panel study of small firms in high-tech industries', *Review of Economics and Statistics*, **76**, 38–51.

Hollingsworth, R. (1993), 'Variation among nations in the logic of manufacturing sectors and international competitiveness', in D. Foray and C. Freeman (eds), *Technology and the Wealth of Nations*, London: Pinter, 301–21.

Holtz-Eakin, D., D. Joulfaian and H.S. Rosen (1994), 'Sticking it out: entrepreneurial survival and liquidity constraints', *Journal of Political Economy*, **102**, (1), 53–75.

Houston, D. (1967), 'The shift and share analysis of regional growth', *Southern Economic Journal*, **33**, 577–81.

Howells J.R. (1987), 'Developments in the Location, Technology and Industrial Organization of Computer Services: Some Trends and Research Issues', *Research Studies* **21**, 493–503.

Ireland, T.C. and R.L. Moomaw (1981), 'The competitive effect in shift-share analysis: a will of wisp?', *The Review of Regional Studies*, **11**, 72–8.

Jacobs, B., R. Nihuis and P.J.G. Tang (1999), 'Sectoral Productivity Growth and R&D Spillovers in the Netherlands', paper presented at an International workshop on Endogenous Growth Policy and Regional Development, Amsterdam, February.

Jacobs, J. (1969), *The Economy of Cities*, New York: Random House.

Jaffe, A.B. (1986), 'Technological opportunity and spillovers of R&D: evidence from firms' patents, profits and market value', *American Economic Review*, **76**, (5), 984–1001.

Jaffe, A.B. (1989), 'Real effects of academic research', *American Economic Review*, **79**, (5), 957–70.

Jaffe, A.B., M. Trajtenberg and R. Henderson (1993), 'Geographic localization of knowledge spillovers as evidenced by patent citations', *Quarterly Journal of Economics*, 577–98.

Jaffee, D.M. and T. Russell (1976), 'Imperfect Information, Uncertainty, and Credit Rationing', *Quarterly Journal of Economics* **90**, (4), 651–66.

James, F. and J. Hughes (1973), 'A test of shift and share analysis as a predictive device', *Journal of Regional Science*, **13**, (2), 223–31.

Jacques Cattell Press (ed.) (1982), *Industrial Research Laboratories of the United States*, 17th edition, New York and London: R R. Bowker Company.

Jensen, M.C. (1986), 'Agency costs of free cash flow, corporate finance, and takeovers', *The American Economic Review*, **76**, 323–9.

Jewkes, J., D. Sawers and R. Stillerman (1969), *The Sources of Invention*, New York: W.W. Norton.

Judd, K. (1985), 'On the performance of patents', *Econometrica*, **53**, 567–86.

Kalbacher, J.Z. (1979), 'Shift-share analysis: a modified approach', *Agricultural Economic Research*, **31**, (1), 12–25.

Kaldor, N. (1934), 'The equilibrium of the firm', *Economic Journal*, **44**, 60–76.

Kamien, M.I. and N.L. Schwartz (1975), 'Market structure and innovation: a survey', *The Journal of Economic Literature*, **13**, 1–37.

Kamien, M.I. and N.L. Schwartz (1982), *Market Structure and Innovation*, Cambridge, Mass.: Cambridge University Press.

Karlsson, C and A. Manduchi (2001), 'Context – a critical review and assessment', Berlin; Springer Verlag, 101–23.

Karlsson and Manduchi (2001), in M.M. Fischer J. Frohlich (eds), *Knowledge, Complexity and Innovation Systems*, 101–20.

Kelly, K. (1994), *Out of Control: The Rise of Neo-Biological Civilization*, Reading, Mass.: Addison-Wesley.

Kindleberger, C.P. and D.B. Audretsch, (1983), *The Multinational Corporation in the 1980s*, Cambridge, MA: The MIT Press.

Kirchhoff, B.A. (1989), 'Creative destruction among industrial firms in the United States', *Small Business Economics*, **1**, 161–73.

Kirzner, I.M.D. (1997), 'Entrepreneurial discovery and the competitive market process', *The Journal of Economic Literature*, **35**, (1), 60–85.

Klaasen, L.H. and J.H.P. Paelinck (1972), 'Asymmetry in shift and share analysis', *Regional and Urban Economics*, **2**, (3), 256–61.

Kleinknecht, A. (1987), *Innovation Patterns in Crisis and Prosperity: Schumpeter's Long Cycle Reconsidered*, London: Macmillan Press.

Kleinknecht, A. (1989), 'Firm Size and Innovation: Observations in Dutch Manufacturing Industry', *Small Business Economics* **1**, (3), 215–22.

Knight, F.H. (1921), *Discovery and the Capitalist Process*, Chicago: University of Chicago Press.

Kraft, K. (1990), 'Are product- and process-innovations independent of each other?', *Applied Economics*, 22, 1029–38.

Krugman, P. (1991), 'Increasing returns and economic geography', *Journal of Political Economy*, **99**, (3), 483–99.

Krugman, P. (1995), *Development, Geography and Economic Theory*, London: MIT Press.

Krugman, P. (1998), 'Space: the final frontier', *The Journal of Economic Perspectives*, **12**, (2), 161–74.

Krugman, P. (1991), *Geography and Trade*, Cambridge, MA: The MIT Press.

Kumon, S. (1992), 'Japan as a network society', in S. Kumon and H. Rosovsky (eds), *The Political Economy of Japan*, volume 3, Stanford: Stanford University Press, pp. 109–41.

Leland, H. and D.H. Pyle (1975), 'Informational asymmetries, financial structure, and financial intermediation', *Journal of Finance*, **32**, 371–87.

Lerner, J. (1999), 'The Government as Venture Capitalist: The Long-Run Effects of the SBIR Program', *Journal of Business* **72**, 285–318.

Levin, R.C., W.M. Cohen and D.C. Mowery (1985), 'R & D appropriability, opportunity, and market structure: new evidence on some Schumpeterian hypotheses', *American Economic Review*, **75**, 20–24.

Levin, R.C., A.K. Klevorick, R.R. Nelson and S.G. Winter (1987), 'Appropriating the returns from industrial research and development', *Brookings Papers on Economic Activity*, **3**, 783–820.

Link, A.N. (1982), 'An analysis of the composition of R&D spending', *Southern Economic Review*, **49**, 342–9.

Link, A.N. (1985), 'The changing composition of R&D', *Managerial and Decision Economics*, **6**, 125–8.

Link, A.N. and B. Bozeman (1991), 'Innovative behavior in small-sized firms', *Small Business Economics*, **3**, (3), 179–84.

Link, A. and J. Rees (1990), 'Firm size, university based research and returns to R&D', *Small Business Economics*, **2**, 25–32.

Lipnack, J. and J. Stamps (1994), *The Age of the Network*, Essex Junction, Vt: Omneo.

Loesch, August (1954), *The Economics of Location*, New Haven: Yale University Press.

Loveman, G. and W. Schenberger (1991), 'The Re-Emergence of Small-Scale Production: An International Comparison', *Small Business Economics* **3**, (1), 1–39.

Lucas, R.E. (1988), 'On the Mechanisms of Economic Development', *Journal of Monetary Economics*, 22, 1–42.

Lucas, R.E. (1993), 'Making a miracle', *Econometrica*, **61**, 251–72.

Lumme, A., L. Kauranen, E. Autio and M.M. Kaila (1993), 'New technology based companies in Cambridge in an international perspective', Working Paper No. 35, Small Business Research Center, University of Cambridge, September.

Lund, L. (1986), 'Locating corporate R&D facilities', Conference Board Report No. 892, Conference Board, New York.

Lundvall, B.A. (1988), 'Innovation as an interactive process: rom user-producer interaction to the national system of innovation', in G. Dosi, C. Freeman, R. Nelson, G. Silverberg and L. Soete (eds), *Technical Change and Economic Theory*, London: Pinter, pp. 349–69.

Lundvall, B.A. (ed.) (1992), *National Systems of Innovation: Towards a Theory of Innovation and Interactive Learning*, London: Pinter.

Lunn, John (1986), 'An empirical analysis of process and product patenting: a simultaneous equation framework', *Journal of Industrial Economics*, **34**, 319–30.

Lunn, J. (1987), 'An empirical analysis of firm process and product patenting', *Applied Economics*, **19**, 743–51.

Maddala, G.S. (1983), *Limited-Dependent and Qualitative Variables in Econometrics*, Econometric Society Monographs No. 3, Cambridge: Cambridge University Press.

Maddison, A. (1987), 'Growth and slowdown in advanced capitalist economies', *Journal of Economic Literature*, **25**, 469–698.

Mairesse, J. and P. Mohnen (1990), 'Recherche-développement et productivité: un survol de la littérature économétrique', *Économie et Statistique*, No. 237–8, 99–108.

Malecki, E. (1981), 'Federal R&D spending in the United States of America: some impacts on metropolitan Économies', *Regional Studies*, **16**, 19–35.

Malecki, E. (1986), 'Research and development and the geography of high-technology complexes' in John Rees (ed.), *Technology, Regions and Policy*, Totowa, NJ: Rowman and Littlefield, pp. 51–74.

Malecki, E. (1991), *Technology and Economic Development*, Essex, UK: Longman Scientific and Technical; New York, US: Wiley.

Malecki, E. and S.L. Bradbury (1992), 'R&D facilities and professional labor: labor force dynamics in high technology', *Regional Studies*, **26**, 123–36.

Mansfield, E. (1981), 'Composition of R&D expenditures: relationship to size of firm, concentration, and innovative output', *Review of Economics and Statistics*, **63**, 610–15.

Mansfield, E. (1984), 'Comment on Using Linked Patent and R&D Data to Measure Inter-industry Technology Flows' in Z. Griliches (ed.), *R&D,*

Patents and Productivity, Chicago: University of Chicago Press, 175–204.

Mansfield, E. (1991), 'Academic research and industrial innovation', *Research Policy*, **20**, 1–12.

Mansfield, E. (1995), 'Academic research underlying industrial innovations: sources, characteristics and financing', *The Review of Economics and Statistics*, **77**, 55–65.

Markusen, A., P. Hall and A. Glasmeier (1986), *High Tech America: The What, How, Where and Why of Sunrise Industries*, Boston: Allen and Unwin.

Marshall, A. (1961), *Principles of Economics*, London: Macmillan. Orig. pub. 1890.

McDonough, C.C. and B.B. Sihag (1991), 'The incorporation of multiple bases into shift-share analysis', *Growth and Change*, **22**, (1), 1–9.

Milgrom, P. (1988), 'Employment contracts, influence activities and organization design', *Journal of Political Economy*, **96**, (1), 42–60.

Miller, M. (1977), 'Debt and taxes', *Journal of Finance*, **32**, 261–75.

Modigliani, F. and M. Miller (1958), 'The cost of capital, corporation finance and the theory of investment', *American Economic Review*, **53**, June, 261–97.

Muizer, A.P. and G.J. Hospers (1998), *Industry Clusters and SMEs*, Zoetermeer: Small Business Research and Consultancy.

Myers, S.C. (1977), 'Determinants of corporate borrowing', *Journal of Financial Economics*, **4**, 147–76.

Naisbitt, J. (1994), *Global Paradox*, New York: William Morrow & Company.

National Science Foundation (1982), 'Academic Science and Engineering R&D Expenditures', Fiscal Year 1982 (Data obtained from GASPAR data files).

Nelson, R. (1959), 'The simple economics of basic scientific research', *Journal of Political Economy*, **67**, 297–306.

Nelson, R. (1982), 'The role of knowledge in R&D efficiency', *Quarterly Journal of Economics*, **97**, 453–70.

Nelson, R. (1986), 'Institutions supporting technical advance in industry', *American Economic Review*, **76**, (2), 186–9.

Nelson, R. (1988), 'Institutions supporting technological change in the United States', in G. Dosi, C. Freeman, R. Nelson, R.G. Silverberg and L. Soete (eds), *Technical Change and Economic Theory*, London: Pinter, pp. 312–29.

Nelson, R. (ed.) (1993), *National Innovation Systems*, New York: Oxford University Press.

Nelson, R.R. and S.G. Winter (1977), 'In search of a useful theory of innovation', *Research Policy*, **6**, (1), 36–76.

Nelson, R. and S. Winter (1982), *An Evolutionary Theory of Economic Change*, Cambridge, Mass.: Belknap Press.

The New York Times (1996), 'A Hometown Feels Less Like Home', *The Downsizing of America*, fourth of seven articles, March 6th, p.1.

Nijkamp, P., and J. Poot (1997), Endogenous technological change, long run growth and spatial interdependence: a survey', in C.S. Bertuglia, S. Lombardo, and P. Nijkamp (eds), *Innovative Behavior in Space and Time*, Berlin: Springer-Verlag, pp. 213–38.

Nijkamp, P. and R. Stough (2000), 'Growth and change', *A Journal of Urban and Regional Policy*, **31**, (4), 451–4.

Office of Management and Budget (1987), Standard Industrial Classification Manual.

Ohmae, K. (1993), 'The rise of the region state', *Foreign Affairs*, **72**, 78–87.

Oinas P. and E.J. Malecki (1999), 'Spatial Innovation Systems' in Malecki, E.J., P. Oinas, (eds), *Making Connections. Technological Learning and Regional Economic Change*, Ashgate, Aldershot 261–75.

Osborne, D. and T. Gaebler (1992), *Reinventing Government*, New York: Addison-Wesley.

O'Toole, J. and W. Bennis (1992), 'Our federalist future', *California Management Review*, **34**, (4), 73–90.

Pakes, A. and Z. Grilliches (1980), 'Patents and R&D at the Firm Level: A First Report', *Economics Letters* **4**, 377–81.

Paquet, G. (1990), 'The internationalization of domestic firms and governments: anamorphosis of a palaver', *Science and Public Policy*, **17**, (5), 327–32.

Paquet, G. (1992), 'The strategic state', in J. Chrétien (ed.), *Finding Common Ground*, Hull: Voyageur Publishing, pp. 85–101. [For a longer version see PRIME Working Paper 94–16.]

Paquet, G. (1994), 'Reinventing governance', *Opinion Canada*, **2**, (2), 1–5.

Paquet, G. and J. Roy (1995), 'Prosperity through networks: the bottom-up strategy that might have been' in S. Phillips (ed.), *How Ottawa Spends 1995–96*, Ottawa: Carleton University Press).

Parker, D.D. and D. Zilberman (1993), 'University technology transfers: impacts on local and U.S. economies', *Contemporary Policy Issues*, **11**, 87–99.

Pavitt, K. (1984), 'Sectoral patterns of technical change: towards a taxonomy and a theory', *Research Policy*, **13**, 343–73.

Pavitt, K., M. Robson and J. Townsend (1987), 'The Size Distribution of Innovating Firms in the UK: 1945–1984', *Journal of Industrial Economics* **55**, 291–316.

Perloff, H.S., E.S. Dunn, E.E. Lampard, and R.F. Muth (1960), *Regions, Resources and Economic Growth*, Baltimore, MD: The Johns Hopkins University Press.

Perroux, F. (1960), *Économie et société*, Paris: Presses Universitaires de France.

Piore, M.J. (1992), 'Fragments of a cognitive theory of technological change and organisational structure', in N. Nohria and R.G. Eccles (eds), *Networks and Organisations*, Boston: Harvard Business School, pp. 430–444.

Piore M. and C. Sable (1984), *The Second Industrial Divide: Possibilities for Prosperity*, New York: Basic Books.

Polanyi, K. (1968 [1957]) 'The economy as instituted process' in K. Polanyi (ed.), *Archaic and Modern Economies*, New York: Anchor Books, pp. 139–74.

Porter, M.E. (1990), *The Competitive Advantage of Nations*, New York: The Free Press.

Porter, M.E. (1992), 'Capital disadvantage: America's failing capital investment system', *Harvard Business Review*, **70**, (5), 65–82.

Porter M. (1998), 'Clusters and the New Economics of Competition', *Harvard Business Review*, November-December, 77–90.

Praskevopoulos, C.C. (1971), 'The stability of the regional share component: an empirical test', *Journal of Regional Science*, **11**, 107–12.

Premus, R. (1982), *Location of High-technology Firms and Regional Economic Development*, Washington, D.C.: US Government Printing Office.

Putnam, R.D. (1993), *Making Democracy Work, Princeton*: Princeton University Press.

Rees, J. (1991), 'State technology programs and industry experience in the United States', *Review of Urban and Regional Development Studies*, **3**, 39–59.

Rees, J. and H. Stafford (1986), 'Theories of regional growth and industrial location: their relevance for understanding high-tech complexes', in J. Rees (ed.), *Technology, Regions and Policy*, Otowa: Rowman and Littlefield, pp. 23–50.

Resnick, M. (1994), 'Changing the centralized mind', *Technology Review*, **97**, 5, 32–40.

Rheingold, Howard (1993), *The Virtual Community*, Reading, Mass.: Addison-Wesley.

Rivlin, Alice M. (1992), *Reviving the American Dream: The Economy, the States and the Federal Government*, Washington, DC: Brookings Institution.

Romer, P.M. (1986), 'Increasing returns and long run growth', *Journal of Political Economy*, **94**, 1002–37.

Romer, P.M. (1990), 'Endogenous technical change', *Journal of Political Economy*, **98**, S72–102.

Romer, P.M. (1994), 'The origins of endogenous growth', *Journal of Economic Perspectives*, **8**, 3–22.

Rosenberg, N. (1963), 'Technological change in the machine tool industry, 1840–1910', *Journal of Economic History*, **23**, 414–43.

Rothwell, R. (1989), 'Small firms, innovation and industrial change', *Small Business Economics*, **1**, (1), 51–64.

Saxenian, A.L. (1994), *Regional Advantage: Culture and Competition in Silicon Valley and Route 128*, Cambridge, Mass.: Harvard University Press.

Scherer, F.M. (1965), 'Size of firm, market structure, opportunity, and the output of patented inventions', *American Economic Review*, **55**, 1097–25.

Scherer, F.M. (1978), 'Technological maturity and waning economic growth,' *Arts and Sciences*, **1**, 7–11.

Scherer, F.M. (1982), 'Interindustry technology flows in the United States', *Research Policy*, 11, 227–45.

Scherer, F.M. (1983), 'The Propensity to Patent', *Journal of Industrial Organization* **1**, 107–128.

Scherer, F.M. (1984), *Innovation and Growth: Schumpeterian Perspective*, Cambridge, Mass.: MIT Press.

Scherer, F.M. (1991), 'Changing perspectives on the firm size problem', in Z. Acs and D.B. Audretsch (eds), *Innovation and Technological Change: An International Comparison*, Ann Arbor: University of Michigan Press, pp. 24–38.

Schmookler, J. (1966), *Inventions and Economic Growth*, Cambridge, Mass.: Harvard University Press.

Schumpeter, J. A. (1934), *The Theory of Economic Development*, Cambridge, Mass.: Harvard College.

Schumpeter, J.A. (1942), *Capitalism, Socialism and Democracy*, New York: Harper Collins.

Science Council of Canada (1984), *Canadian Industrial Development: Some Policy Directions*, Ottawa: Supply & Services Canada.

Science Council of Canada (1990), *Grassroots Initiatives, Global Success: Report of the 1989 National Technology Policy Roundtable*, Ottawa: Science Council of Canada.

Scott, J.T. (1984), 'Firm versus industry variability in R&D intensity', in Zvi Griliches (ed.), *R&D, Patents and Productivity*, Chicago: University of Chicago Press.

Shachar, A. and D. Felsenstein (1992), 'Urban economic development and high technology industry', *Urban Studies*, **29**, (6), 839–55.

Shane, S. and S. Venkataraman (2000), 'The promise of entrepreneurship as a field of research', *Academy of Management Review*.

Shankerman, M. and A. Pakes (1986), 'Estimates of the value of patent rights in European countries during the post-1950 period,' *The Economic Journal*, **96**, 1052–76.

Soete, L.L.G. (1979), 'Firm size and inventive activity: the evidence reconsidered', *European Economic Review*, **12**, 319–40.

Solow, R. (1957), 'Technical change in an aggregative model of economic growth', *International Economic Review*, **6**, 18–31.

Sternberg, R. (1999), 'Innovative Linkages and Proximity: Empirical Results from Recent Surveys of Small and Medium Sized Firms in German Regions', *Regional Studies* 33, 529–40.

Stiglitz, J., and A. Weiss (1981), 'Credit Rationing in Markets with Imperfect Information', *American Economic Review* 71, (3), 393–410.

Stoffaes, C. (1987), *Fins de mondes*, Paris: Editions Odile Jacob.

Stohr, W. (1986), 'Regional innovation complexes', *Papers of the Regional Science Association*, 59, 29–44.

Stoneman, P. (1983), *The Economic Analysis of Technological Change*, Oxford: Oxford University Press.

Storper, M. (1992), 'The limits of globalisation: technology districts and international trade', *Economic Geography*, 68, (1), 60–93.

Storper, M. (1993), 'Regional worlds of production: learning and innovation in the technology districts of France, Italy and the USA', *Regional Studies*, 27, (5), 433–55.

Storper, M. (1995), 'The resurgence of regional economies, ten years later: the region as nexus of untraded interdependencies', *European Urban and Regional Studies*, 2, (3), 191–222.

Storper, M. and R. Walker (1989), *The Capitalist Imperative: Territory, Technology and Industrial Growth*, Oxford: Basil Blackwell.

Stough, R., S.V. Lall, and M.P. Trice (1999), 'Regional endogenous growth and policy', paper presented at the International Workshop on Endogenous Growth Policy and Regional Development, Amsterdam, February.

Suarez-Villa, L. (2000), *Invention and the Rise of Technocapitalism*, New York: Rowman & Littlefield Publishers.

Talen, E. and L. Anselin (1996), 'Assessing spatial equity: the role of access measures', Regional Research Institute Research Paper 96–03, West Virginia University, Morgantown, WV.

The Economist (1994), 'Canada: Welcome to Cascadia', 331, (7864), 52.

Titman, S. (1984), 'The effect of capital structure on a firm's liquidation decision', *The Journal of Financial Economics*, 13, 137–51.

Titman, S. and R. Wessels (1988), 'The determinants of capital structure choice', *The Journal of Finance*, 43, 1–19.

Todtling, F. (1994), 'The uneven landscape of innovation poles: local embeddedness and global networks', in A. Amin and N. Thrift (eds), *Globalization, Institutions and Regional Development in Europe*, Oxford: Oxford University Press, pp. 68–90.

US Bureau of the Census (1982), County Business Patterns (Data obtained from ICPSR online data services).

Varga, A. (1988), *University Research and Regional Innovation: A Spatial Econometric Analysis of Academic Technology Transfer*, Boston: Kluwer.

Venkataraman, S. (1997), 'The distinctive domain of entrepreneurship research, in advances in entrepreneurship', *Firm Emergence and Growth*, **3**, 119–38.

Von Hippel, E. (1988), *The Sources of Innovation*, New York: Oxford University Press.

Warner, J. (1977), 'Bankruptcy costs: some evidence', *The Journal of Finance*, **32**: 337–47.

Webber, A.M. (1993), 'What's so new about the new economy?', *Harvard Business Review*, **71**, (1), 24–42.

Westhead, P. and D.J. Storey (1995), 'Links between higher education institutions and high technology firms', *International Journal of Management Science*, **23**, (4), 345–60.

White, H. (1980), 'A heteroskedastic-consistent covariance matrix estimator and a direct test for heteroskedasticity', *Econometrica*, **48**, 817–38.

Wijst, D. van der and R. Thurik (1993), 'Determinants of small firm debt ratios: an analysis of retail panel data', *Small Business Economics*, **5**, 55–65.

Williamson, O. (1968), 'Economics as an Antitrust Defense: The Welfare Tradeoffs', *American Economic Review* **5891**, 18–36.

Williamson, O.E. (1975), *Markets and Hierarchies: Antitrust Analysis and Implications*, New York: Free Press.

Williamson, O. E. (1988), 'Corporate finance and corporate governance', *The Journal of Finance*, **43**, 567–91.

Winter, S.G. (1984), 'Schumpeterian competition in alternative technological regimes', *Journal of Economic Behavior and Organization*, **5**, 287–320.

Wriston, W.B. (1992), *The Twilight of Sovereignty*, New York: Scribner's.

Index